The Mary Rose

The Mary Rose

The Excavation and Raising of
Henry VIII's Flagship

Margaret Rule

Foreword by HRH The Prince of Wales

WINDWARD

Dedication to
Arthur and Nicolas, without whose support none of the past
seventeen years would have been possible, and to the memory of
Keith Muckelroy, with whom, for too short a time, I shared a
dream.

© Margaret Rule 1982
First published in Great Britain 1982 by
Conway Maritime Press Ltd
Revised Second Edition 1983

Windward
an imprint owned by W H Smith & Son Limited
Registered No 237811 England
Trading as WHS Distributors,
St John's House, East Street, Leicester, LE1 6NE

ISBN 0 7112 0323 7

Designed by Richard Johnson
Typesetting by Sunset Phototype, Barnet
Artwork by Letterspace, Barnet
Printed by Jolly & Barber Ltd, Rugby
Bound by R J Acford, Chichester

FRONTISPIECE
A watch bell, found in June 1982, was one of the last objects to be raised from the Mary
Rose. *The inscription, in Dutch, reads 'IC BEN GHEGOTEN INT YAER MCCCCCX'*
— I was cast in the year 1510 (the year the ship was completed).

PAGE SIX
Margaret Rule surrounding the ephemeral stain of a corroded steel sword with a wall of sheet
aluminium before pouring liquid plaster over the sword which when set reinforced the fragile
steel so that it could be recovered.

PAGE TEN
A Royal Cipher on a gun cast for Henry VIII recovered from the upper deck of the Mary Rose
in 1980.

Contents

Acknowledgements

Foreword by HRH Prince Charles, Prince of Wales   11

Chapter 1: The Place of the Mary Rose in History   13

Chapter 2: The Search of the Ship   39

Chapter 3: The Work of the Mary Rose 1979-1982   73

Chapter 4: The Hull   103

Chapter 5: The Decks   117

Chapter 6: The Running and Standing Rigging   136

Chapter 7: Ordnance   149

Chapter 8: The Crew, Officers and Life on Board   184

Chapter 9: Salvage and Recovery   202

Appendix: Remote Sensing and Survey Methods used on the   231
    Mary Rose site

References   234

Glossary   236

Bibliography   238

Index   239

Acknowledgements

Any excavation which takes seventeen years to complete must have relied on the goodwill, financial support and physical and mental effort of a very large number of people. The *Mary Rose* project is no exception.

From its inception in 1965 it relied heavily on 'amateur' workers who gave their skills and their time without any thought of reward. These included innumerable amateur scuba divers from civilian and service diving clubs who gave their time as well as archaeologists, scientists, conservators and historians who gave their advice.

Without the support of people like John Barber and Tony Glover the dream of finding the *Mary Rose* would have remained nothing more than a dream and their generous loan of boats like *High & Dry, Roger Grenville,* MFV *Julie-Anne* and MFV *Sand-Julie* was essential to the operation in the years before the formation of the Mary Rose Trust in 1979.

Tony Glover's generosity extended to sharing with me some of his wealth of knowledge of the waters of the Solent thus helping me to understand the natural factors of wind and tide which dictated any management of the diving operations in later years.

From the earliest days the names of divers like George Clark of Hampshire Fire Brigade, Morrie Young, Pete Powell, Reg Cloudesdale and Percy Ackland of Southampton Branch of the British Sub-Aqua Club, Don Bullivant and Eric Sivyer of Southsea Branch of the BSAC, Norman Robinson, Tom Hale, Andy Gallagher, Alan Baldwin and Artie Shaw shine out like beacons, but many others are recorded in the logs and each and every one deserves our thanks for ensuring the ultimate success of the project by their tireless and dogged commitment to the initial search and survey.

Andrew Fielding and the late Keith Muckelroy brought a different sort of commitment: in addition to being experienced and competent divers they had the necessary professional approach to standards of recording and when, in later seasons, they were joined by Jon Adams I had the nucleus of a team of professional diving archaeologists to control the excavation and ensure that evidence was properly recorded.

The Archaeological Supervisors, Adrian Barak, Alex Hildred, Chris Dobbs, Barrie Burden, Berit Mortlock and Bob Stewart, wrestled with the herculean tasks of training volunteer divers and enthusing them with our determination to wring the maximum amount of information from the stratified deposits within the hull and in the surrounding scourpits.

In the four seasons since the Trust was formed in 1979, a total of 24,640 dives have been made on site by members of the archaeological team and 9 man-years have been spent on the seabed. Corners have been cut and the task of excavation and survey would have benefited from being spread over a longer period of time, but an invisible enemy was constantly on our heels and the results of degradation by silt-laden currents, micro- and macro-biological organisms was plain for all to see.

Biological surveys to study colonisation of the site and investigate biological degradation were undertaken as an undergraduate project by Corinne Roots and Tony Wainwright of the University of Aberystwyth in 1975 and 1976, and Dr Ken Collins and Jennie Mallinson of the Department of Oceanography, University of Southampton, are continuing this work which will be published as part of the overall site report.

Dr John Levy and Professor Pratt of the Imperial College of Science and Technology have provided a stable and remarkably civilised background for a study of the longbows and arrows from which the ebullient 'team leader' Robert Hardy, an acknowledged authority on the longbow, and I have benefited and I hope that this team will continue to evaluate the material as it becomes available and that we will see true replica bows shot over a range in due course.

Planning the ultimate museum at Eastney was made more pleasurable by the innate courtesy and professionalism of Peter Ahrends, Robin Wade and Alan Falkner and current discussion with civilian and service officers about plans to house the *Mary Rose* are greatly facilitated by the personal enthusiasm of Admiral Eberle, Commander-in-Chief Home Fleet, Admiral Tippet, Flag Officer Portsmouth, and the professionalism of Robert Hack, Civil Advisor to the Port Admiral.

British Industry has supported the project since its inception with gifts and loans of essential equipment and the support of the BP Group of Companies with technical advice on matters ranging from conservation of water-logged wood to sonic ranging has been invaluable and I am particularly grateful to Michael O'Hanlan and Len Dolan for their cheerful support and expert advice at innumerable press conferences held on behalf of The Mary Rose (1967) Committee.

The project has almost come to a halt on many occasions but each time fate has stepped in to provide a new stimulation. In 1970 it was the discovery of the first iron gun by Alexander McKee, and in 1973, when spirits and funds were particularly low, a visit by His Royal Highness the Duke of Edinburgh to see objects recovered from the wreck injected a new enthusiasm and stimulated the support from industry and local government. The support of the late Lord Mountbatten of Burma was a sheet anchor which remained with us from the early years of the project until his tragic death in 1980. Always one of the first to define a problem he then did his utmost to help with a solution and I feel that to bring the *Mary Rose* into No 3 dock alongside HMS Victory will fit neatly into his concept of tradition and naval history.

What can I say of the inspiration and involvement of His Royal Highness Prince Charles, Prince of Wales, President of the Mary Rose Trust, Scuba Diver, archaeologist and heir to the throne of the United Kingdom of Great Britain and Northern Ireland? Our confidence in, and loyalty to our President can only equal that of Henry VIII's Admiral to his king who wrote 'I remit all this to the order of your most noble Grace who I pray God preserve from all adversity and send you as much victory of your enemys as ever had any of your noble ancestry' (written in the Downs on board the *Mary Rose*, 22 March 1513).

We, of the Mary Rose Trust, can only re-echo that sentiment and humbly dedicate it to His Royal Highness.

I have enjoyed the benefit of endless discussions over the years with many colleagues and friends including Jim Clark, Colin Carpenter, Howard Blackmore, Dr Basil Greenhill, Dr Sean McGrail, Peter Marsden, Robert Grenier, Ken Barton, the late Paul Johnson, Joan du Plat Taylor, A H (Bill) Corney, Lars Barkman, Colin Mudie, the late George Naish and Councillor John Marshall. I am grateful to them all for their generous scholarship and wisdom, but any mistakes are my own and in mitigation I can only plead a natural wish to recover the maximum evidence before the ship was destroyed and the evidence lost for ever.

As the *Mary Rose* project goes forward into the final phase of recovery, I can only wish my colleagues success. To every diver whether he be a civilian diver employed by the Mary Rose Trust or a service-trained diver from the Royal Engineers, I wish good luck and happy returns.

As the ship comes ashore we move to a new stage of the project and I look forward to sharing the rediscovery of a Tudor moment in time with visitors from all over the world. Many questions remain to be answered and there are problems still to be solved, but all that was possible underwater in 0.5m visibility will be matched and surpassed once the ship is ashore.

In conclusion, I humbly thank all those too numerous to mention who made the project possible. The Roll of Honour is too long to be recorded at this time but their names are enshrined in the dive logs and the correspondence files. I hope that their reward will be the successful conclusion of an enterprise which will probably never again be equalled.

Margaret Rule
June 1982

ACKNOWLEDGEMENTS TO SECOND EDITION

On Monday 11 October the *Mary Rose* came home to Portsmouth. Since then we have had a new task, but one no less demanding than the old one. Andrew Fielding and his small team have worked twenty-four hour shifts to keep the hull wet and Arthur King of Alexander Towing and John Wilson and his colleagues of ITM Offshore have had sleepless nights preparing the barge *GW92* to receive the cradle and the hull. Today they completed the transfer of the hull from the 150ft long barge *TOW 1* to the 100ft long *GW92* using modular hydraulic bogies incorporating 192 wheels. The whole 'package' is now ready for docking in No 3 Dock alongside Nelson's flagship *Victory*.

Colleagues within the naval base have advised us and they were responsible for removing the ULF and the superfluous steel supports beneath the cradle. The goodwill has been immense and it is a pleasure to record how many people found time in a bad economic climate to assist a project which has little more to commend it than the fact that our history is our heritage and that the *Mary Rose* now belongs to everyone.

Margaret Rule
23 November 1982

Picture Credits

One of the reasons I am writing this foreword is that I am a great admirer of Margaret Rule. The way in which she has carried out, and _is_ carrying out, the excavation and eventual raising of the Mary Rose is a remarkable record of professional dedication on a grand scale.

Marine archaeology is still a comparatively new specialization and working on the seabed in the dirty, tidal waters of the Solent makes traditional "surface" archaeology seem like the proverbial picnic! All sorts of unforeseen problems arise which have to be overcome by ingenious, and often improvised, techniques from which future marine archaeologists will no doubt learn some very useful lessons.

Margaret Rule has taken me down to the site of the wreck every year for about five years and it has been fascinating to see the progress she and her team of divers, many of them enthusiastic volunteers, have made in revealing the timbers of King Henry VIII's great fighting ship. Only now, after some four or five years, am I beginning to make a little sense of the excavations. With the ship lying at an angle of 60° on the seabed it is extraordinarily hard, even for a former Cambridge student of archaeology, to orientate oneself to the location of the timbers. The fact that other people, like Margaret Rule, _can_ orientate themselves properly and can carry out such a professional operation in far from advantageous conditions is worthy of the warmest praise.

The result of all this hard work and expertise is that future generations, we hope, will be able to glimpse a small part of Britain's maritime heritage; will be able to see history "come alive" and to step, as it were, into the shoes of a Tudor seaman in the reign of Henry VIII. The only real way of understanding and coping with the present is, I believe, through an adequate knowledge and interpretation of the past. From that point of view we are able, for once, to transform a contemporary naval disaster into a victory in terms of human awareness. But it is not all as simple and exciting as it may sound. Excavating and raising the ship is proving to be a terrifyingly expensive business. The actual raising operation is going to be a most complicated engineering problem, requiring last minute improvisation owing to the delicate state of the ship's structure. Building the museum for the Mary Rose to be displayed is another expensive undertaking. So Margaret Rule and the Mary Rose Trust need all the help they can obtain. All I can say is that they certainly have my support.

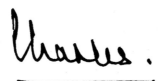

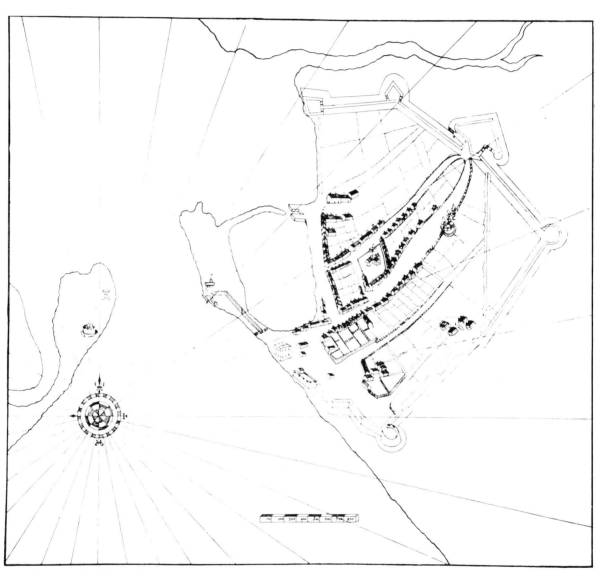

Map of Portsmouth before 1540.
The Round Tower, the Square
Tower and the Long Curtain
Battery which guarded the deep
water channel at the entrance to the
harbour are shown as they must
have been when the Mary Rose
sank.

CHAPTER 1

The Place of the Mary Rose in History

WHEN HENRY VIII BECAME King of England in 1509 he was a vigorous, well-educated young man of eighteen with a single-mindedness that later matured into obstinacy. He had inherited a small fleet of ships from his father Henry VII but his kingdom was small with a population of scarcely four million and an agricultural policy which depended on the wool trade for economic viability. The last thing England could afford was expensive military campaigns but it was essential that the Channel be kept open and a foothold on the French coast was necessary not only for royal prestige but also to ensure free passage for English merchant ships. Calais remained under English rule, the last piece of debris left from English territories in France after the Hundred Years War. In Europe two major powers, France and Spain, jostled for control and the Pope backed first one and then the other. Henry allied himself with both by marriage — first his own to Catherine of Aragon, the aunt of Charles V, Emperor of Spain, and then by arranging the marriage of his favourite sister Mary to the elderly King of France, Louis XII. But more and more he concentrated his efforts on building capital ships, improving existing coastal forts and constructing new ones until, by the middle of the sixteenth century, he had a chain of coastal defences the like of which had not been seen in England since the days of the *Classis Britannica* and the Saxon Shore forts in the third century AD.[1] In order to defend his forts and his ships Henry VIII had to bring about a rapid improvement in the art of gunfounding in England. Early English monarchs including Henry IV had taken a personal interest in the manufacture of ordnance but Henry VIII was stimulated by the example of his brother-in-law, James IV of Scotland, who had established a small but efficient navy and had provided cannon foundries at Edinburgh and Stirling to provide his ships and his castles with the most modern weapons.

Henry appointed his father's gunner, Humphrey Walker, as the King's gunfounder[2] and in 1510 Lorenzo Pasqualigo reported to the Venetian Senate that the price of tin had increased rapidly because Henry had bought enough to cast 100 cannon.[3]

This effort was not sufficient to meet the demands of defence and Henry ordered 24 curtows (weighing 4000lbs each) and 24 serpentines (weighing 1100lbs each) from Hans Poppenruyter of Malines, Belgium.[4] These were delivered and paid for in 1512 and later Hans Poppenruyter made more guns for Henry, but even this was not enough and by 1514 Simon Giles, an immigrant from Malines, was manufacturing guns in a London foundry for the King. An inventory dated February 1514 lists guns 'remaining in the Tower of London and at Hunsdyche' (Houndsditch in East London) including guns 'of Umfrey Walker's making being in the Tower' and of 'Symondes making being at Hunsdyche'.[5]

Later Henry imported other craftsmen, including Francesco Arcanis, who joined the King's service as Engineer, or Master of Mines, in 1522,[6] and later two more members of his family, Rafaelo and Arcangelo, began to cast guns in London and at Calais. A Frenchman, Peter Baude, also entered Henry's service in the late 1520s and he worked both at the Tower and at Houndsditch casting guns for the King.[7] This injection of new blood and improved technology was vital. The new range of cast bronze muzzle-loading guns now being made in the King's foundries meant that if treaties failed he could defend his country.

Among the ships inherited from his father were the *Regent* of 1000 tons and the *Sovereign* of 800 tons.[8] Little is known of these ships or their armament although an extensive inventory of the *Sovereign* in 1495 suggests that all 141 guns listed were relatively small and that they were probably carried high up in the ship either in the waist or in the high castles in her bow and stern.[9]

It was customary in the fifteenth century to consider larger ships as having a dual purpose, enabling them to be hired out as merchant ships in time of peace but allowing them to be fitted with guns above the bulwark rail whenever necessary in time of war. The function of such ships in wartime was either to carry troops to fight a land battle ashore or to engage the enemy at close quarters at sea, allowing the soldiers to use light hand guns to sweep the enemy decks and then to carry the battle to the decks of the enemy ship with hand guns, pikes, bills, swords and knives all playing their part. The advantage of height to a gunner in the lofty castles or in one of the fighting tops is obvious but strategic warfare at sea was impossible until a coordinated battery of large-calibre guns of long range, relatively high velocity and low windage could be carried on board a warship. The fire-power of fifteenth century ships was limited by the weight of guns which could be carried without seriously affecting the stability of the ship. Unless the weight of the heavy, large-calibre

OPPOSITE
The Mary Rose *was named after the King's favourite sister, who married Charles Brandon, Duke of Suffolk, after the death of her first husband Louis XII of France. A wedding portrait painted in 1515.*

See p17.

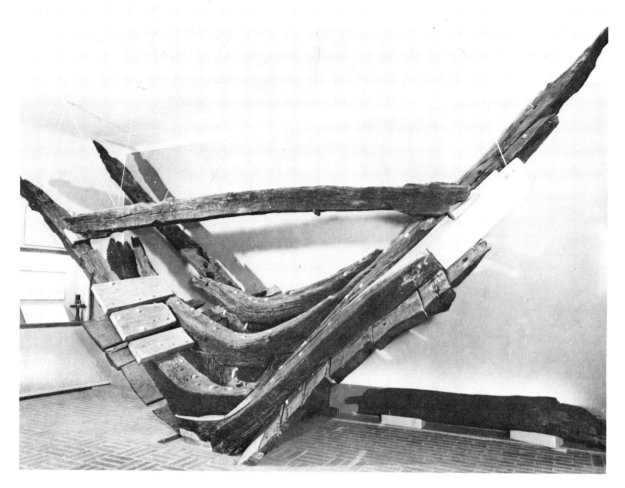

A section of the structure recovered from the Swedish warship Elefanten *of 1559,* a very large ship which provides the closest comparative evidence for a ship of the Mary Rose *period. She is of smooth-skinned carvel construction with bands of 'thick stuff' and heavy grown riders bracing the hull athwartships.*

Mid-fifteenth century model of a two-masted sailing ship which once hung in the church at Mataro in Spain, now in the Maritime Museum Prins Hendrik in Rotterdam. The deck beams for the main- and quarterdecks pass right through the hull; the same construction is found in the upper deck beam of the Mary Rose *at the forward end of the sterncastle.*

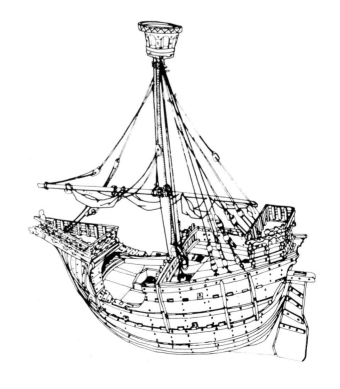

SOVEREIGN GUN INVENTORY

Serpentynes of yron in the forecastell aboue in the Dekke yche of them with his miches & forloke of yron	*xvj*
Chambers of yron to the same	*xlviij*
Serpentynes of yron in the Somercastell alawe ych of them with his miche & foreloke of yron	*xxiiij*
Chambers of yron to the same	*lxxij*
Stone gonnes of yron in the Wast of the seid Shipp with miches & forlokkes to the same	*xx*
Chambers of yron to the same	*lx*
Serpentynes of yron in the Somercastell with miches & forlokkes to the same	*xx*
Serpentynes of Brasse with his miche & forloke in the seid Somercastell	*j*
Stone gonnes in the seid Somercastell ych of them with his miche & foreloke	*xj*
Chambers to the seid Serpentynes & Stone gonnes	*iiijxij*
Serpentynes of yron in the Sterne of the seid ship with miches and forlokes to the same	*iiij*
Chambers of Yron for the same	*xij*
Serpentynes of yron in the Dekke ovyr the Somercastell with miches & forlokkes to the same	*xxv*
Chambers to the same	*lxxv*
Serpentynes of yron in the poppe of the seid shipp with miches & forelokes to the same	*xx*
Chambers of yron to the same	*lx*

guns could be brought down into the hull itself it was virtually impossible to carry many on board the ship. The main problem was how to cut gunports close to the waterline and provide an effective watertight seal when at sea. It was difficult to do this satisfactorily as long as the ships were clinker-built of overlapping planks, giving an uneven skin to the hull. Although some clinker-built medieval hulls are illustrated with a port cut high above the waterline and the late fifteenth century carrack drawn by the Flemish artist 'W A' has a large open port close to the waterline at the stern, it is clear that these were loading ports which would be securely battened down before leaving harbour. Gunports were a more difficult proposition. They had to be opened swiftly to allow the guns to run forward and they had to be securely closed even

See p 18.

more swiftly if the guns were brought inboard for the ship to go about or if the weather suddenly worsened. Such ports had to be totally water-tight even in the heaviest of seas.

The radical change necessary to replace overlapping clinker planks on large ships with smooth planks placed edge-to-edge began to take place in England at the beginning of the sixteenth century. In many ways it is surprising that the change took so long. The native ships of the Veneti described by Julius Caesar in 56 BC, and the Romano-British merchantmen excavated by Peter Marsden at Blackfriars on the River Thames, were sturdy edge-to-edge planked vessels with smooth hull planking secured to the ribs of the ship with large iron bolts. These were quite unlike the lightly-built longships which dominated the Baltic at that time, and later developed into the clinker-built merchantmen so common in Northern Europe, as shown by the ship with a central stern rudder on the early thirteenth century town seal of Ipswich.

In the first half of the sixteenth century ships got larger and the need to carry heavy guns became more pressing. The change from clinker to carvel took place and it appears to have occurred almost simultaneously along both shores of the English Channel and on the Atlantic coasts of Spain and Portugal. Although the invention of the gunport lid is traditionally thought to be due to the efforts of a French shipwright, Descharges, who worked in Brest at the beginning of the sixteenth century, the painting of the departure of Henry VIII for the Field of

OPPOSITE

Flemish carrack from about AD 1470, drawn by the artist known only by his initials, 'WA'. The main shrouds are attached to the chain-wale with deadeyes and lanyards in a similar fashion to the Mary Rose *but the vertical standards which brace the chain-wale against the upward pull of the shrouds are absent from the illustration. The open loading hatch on the port quarter would have been battened down securely before the ship left port.*

The first common seal of Ipswich, Suffolk, dating from AD 1200. The obverse bears the inscription: S'COMVNITATIS VILLE GYPEWICI and the earliest representation on a European ship of a rudder slung to the aft side of the sternpost with pintles and gudgeons. The sternpost rudder greatly improved sailing efficiency and transformed the shape of the double-ended hull to one with a distinctly different bow and stern.

Cloth of Gold in France in 1520 clearly illustrates large carracks with batteries of guns in the castles as in the previous century, but also with heavy guns protruding through ports below the weather deck on what appears to be a continuous gundeck. When this change came about in England is still uncertain but certainly it was commonplace for English warships to carry continuous batteries of guns on the main gundeck below the bulwark rail by the 1540s. Examination of the hull of the *Mary Rose* after she is ashore may answer the question — was she originally built with lidded gunports and a continuous gundeck in 1509

or did this transformation occur when she was rebuilt in 1536? Limited examination of the frames and plankings at the maindeck level on the starboard quarter shows that in this place at least the clinker planks had been removed and replaced by edge-to-edge carvel planks; the frames had been adzed to remove the sharp angle of a land, or notch, which originally housed the edge of the clinker plank, but it had been impossible to do this completely without weakening the frame to an unacceptable degree so that the shipwright had inserted a fillet of wood to accommodate the gap.

The principal ships in Henry VIII's navy pictured in Dover harbour in 1520 when the King and Queen embarked for Boulogne and their meeting with the French King Francis I. The Kathryn Pleasaunce *had been especially built to provide reasonable accommodation for the King and Queen but over 5000 men and women had to be transported across the Channel and even on the largest ships, living conditions would have been cramped. The ship at the lefthand side of the picture, with gunports on a maindeck close to the waterline, a continuous chain-wale and standards along the whole length of the starboard quarter, bears a strong resemblance to the* Mary Rose.

General view of the excavation at Roff's Wharf on the site of Woolwich Power Station in London in 1912 which revealed the remains of a large carvel-built ship believed to be the Sovereign. *The* Sovereign *was built in 1488 and rebuilt in 1509 in Portsmouth shortly before the* Mary Rose *was built. In 1621 she was abandoned in a dock at Woolwich.*

The remains of a sixteenth century ship believed to be the *Sovereign* – an 800-ton warship built in 1488 and rebuilt in Portsmouth in 1509, only a few months before the keel of the *Mary Rose* was laid in the same dock – were discovered at Roff's Wharf in Woolwich in 1912.[10] As with the *Mary Rose*, there was clear evidence that clinker planking had been removed and that notches in the frames had been adzed smooth and carvel planking added in its place. If this change took place during her rebuild in 1509 one wonders why the *Mary Rose* was built in the 'old style'. Careful examination ashore may provide the answer. It is always possible that the only section of frame and plank examined underwater is anomalous and may simply be a case of rebuilding with secondhand timbers.

In 1509 the small south coast town of Portsmouth in Hampshire was a bustling lively place thronged with craftsmen and travelling pedlars. The King's ship *Sovereign* was being built in the great dock completed by his father fourteen years before at a cost of £193 0s 6¾d.[11] Wagon-loads of wood trundled into town from the Forest of Bere and blacksmiths in nearby Havant were busy supplying nails and bolts for the new ship. As soon as she was finished the keel of two new ships were laid, the *Mary Rose* and *Peter Pomegranite* – a major programme of rearmament was underway. Between 1509 and 1512 Henry ordered 9

other ships to be built, 2 more to be rebuilt, and he captured or purchased 10 others. Fragmentary details survive of purchases made and food and fittings supplied, but unfortunately no plans or drawings survive from this period to show exactly how these ships were built.

Oppenheim records that shipwrights were paid 2d to 6d per day[12] but that they were bedded and boarded as well, being issued with coats and an allowance of 2½d per day for victuals including bread, beef and beer. Cooks were engaged to prepare their meals and a chamberlain to make their beds, which were furnished with flock mattresses, sheets, bolsters, blankets and coverlets. This compares favourably with life on board the diving salvage vessel *Sleipner* in 1982 except that in the sixteenth century the shipwrights had to sleep three in a bed.

Presumably all this activity brought profit to the town, and ale-houses and stores quickly grew up behind the urban embankment which fronted the town walls. The tradition of hiring the King's ships to merchants in peacetime continued with the *Anne* being hired to trade between the Baltic and Bordeaux in 1511,[13] but after 1533, when war became almost inevitable, hiring ceased until the profit-sharing entre-preneurial activities of Elizabeth I, Drake and Hawkins. Nevertheless, soon after the *Anne* was fitted out, the *Peter Pomegranite* was hired for a merchant voyage to Barrow.[14] The first reference to the *Mary Rose* at sea

Detail of a section through the 'Woolwich Ship' showing the adzed lands and fillets of wood which were inserted to accommodate the change from clinker to carvel planking. The seams are covered with seam battens similar to those which cover the seams between the lower strakes of the Mary Rose.

dates from 29 July 1511 when Robert Brygandyne, the Clerk of the King's Ships, was paid £120 for the conveyance of two new ships, the *Mary Rose* and the *Peter Granade*, from Portsmouth to the Thames.[15] The following September he was paid a further £80 for expenses incurred on these 'new ships'. On 24 September Richard Palshidde of Southampton was paid for supplies including twenty-four coats of white and green (the King's colours) for twenty-four soldiers employed for the safe conduct from Portsmouth to the Thames of London and six similar coats for the master, four for the quartermaster and four for the boatswain, at 6s 10d per coat.[16]

By 1 October payments were being made for eight loads of wood for fitting of stocks of ordnance on board the *Mary Rose*[17], and Thomas Sperte, master, and David Boner, purser, were paid for decking and rigging the ship.[18] This work continued throughout November with charges being recorded for fitting guns and ships, but by Christmas the work takes on a lighter note when William Botrye, a mercer in the City of London, received payment for 'tukes, bokerams, brussells cloths and chamletes' to make streamers and banners for the ship, and John Brown, a painter, was paid for painting and staining the streamers and banners.[19] All was now ready; the *Mary Rose* lay in the Thames close to the Royal palace at Greenwich, fitted out and complete, ready to go to war with pennants and banners streaming.

By September 1511 the Pope and the King of Aragon had entered an alliance against Louis XII of France and on 25 January 1512 the English Parliament decided to join battle with the Spanish against the French. Seamen had to be recruited to man the ships and the master, Thomas Sperte, scoured the country for suitable recruits, going as far as Bristol and Norfolk to find suitable sailors, and luring them to Portsmouth with the promise of 'conduct money' of 6d a day for travelling (at a rate of 12 miles per day). The wages he offered were probably good by contemporary standards with the Admiral, Sir Edward Howard, being paid 10s a day, the master, Sir Thomas Wyndham, receiving 1s 6d a day, the pilots £1 a month and 411 soldiers, mariners, gunners and servants receiving 5s a month. In addition to these wages the men received their food and their uniform, and during a 10-day period in the spring of 1515 the King paid £33 for victualling 300 mariners on board the *Regent*, supplying them with biscuit, beer, beef and fish — a good wholesome diet.

The task the King set the Admiral, Sir Edward Howard, in 1512 was to hold the Channel clear of enemy ships and then to ensure an easy and safe passage for ships and men attempting to capture Boulogne. Using the *Mary Rose* as his flagship, Sir Edward Howard left London river in April with 17 other warships and 2 supply vessels and during the next two months he had cleared the Channel and returned unscathed to Portsmouth to take part in a Royal Fleet Review in July. On 10 August the Admiral left Portsmouth in his flagship, the *Mary Rose*, to lead a fleet of 25 ships in an attack on the major French fleet anchorage at Brest. The crew list of the *Mary Rose* was swollen by the addition of the Admiral's staff and those of Sir Thomas Wyndham, 'Treasurer of the Army at Sea', as well as 5 trumpeters who had the job of sounding battle orders. The main French fleet of 222 ships was anchored close to the shore, with their crews celebrating the feast of St Lawrence, and the two capital ships, the *Grande Louise* of 790 tons, with Admiral René de Clermont on board, and the 700-ton *Marie la Cordelière*, in a vulnerable position. Howard immediately set upon the French flagship and bombarded her with his heavy guns until she retreated to the shelter of the French battery on the shore. Meanwhile Captain Anthony Ughtred in a small English ship, the *Mary James*, was engaging *La Cordelière* and archers from the *Regent* were close-engaged, sweeping the French ship with arrows. During this engagement the *Cordelière* was set on fire, either accidentally or by fire arrows, and locked tight alongside the *Regent*; both ships burnt out to the waterline with devastating loss of life. Howard remained in the area for a further two days and then returned home after burning and taking 32 vessels and capturing 800 men. The *Mary Rose* had seen her first battle.

After wintering in the Thames, the English Fleet was ready for sea again and on 19 September 1513 Henry reviewed his fleet in the Thames, wished them 'God Speed' and watched them sail eastwards to the Channel. Once round the Foreland and into the Channel, Sir Edward Howard decided to put his fleet through their paces and he conducted a race, or time trials, to measure the sailing efficiency of his ships. If any of them were tender or sluggish now was the time to find out. Included in his fleet were great ships such as the *Sovereign* of 1000 tons, the *Gabryell Royal* of 800 tons purchased from Italy, and the *Catherine Forteleza* of 700 tons purchased from Spain, but when he wrote his report to the King in the great cabin on board the *Mary Rose*, he declared: 'The *Mary Rose*, Sir, she is the noblest ship of sail and a great ship at this hour that I trow to be in Christendom. A ship of 100 tons will not be sooner about than she.' He was not so complimentary about all of the ships in his command, saying that the 300-ton *Christ* 'was one of the worst that day, Sir, she be overladen with ordnance beside her heavy tops which are big enough for a ship of 800 or 900 tons.'

During the years that followed the *Mary Rose* campaigned at sea with the fleet and in 1536 she was refitted and partially rebuilt in the

THE MARY ROSE

For the Mary Rose

ORDNANCE	GUNS OF BRASS		GUNS OF IRON		GUNPOWDER		SHOT OF IRON		SHOT OF S
ARTILLERY	Cannons	2	Portpieces	12	Serpentine		for cannon	50	AND LEAI
MUNITIONS	Demi Cannons	2	Slings	2	powder in	2 last	for demi cannon	60	for portpieces
EQUIPMENT	Culverins	2	Demi Slings	3	barrels		for culverin	60	for fowlers
FOR THE WAR	Demi Culverins	6	Quarter Slings	1			for demi culverin	140	for toppieces
FOR THE ARMORY	Sakers	2	Fowlers	6	Cornepowder		for sakers	80	for bases
AND IN THE DEFENCE	Falcons	1	Bases	30	in Barrels	3 last	for falcons	60	shot of lead
OF THE SAID SHIP			Top pieces	2			for sling	40	for handguns
TO THE SEA			Hailshot	20			for demi sling	40	shot of lead
			Handguns				for quarter sling	50	
			complete	50			Dice of iron for		
							hailshot		

The only contemporary picture of the Mary Rose comes from the Anthony Roll, a list of the King's ships completed in 1546. It shows the ship as she was after her rebuild in 1536 and clearly depicts a purpose-built ship of war. The ship carried 91 guns and two heavy guns can be seen protruding through open lidded gunports on either side of the rudder in the square stern. A battery of five large guns project through lidded gunports cut through the main hull close to the waterline on the starboard side of the ship and it may have been a sudden ingress of water through these open ports when the ship went about which caused the fatal accident.

	MEN			
unage 700		*Soldiers*	*185*	
		Mariners	*200*	*415*
		Gunners	*30*	

BOWS BOWSTRINGS ARROWS MORRIS PIKES BILLS, DARTS FOR TOPS		*MUNITIONS*		*EQUIPMENT FOR WAR*	
		Pickhammers	*12*	*Ropes of hemp*	*10 coils*
Bows of yew	*250*	*Sledges of iron*	*8*	*Nails*	*1000*
Bowstrings	*6 gross*	*Crowes of iron*	*12*	*Bags of lead*	*8*
Lynere-arrows		*Comanders*	*12*	*Fyrkins with pinsys*	*6*
in sheaves	*400*	*Tompions*	*14*	*Irine pots*	*10 dozen*
Morris pikes	*150*	*Canvas for*		*Spare wheels*	*4 pairs*
Bills	*150*	*cartridges*	*20 ells*	*Spare trucks*	*4 pairs*
Darts for tops		*Paper for*		*Spare axel trees*	*6*
In dozens	*40*	*cartridges*	*1 quire*	*Sheep skins*	
		formers for		*for sponges*	*12*
		cartridges	*6*	*timber for fordocks*	
				and	*100 feet*

Medway. Little is known of this rebuild but a study of the list of ordnance on board in 1514 and 1545 suggests that modification must have been made to her gundecks to enable the great cannons and demi-cannons to be housed efficiently. The only contemporary picture of the *Mary Rose* dates from after her rebuild; indeed, the actual document dates from the year after the ship sank in 1545. It comes from a list of the King's ships compiled by Anthony Anthony, an officer in the Board of Ordnance, in which is listed every one of the King's ships together with 'ordnance, municions and habillments of war'.

The artist is illustrating the second largest ship in the King's Navy and he is intent on showing us a fighting machine, but the details which would make the painting a portrait are missing or altered. When the time came to meet the threat of invasion in 1545, the ships illustrated on the Anthony Roll and the new fortifications which had been studied, devised, planned and finally built since 1539 were there to meet the challenge.

See p12.   Portsmouth was a town of barely 55 acres within the town walls, with its raison d'être and its life blood, the dockyard, situated outside the town. The old Roman naval base at Portchester had gone out of use in the third century to be superseded by *Clausentum* (Southampton) and during the medieval period the fort had enjoyed the curious distinction of having an Augustinian priory and a Norman castle inserted within its wall, but as Portchester Reach silted up and became unnavigable, a new base was created nearer the harbour mouth.

In 1194 Richard the Lionheart gave Portsmouth the Royal charter,[20] and he may have created a wet dock or shipbuilding slip at the Pond of the Abbess roughly where HMS *Vernon*, the naval diving school, now stands on reclaimed land. Eighteen years later King John ordered these 'docks to be enclosed by a good and strong wall for the preservation of our ships and galleys and likewise to cause penthouses to be made to the same wall in which our ships' tackle may be safely kept.'

When Henry VII bought 8 acres of land at the harbour entrance to build the first dry dock in the world he laid the foundations for a great naval base which has flourished for nearly 500 years.

The entrance to the harbour could be sealed off by a chain boom which extended from the Gosport shore, where a wooden watchtower probably housed a gun battery, to the Round Tower which dominates the harbour entrance. In 1484 the Square Tower and the Curtain Battery were built to complete the line of defences at the harbour entrance and by the sixteenth century the Round Tower had gunports at ground level for heavy guns capable of firing at point blank range at any enemy ships entering the harbour.[21]

The threat of a combined attack by France and Spain in 1538 led to an intensive programme of coastal defence. Strategic castles were built to protect the fleet anchorages in the Downs, at Rye (Camber Castle), and in the Solent; blockhouses were built at East and West Cowes to control the entrance to the River Medina, which provided a waterway to the heartland of the Isle of Wight. Calshot Castle was built to control the entrance to Southampton Water and later, in 1542, Netley Castle was built to guard the eastern shore of Southampton Water. Hurst Castle dominated the western approach into the Solent via the Needles channel and in 1544 Southsea Castle was completed to cover the deep water channel into Portsmouth harbour.

The scene was set, the defences were ready, and Henry launched his battlefleet across the Channel to seize and capture the French town of Boulogne. Cardinal Wolsey, who had advised the King for so long, had been disgraced in 1529 and died the following year. Wolsey had always seen the advantages of an alliance between Henry and the powerful Emperor, Charles V of Spain. Spain, after all, controlled the vital ports in the Netherlands through which the lucrative trade in wool had to pass to reach the continental market and, ever ambitious, Wolsey must have hoped for the Emperor's support in the next Papal elections.

After the excommunication of Henry VIII from the Church of Rome in 1533 and the annulment of his marriage to the aunt of Charles V, Catherine of Aragon, Henry stood alone without Wolsey's advice and with Pope Clement openly encouraging Francis I and Charles V to join forces against him. French support for James V of Scotland was open and irritating and Henry had constantly to stretch his resources to deal with two threats at once; his armies were needed to counter attacks on the south coast and on the Scottish borders. Home defence was the responsibility of a local militia raised on a regional basis and under the command of Lieutenants who were responsible for the defence of their region in an emergency. At best the militia could only raise some 120,000 men to defend the coasts of Kent, Essex, the West Country and the Scottish borders. Bad roads and attenuated supply lines meant that a successful campaign had to be victualled and supplied by sea. For the English campaign in Scotland, which culminated in the capture of Edinburgh in the spring of 1544, 212 ships had to be mustered to convey 15,000 men with supplies of food, munitions and horses for a two-month campaign and extra sailors had to be recruited from the fishing fleets of the east and south coasts of England to man these ships.[22]

French pirate raids across the Channel had become almost an annual event since the beginning of the century and the citizens of Seaford and Brithelmstone (Brighton) asked to be excused from the payment of tithes because 'the French have yet again burned the harvest'. Although appeals against payment of taxes were as common then as they are today, the late-summer raids across the Channel were having an effect on the local population, who depended on agriculture and fishing for their livelihood.

The claim of Francis I to the Kingdom of Milan in northern Italy led to a break in the uneasy alliance between France and Spain, and Henry joined forces with Charles to settle the French question once and for all. The preparations for the invasion of France in 1544 were detailed. This was never intended to be a mere raid of retaliation for some localised provocation on the south coast of England. Detailed estimates of men, artillery and provisions needed for a successful campaign were drawn up, and even the relative costings of transporting horses, carriages and harness together with oxen, carriages, yokes and chains from England, were set against the cost of hiring them in Flanders. The economics of purchase against hire were recognised with the remark that 'take all from England' would cost £9400 less 'and yet all the oxen, horses and carriages remain the King's majesties', so, not surprisingly, it was decided to take all the provisions and supplies from England.

The detailed list covers many of the stores found within the *Mary Rose* today, including '6000 arrows in 120 chests, 3000 bows in 64 chests, lanterns, tallow candles, spare axle trees and carriage wheels'. The nameless fighting men, including the ten archers supplied by Sir Thomas Wryothesley, Constable of Portchester and Lieutenant of the Forest of South Bere, may have been the cousins or brothers of the archers and soldiers who drowned on board the *Mary Rose* less than a year later.

The campaign in France culminated in the capture of Boulogne, providing Henry with a second port from which to control the Channel – but within four days Charles V had concluded a separate peace treaty and Henry was left to fortify the town against seige and withdraw his navy for the winter.

In the spring of 1545 Henry stood alone and Francis I began to assemble a fleet for the invasion of England. The French plan was clear: to attack Portsmouth, the premier naval base on the south coast, and cut off essential supply lines to Boulogne. In order to do this a major naval force had to be assembled in the estuary of the Seine between Le Havre and Honfleur, and in June Henry sent two task forces across the Channel in an abortive attempt to destroy the newly-assembled French fleet. By July the French fleet was ready, fully-equipped and loaded with 30,000 men, ready to attack Portsmouth and to destroy the King's ships in their own anchorage; at the same time Marshal de Briez with a land army was ordered to recapture Boulogne. The attack was to be on two fronts, by land and by sea, with the recapture of Boulogne the real objective in both cases and on 6 July Francis I dined on board the French flagship, the 800-ton *Carraquon*, and went ashore to watch his fleet leave the anchorage. The disaster that followed may have been the direct result of that farewell dinner party. Fire spread through the ship, probably from the galley, and the French Admiral – Claude d'Annebault, Baron de Retz, Admiral of France, Marshal of France and Governor of Normandy – had to beat a hasty retreat before the guns began to explode and the ship to burst into flames.

Abandoning the *Carraquon*, the Admiral established himself in another carrack, *La Maitresse*, but once more mishap caused a new disaster when the *Maitresse* grounded near Honfleur. However, the fleet finally left the anchorage and after a fair passage across the Channel dropped anchor in St Helens Roads on the north-east corner of the Isle of Wight on Saturday 18 July.

A portrait by Holbein of Sir George Carew, the Vice Admiral who drowned on board the Mary Rose.

Henry had good intelligence reports of the threatened invasion and
he was in Portsmouth from 15 July as Commander-in-Chief of the
army and navy. On land the defences were prepared and Henry controlled the action from a headquarters close to the tented army
encampment clustered around Southsea Castle. There Charles Brandon, the King's brother-in-law, prepared his men to repel any land-
ings should the French breech the sea defences or land on the marshy
low ground around Langstone harbour. Barely 60 ships, carracks,
galliasses and galleys waited in Portsmouth harbour under the command of John Dudley, Viscount Lisle, Admiral of England; but the
defensive position was good. The channel into Portsmouth harbour
winds close to the shore at the harbour mouth following the bed of an
ancient river system and it is bounded by vast areas of shallow water
with Spit Bank, Horse Sands and No Mans Land Sands on either side
all the way from St Helens Roads where the French fleet lay an anchor.
In front of the entrance itself lay the 'Spyte', or the Hamilton Bank,
where many an unwary yachtsman goes aground today, and with the
great gun batteries at Southsea Castle, the Square Tower and the
Round Tower commanding the deep water channel from the shore,

*The eighteenth century Cowdray
engraving representing the scene in
the Solent on 19 July 1545 when
the Mary Rose sank. (The
original contemporary painting in
Cowdray House was destroyed by
fire a few years after the engraving
was commissioned by the Society of
Antiquaries.) The main French
invasion fleet is lying off St Helens
(at the top left of the picture) but
four small galleys have gone
forward to engage King Henry's
flagship the Henry Grace à
Dieu. Few of the ships carry much
sail and the weather is described as
'light airs', but in the centre of the
picture the Mary Rose can be seen
sinking rapidly, with only two
masts and fighting tops above the
water. Henry VIII is on his horse
just to the right of the castle
entrance, richly clothed in cloth of
gold and velvet*

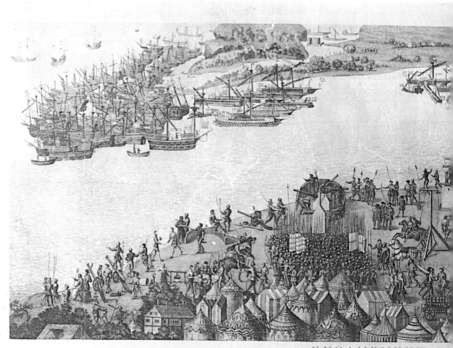

THE ENCAMPMENT OF
TOGETHER WITH A VIEW OF THE ENGLISH AND FRENCH
ENGRAVED FROM A COEVAL PAINTING

Henry had only to sit tight and draw the enemy onto the shallows or within range of the gun batteries.

While he was playing a waiting game, Henry's reinforcement of 60 ships were under way from the Thames and from ports in the West Country, but even when his forces were complete Henry's fleet of 100 ships and 12,000 men would be outmatched and outmanned by the French fleet of 225 ships with 30,000 soldiers. The strategy had to be defensive and after dining with his senior captains on board the flagship, the *Henry Grace à Dieu*, the King gave his Admiral, Lord Lisle, and his Vice-Admiral, Sir George Carew, their orders and placed a gold whistle on a chain around Sir George's neck as his badge of office.[23] Shortly afterwards a lookout reported a large number of sails which he supposed to be men-of-war and the King bade his captains farewell and left for the shore, leaving each commander to report to his own ship and his own duties.

As the English fleet left the harbour they passed fortifications which have changed very little to the present day. As we go out to the excavation site a mile away in our small twelve-man tender we can half close our eyes in order to exclude the modern monuments to mammon

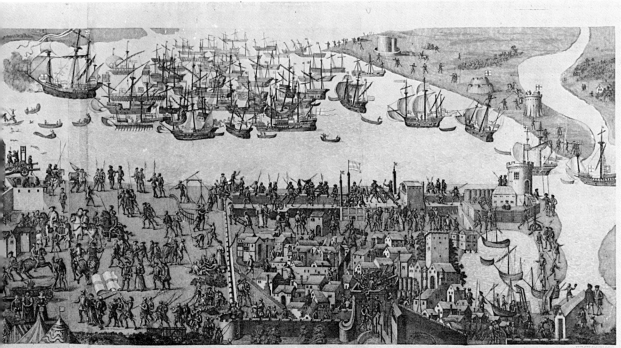

NGLISH FORCES NEAR PORTSMOUTH,
'S AT THE COMMENCEMENT OF THE ACTION BETWEEN THEM ON THE XIX.TH OF JULY MDXLV.
SUSSEX THE SEAT OF THE RIGHT HONOURABLE ANTHONY BROWNE LORD VISCOUNT MONTAGUE

A modern view of Portsmouth harbour and Spithead, where the Mary Rose *sank, taken from Portsdown Hill.*

and the municipal blocks of flats and see again the mellow lines of the fortifications and the higgledy-piggledy cluster of ale-houses around Portsmouth Point. Doubtless friends and sweethearts clustered on the beach below the urban ramparts just as they did 400 years later in 1945.

Once through the harbour entrance and abreast of the castle, the English fleet turned south with Spit Sand to starboard and Horse Sands to port. Today the channel is well marked with buoys just as it was in Henry's day, but to confuse the enemy those vital buoys had been removed and the English pilots had to rely on their local knowledge and information provided by their leadsmen. Sir John Oglander, the deputy Governor of Portsmouth, writing in 1610 described the battle that day as 'a little skirmish between our ships being in number 60 but it is true we were too weak and withdrew to the Horse.'[24]

The Solent area and the site of the Mary Rose excavation.

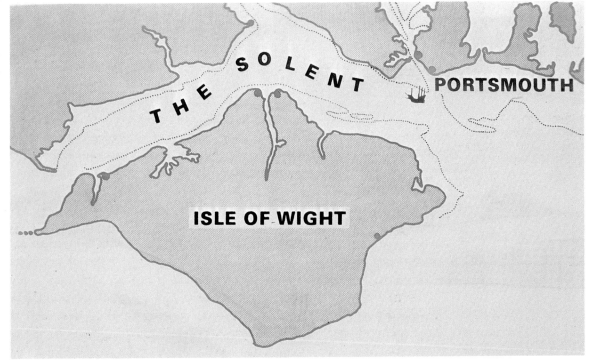

Gawin Carow.   Knight.

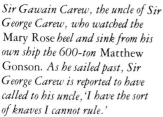

Sir Gawain Carew, the uncle of Sir George Carew, who watched the Mary Rose *heel and sink from his own ship the 600-ton* Matthew Gonson. *As he sailed past, Sir George Carew is reported to have called to his uncle, 'I have the sort of knaves I cannot rule.'*

Sieur Martin du Bellay, an officer with the cavalry force embarked in the invasion fleet, reported: 'After a long fight with gunshot the enemy began to slip to the left to the shelter of the land. This was the place where the ships were defended by a few forts which stood on the cliff behind them and on the other side by hidden shoals and rocks, with only a narrow and oblique entrance for a few ships at a time. This withdrawal and the approaching night put an end to the first day's fighting without our having suffered notable loss from their cannon shot.'

The following day, 19 July, was calm and still, and the English carracks were immobilised with scarcely a breath of wind to fill a sail. D'Annebault, the French Admiral, ordered his galleys to advance upon the English ships but as the morning wore on an offshore breeze sprung up and the carracks began to hoist sail. Lediard in his *Naval History* records D'Annebault's version of events:

It was ordered that at daybreak the galleys should advance upon the British whilst at anchor and, by firing at them with all fury, provoke them into engagement and then retreating endeavour to draw them out of their hold towards the main battle. This order was executed with a great deal of intrepidity and the weather favoured our attempt beyond our wishes for it was proven in the morning a perfect calm. Our galleys had all the advantages of working which we could desire to the great damage of the English who for want of wind not being able to stir laid exposed to our cannon and being so much higher and bulkier than our galleys hardly a shot missed them while they, with the help of their oars, shifted at pleasure, and thereby avoided the danger of the enemy's artillery. Fortune favoured our fleet in this manner for above an hour during which time, among other damages the English received, the *Mary Rose*, one of their principal ships, was sunk by our cannon and of 5 or 600 men which were on board only 5 and 30 escaped.[25]

This account differs widely from the contemporary English versions of the action, notably that of Sir Peter Carew, who wrote in his memoirs a full description of the action between the English and the French fleets off Portsmouth.

The King who upon hearing the news thereof [the arrival of the French fleet] was come to Portsmouth he fretted and his teeth stood on an edge to see the bravery of his enemies who come so near his nose and he not able to encounter with them, whereof immediately the beacons were set on fire throughout the whole coasts and forthwith such was resort of the people as was sufficient to guard the land from the entrance of the Frenchmen. Likewise commandments were sent to all the King's ships and all other ships of war which were at London and at Queenborough and elsewhere that they should with all speed possible make haste and come to Portsmouth, which things were accordingly performed. The King as soon as his whole fleet was come together willed them to set things in order and to go to sea, which things being done and every ship cross sailed and every captain knowing his charge it was the King's pleasure to appoint Sir George Carew to be Vice Admiral of that journey and had appointed him to a ship named the *Mary Rose* which was as fine a ship as strong and as well appointed as none better in the realm, and at their departure the King dined onboard with the Lord Admiral, Sir George Carew, Sir Peter Carew and their uncle, Sir Gawain Carew and with such others only as were appointed to that voyage and service. The King being at dinner willed some one to go up to the top and see whether he could see anything on the seas but the word was no sooner spoken but that Peter Carew was as forward, and forthwith, climbing up to the top of the ships and there sitting the King asked of him what news who told him that his thoughts had sight of 3 or 4 ships but as he thought they were merchants, but it was not long but he ascried a great number and then he cried out to the King that there was he thought a fleet of men of war. The King then took up his boat and rowed to the land and every other captain went to his ship appointed under him. Sir George Carew being entered into his ship commanded every man to take his place and the sails to be hoist but as the same no sooner done than that the *Mary Rose* began to heel, that is to lean over to one side. Sir George Carew being in his own ship and seeing the same called for the master of his ship and told him thereof and asked him what it meant who answered that if she does heel she is like to be cast away. Then the said Sir Gawain passing by the *Mary Rose* called out to Sir George Carew asking him how he did, who answered he had the sort of knaves whom he could not rule and it was not long after that the said *Mary Rose* thus heeling more and more was drowned with 700 men which were in her with very few escaped. He had in the ship a 100 mariners, the worst of them being able to be master in the best ship within the realm, and those so maligned and distained one another that refusing to do that which they should do were careless to do that which they ought to do and so contending in envy perished in frowardness.[26]

Certainly the loss of the *Mary Rose* was sudden and unexpected. It would appear from the English accounts that while hoisting sail and getting under way to assist the *Henry Grace à Dieu,* which was being challenged by the mobile French galleys, she suddenly heeled while going about. Her gunports were open, her guns run forward ready for action. As soon as this happened water began to pour over the gunport sills and the inevitable loss of stability with the additional weight of the insurging water caused the heel to become a capsize. The *Mary Rose* went rapidly to the bottom and it would appear that less than 40 men were saved from her. Guns broke loose from their lashings, ballast and spare ammunition broke free from the lockers and poured across to the starboard side of the ship. The ship sank so rapidly that she embedded herself deeply into the soft upper sediments of the seabed until her keel rested on the intractable geological clay 2 to 3 metres below.

It was a great loss to the King, but the battle was inconclusive. The French withdrew to the Isle of Wight, where they entered Brading, Sandown and Bonchurch and set fire to some village houses. There was a great loss of life, but the Isle of Wight militia and the Hampshire militia were able to defend themselves sufficiently and what might have been an invasion, became a skirmish. The French fleet then withdrew from the Isle of Wight without effecting a fully-manned landing, attacked Seaford, causing some casualties, and finally sailed back across the Channel. The potentially great and bloody invasion had been reduced to a skirmish at sea, with a few raids of nuisance and attrition.

CHAPTER 2

The Search for the Ship

IMMEDIATELY AFTER the *Mary Rose* sank, naval and military commanders Viscount Lisle, the Lord Admiral, and Charles Brandon, the Duke of Suffolk, were faced with two tasks: firstly to explain why she had sunk; and secondly to recover the hull as quickly as possible. The first task was relatively easy and the eye-witness account of Sir Peter Carew and Lord Russell's letter to Sir William Paget paved the way to a general verdict of 'indiscipline and mishandling', although Walter Raleigh, years later, attributed the disaster mainly to a design fault and the fact that there was too little freeboard between the lower gunport sills and the water.[1] Archaeological evidence shows that the lower ports were certainly open and the lids were lashed upwards against the side of the hull when the ship sank and this certainly could have been a contributory factor.

The second, and much more formidable, task was delegated to the Venetians Peter de Andreas and Simon de Marine who received 40 marks from the Treasurer of the Chamber for their efforts in trying to recover the sunken ship from the seabed. The proposed salvage was put in hand immediately and Charles Brandon, the King's brother-in-law,

The Jesus of Lubeck *(700 tons) from the Anthony Roll portrait 1546. Although rated as the same capacity as the* Mary Rose, *the* Jesus of Lubeck *carried fewer guns and longbows and 110 fewer soldiers and mariners, and with only 6 bronze guns against the 15 listed in the* Mary Rose *inventory she may have been more stable. In 1545 the empty ships* Jesus *and the* Samson *were used as hulks in an attempt to salvage the* Mary Rose *by attaching ropes to her at low water and lifting her from the seabed on the rising tide. In September 1567, dismasted and leaking badly, the* Jesus *was captured by the Spanish from John Hawkins at San Juan de Ulva and sold for 601 Ducats as unseaworthy.*

in a letter to Sir William Paget dated 1 August, only twelve days after the disaster, listed the equipment needed to raise the vessel:

Charles Brandon, Duke of Suffolk, to Sir William Paget, Secretary of State, Portsmouth, 1 August 1545.

As for concerning *Mary Rose*, we have consulted and spoken together with them that have taken upon them to recover her and are desirous to have for the saving of her, such neccessaries are mentioned in the schedule herein enclosed; not doubting, God willing, but that they shall have all things ready accordingly, so that shortly she shall be saved. A remembrance of things necessary for recovery, with the help of God, of the *Mary Rose*:

First: Two of the greatest hulkes that may be gotten; more [of] the hulkes that rideth within the haven.

Item: Four of the greatest hoys within the haven.

Item: Five of the greatest cables that may be had.

Item: Ten great hawsers.

Item: New capstans with twenty pulleys.

Item: Fifty pulleys bound with iron.

Item: Five dozen ballast baskets.

Item: Forty tons of tallow.

Item: Thirty Venetian maryners and one Venetian carpenter.

Item: Sixty English maryners to attend upon them.

Item: A great quantity of cordage of all sorts.

Item: Symond, patron and master in *Foyst*, doth agree that all things must be had for the purpose aforesaid.

Charles Brandon's confidence in his method must have cheered the King. In another letter of the same date Brandon says, 'I trust by Monday or Tuesday at the furthest the *Mary Rose* shall be weighed up and saved. There be two hulkes, cables, pulleys and other things made ready for weighing her.' The plan was feasible and it had been used many times before to lift vessels in shallow tidal waters. Two empty ships, each of 700 tons burthen, the *Jesus of Lubeck* and *Samson*, were moored on either side of the *Mary Rose* and secured to her by strong cables. At low water the cables would be hauled tight on the capstans and as the tide rose the buoyant empty ships would rise with it, bringing the *Mary Rose* off the bottom. This salvage method is gentle and controllable in calm weather, and conditions on the *Mary Rose* site are ideal with relatively weak currents even at high tide and a tidal range of 14ft (4.25m) on the spring tides. By 1 August all was ready and on 5 August the sails, rigging and yards were ashore and three cables had been tied to the masts. On 9 August Viscount Lisle reported that the Venetian salvors had asked for six more days to try and drag the vessel into shallower water. It may be that during these operations the mainmast was torn out of the mast-step in the keelson. Certainly it is clear from the stratified sediments inside the hull that the mainmast was

OPPOSITE

An artist's impression of what the ship may have looked like at the beginning of the seventeenth century. When the Mary Rose *sank the momentum carried the hull through the light upper sediments and the keel settled on the intractable geological clay. Immediately the silt-laden currents carried fine sediments into the hull through the open gunports and settlement occurred within the calm waters inside the hull. At the same time currents hit the exposed upper hull, vortexing and eddying around the protecting superstructure, and scouring away a moat or scourpit in the seabed on the port side of the hull. A shallow scourpit was also found beneath the sterncastle on the starboard side of the ship but this quickly filled with fine sediments which smothered and killed the developing young oysters on the outside of the hull. After several decades of tidal attack, the exposed hull structure became weakened by the attrition of the silt-laden tides and it collapsed into the scourpits around the ship. Once this obstruction was removed the currents could flow freely across the relatively flat site and although minor scourpits were found from time to time around individual deck beams or frames, the site remained stable until archaeological excavation began in 1971.*

torn out very soon after the ship sank and well before the hull filled with silt. If this is so it would explain why attempts to salvage the hull were abandoned. Unless swimmers could attach cables to a secure fastening, salvage was not possible and with the loss of the mainmast the main point of attachment was gone. The ideal method would have been to pass cables underneath the hull but this was probably beyond their abilities, although a lung dive to the seabed was well within the capabilities of a Mediterranean sponge fisherman – and a large cable found during excavations beneath the hull in the summer of 1982 may have been placed there by the Venetian salvors. Individual items including guns were recovered during the next four years and in 1547 and again in 1549 payments amounting to £107 11s 5d were made to Peter Paul, an Italian, for recovering guns from the ship. After this, all attempts to salvage the ship or her contents were abandoned, but the ship was not forgotten and the Elizabethan Admiral, Sir William Monsom, reported that he saw part of the ship 'with his own eyes'. Archaeological evidence shows that the ship lay heeled at 60 degrees from the vertical with the port side uppermost and Monsom may well have seen the upper works of the port side through the clear sparkling waters of the sixteenth century unpolluted Solent.

NINETEENTH CENTURY SALVAGE

A contemporary painting of John and Charles Deane working on the wreck of the Royal George *which foundered at Spithead in 1782. The Deanes operated as 'submarine engineers' all round the south coast of Britain, salvaging and demolishing underwater wrecks. While working on the wreck of the* Royal George *they were invited by some local fishermen to investigate a new area where their lines frequently snagged on an underwater obstruction. A brief inspection revealed the tops of eroded ancient timbers and from the seabed the Deanes recovered guns and other objects dating from the middle of the sixteenth century.*

After the abortive attempts to raise the hull in the sixteenth century the *Mary Rose* lay abandoned. Gradually over the next 150 years the structure exposed above the seabed collapsed and the site was forgotten. Shells and gravel settled over the site to form a compact seabed through which from time to time the tops of the timbers were exposed, covered and re-exposed. It was one of these chance exposures that led to the rediscovery of the wreck by John and Charles Deane in 1836. The Deanes were pioneers: sons of a Deptford shipbuilder who had patented a breathing apparatus for use in fire-fighting after successfully using the helmet from a suit of armour and air piped into the helmet from a hand pump to rescue a group of horses trapped in a burning barn. Deane's patented helmet, pump and fire-fighting suit became the basis of the open diving helmet and standard diving dress. By 1836 they had considerable experience in marine salvage and demolition using a suit perfected in 1828. The diving apparatus consisted of an open helmet, supported on the diver's shoulders and weighted back and front by heavy weights which could be jettisoned in an emergency. Air was

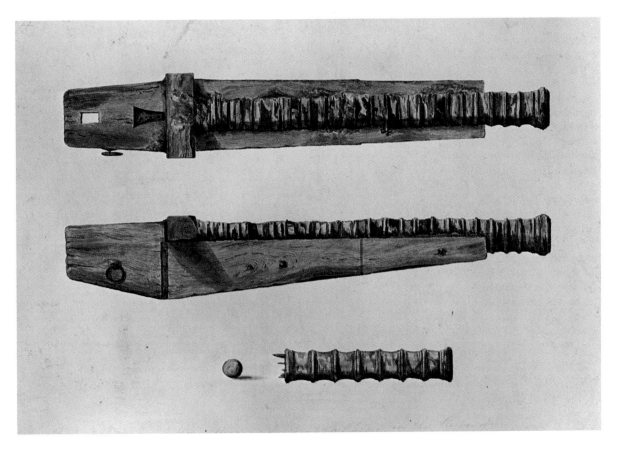

introduced into the helmet via a hose from a pump on the deck of the surface support vessel and the diver wore a rubber undersuit of Mackintosh's patent waterproof cloth beneath heavy calico trousers and jacket. Heavy boots completed the kit and the diver was warm, dry and able to breathe with ease as long as he stayed upright, as Colonel C W Pasley, Royal Engineers, reported to the Inspector General of Fortifications in 1840:

> Whilst the diver's head is upright or nearly so the helmet acts as a portable diving bell and the water cannot possibly get in by the bottom of it though open on account of the compressed air above . . . but Deane's apparatus which is the simplest of all, though very efficient for common purposes and highly approved by many of the best divers, does not admit of a man lying down or stooping with his head lower than his body without the risk of his helmet filling with water and if he should by accident or by neglect of his assistants fall over into a hole or down from the side of a wreck head foremost he will be drowned if not hauled up immediately.

All of the finds recovered by the Deanes were meticulously recorded in watercolour paintings and they included stave-built guns of wrought iron still mounted on the beds of their carriages (one is shown here). Modern excavation has shown that the Deanes never penetrated within the hull of the ship and all the objects they recovered must have come from the collapsed port side of the ship.

The erosion pattern (1)

After the ship sank, it lay on its starboard side at 60 degrees from the vertical and current-born silt was deposited in the relatively calm water within the hull. The ship lay broadside to the strongest currents which run from the east and from the west interspersed by minor currents from the north-east and south-west. As these currents hit the hull exposed above the seabed, they vortexed and eroded a deep wide scourpit on the port side and a narrow scourpit on the starboard side of the hull. The starboard scourpit quickly filled with silt and young oysters which had settled on the exposed hull were smothered and killed. The portside scourpit remained open for much longer and the planks and frames were thinned and weakened by the abrasive action of the silt-laden currents.

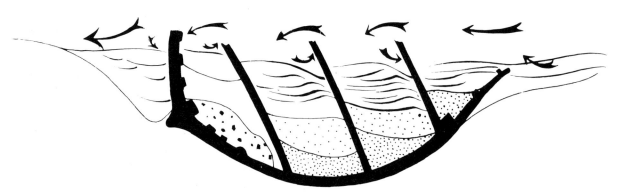

The erosion pattern (2)

After a period of time, the exposed upper structure became so weak that it collapsed downwards, filling the scourpits and thereafter only small secondary scourpits were formed around the ends of the deck beams and the tops of the eroded frames.

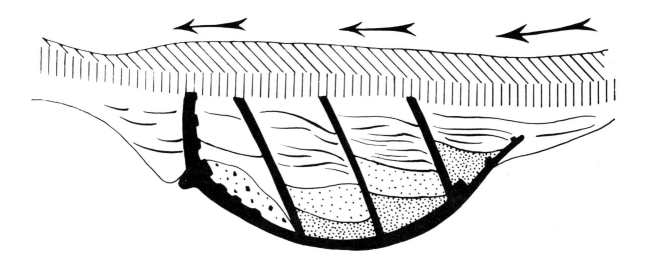

From 1832 the Deanes based their business as 'submarine engineers' in the Portsmouth area and in 1836, while they were working on the wreck of the *Royal George* which had sunk 54 years before in 75ft (23m) of water at Spithead, they were invited by some local fishermen to investigate an area where their lines frequently tangled in some seabed obstruction. On 16 June they dived on the site of the obstruction and found some old timbers protruding from the seabed, which they described as sand to the local historian Horsey. They also found to their delight a large bronze gun 11ft (3.4m) long with a bore of 6.4in (0.16m). In August John Deane brought up three more guns reporting that he had found them resting on 'some wreck completely buried in sand'. All the finds were handed over to the Board of Ordnance, who set up a Committee under the chairmanship of Major General Sir William Miller to decide the identity of the wreck from which the guns had come. In September the Committee reported:

On the whole subject it appears quite certain that the *Mary Rose* was lost at Spithead and that the ship was never weighed up and from the description of the guns lately discovered there is every reason to suppose that they

The erosion pattern (3)
A hard layer of shelly clay was deposited over the site, sealing the Tudor levels, some time in the late seventeenth century or early eighteenth century and above this a mobile 'modern' seabed was formed which was wholly or partially removed from time to time. It was probably as a result of one of these temporary exposures that the Mary Rose *was discovered in 1836, and rediscovered in 1971.*

formed part of her armament. It may fairly be presumed therefore if the wreck the guns were lying on could be displaced in some degree that more guns and other articles of an interesting character might be discovered and weighed up. Indeed the same observation holds good with regards to the *Edgar* and other vessels that have perished in the sudden and violent manner in shallow water to which it would be advisable that the attentions of Mr Deane be called and that every encouragement be given to him.

William Miller, Major General, Woolwich, 30 September 1836.

The Deanes received the full scrap metal price of £220 19s for the brass demi-cannon recovered on 16 June but clearly the thought of clearing sand and silt on the chance of recovering more guns did not encourage them to spend very much more time on the wreck. On 5 December 1840 Deane and William Edwards, the owner of the smack *Mary*, reported to the Ordnance Board: 'In accordance with authority and privilege granted to us by the Lords Commissioners of the Admiralty and approved by your Honourable Board we have at various favoured intervals pursued our diving operations in searching and surveying the place where the *Mary Rose* is supposed to have sunk at Spithead and we have the honour and satisfaction of acquainting your Honourable Board that our exertions have at length been crowned with success.'

During the intervening four years Deane had recovered wrought iron breech-loading guns, cast muzzle-loading brass guns, yew longbows, pottery, cloth, several human skulls and a variety of timber. He requested and received six unserviceable 13in bombshells to enable him to blow a crater in the seabed to expose more of the wreck and on

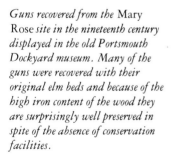

Guns recovered from the Mary Rose *site in the nineteenth century displayed in the old Portsmouth Dockyard museum. Many of the guns were recovered with their original elm beds and because of the high iron content of the wood they are surprisingly well preserved in spite of the absence of conservation facilities.*

30 October he reported that he had recovered two more large iron guns and parts of several others and that they were discontinuing operations on the site. Horsey relates, 'Mr Deane with a spade, shovel, etc, then excavated a portion of the sand and fired a charge of gunpowder and found on descending again that he had got into the hold of the unfortunate ship, having made a crater of large dimensions by this explosion.' Unfortunately for him and fortunately for us this cannot be true. Either Horsey misunderstood what he was told or Deane was exaggerating. The hard shelly clay which underlies the mobile upper sediments and seals the Tudor levels is unbroken by either crater or spade. Clearly the Deanes recovered the broken-up redeposited material from the port side of the hull. The absence of axles, wheels and trucked carriages suggests that the guns lay as they fell on the seabed when the superstructure broke up and the evidence of the sealing layer of hard shelly clay over the stratified Tudor levels is indisputable.

In 1836 the Deanes saw what we saw in 1976 — a few timbers protruding from the seabed, softened and eroded by exposure and re-exposure at intervals over 400 years, but well-preserved below the seabed level and surrounded by an incoherent jumble of eroded super-structure, human bones, stone shot, glass bottles and heavily-concreted negative casts of lost iron fastenings. I believe that the guns recovered in the nineteenth century were the ordnance from the port side of the ship collapsed down into the silts of the mobile seabed and lying on the hard shelly clay. There are some records by historians that after the Deanes ceased work on the *Mary Rose* in 1840 she was successfully blown up by Colonel Pasley's team of Sappers in 1844, but this story can also be dismissed. The ship lies, as she always has, on her side and is well preserved below the seabed level, but with the upper timbers so weakened by biological attack in the sixteenth and seventeenth cen-turies that eventually they were swept away by the tides of time so that by 1971 only a cut-away half section of the hull remained preserved in the mud.

THE SEARCH 1965–1971

In 1965 Alexander McKee, a journalist and amateur diver, invited a group of divers from the Southsea branch of the British Sub-Aqua Club to join him on 'Project Solent Ships', which was designed to discover and survey several known and well-documented historic wrecks which lie beneath the murky waters of the Solent.

The team consisted of well-trained and experienced divers but none of them had any archaeological experience beyond a survey of an im-mersed land site at Church Rocks, Hayling Island. Their inexperience

Alexander McKee and members of the 'Fire Brigade' team, 1968. In the 1960s the Mary Rose *team hired fishing vessels to visit the site and 'excavation' was done using water jets to remove the over-burden of silts from the area where the ship was believed to lie.*

made them cautious and very properly they limited their initial programme to diving and recording what they saw. There were no plans to excavate or to survey – just to look and learn. I was invited to join the team as a non-diving archaeologist and I was desperately keen to see if it was possible to work underwater and to record in a manner which would be acceptable to conventional land archaeologists. At that time I was heavily committed to a series of excavations of Roman sites at Fish-bourne and Chichester, but since work on 'Project Solent Ships' only happened on one or two days on alternate weekends during the summer months I was easily able to get away from my dusty land sites to tackle the problems of objective recording underwater.

At that time it was widely believed that in the tidal waters of the coast of Great Britain wrecks were unlikely to be well-preserved. Alexander McKee and I did not believe this was necessarily so. If we had strong tides to contend with then we also had plenty of mud in the harbours and estuaries of Chichester, Portsmouth and Southampton Water and I rather hoped that in these conditions the ship might dig her own grave in much the same way as a pebble on the beach. The tides scour out a moat or a scourpit around any obstruction above the seabed level, undercutting and eroding the supporting muds beneath any overhanging structure. Gradually the solid mass settles down into the pit and once the mass is below the seabed the whole situation stabilises and the wreck remains concealed by the silts and the muds. The lack of oxygen which then occurs halts or slows down the process of micro-biological degradation by aerobic organisms which are mainly responsible for the decay of organic materials.

'Project Solent Ships' was designed to examine several wrecks ranging in date from the sixteenth century to yesterday and to record in detail what had happened to them. As a journalist McKee was the ideal man to lead an operation of this type. He had imagination, energy and the enthusiasm to recruit a multi-discipline team and inspire them to persevere with what was a pretty unglamorous project in spite of the obvious lure of superb diving conditions only 60 miles away down the coast to the west.

At first all our attention concentrated on the *Royal George,* a First Rate ship of the line with 108 guns which sank with disastrous loss of life at Spithead in 1782. Another target was the *Boyne,* a Second Rate ship carrying 98 guns which sank in relatively shallow water on the eastern side of the main channel leading into Portsmouth. Both of these ships were researched and each had a well-documented history of sinking, salvage and demolition. The *Boyne* had blown up, and burnt down to the waterline before she sank in 1795 and 37 years later both Abbinett and Deane had carried out the salvage work on the wreck. In spite of this, when the *Mary Rose* team of divers dived on her they reported a mound of seaweed-festooned wreckage 10ft (3m) high and about 200ft (60m) long.[2] Even today she is still marked by a wreck buoy and she is a considerable hazard to any boat that strays out of the deep water channel leading to the harbour entrance.

The *Royal George* proved to be a very different proposition. She had sunk in 75ft (23m) of water and had been recognised by the Navy as a hazard in a naval anchorage and both the Deanes and Colonel Pasley of the Royal Engineers had worked on the wreck for several years until finally in 1843 Colonel Pasley reported that the site was now clear of wreck.[3] In spite of this extended programme of professional demolition McKee and his team found low mounds of wreckage on the site of the *Royal George* with fragments of eighteenth century pottery and ship's fittings recognisable in a linear series of mounds, some of them as much as 5–6ft above an otherwise level seabed. Around the ship on a relatively hard unyielding seabed lay the usual anchorage rubbish: teacups, egg-cups, boiler scale and cutlery. From these two surveys it was clear that evidence of wrecks could survive in the Solent in spite of the worst that man and currents could do to them.

Stage 2 of 'Project Solent Ships' according to McKee was 'therefore aimed primarily (but not entirely) at the *Mary Rose* and consisted of visual surveys without instruments of points within the logically indicated area which judging from markings on large scale charts might be

See p32-33.

wrecks or wreck mounds.'[4] What this meant in practice was using amateur divers to swim circuits either around an anchor chain or weighted marker or else swimming on a compass bearing in the area of charted mounds or depressions. Interpretation was difficult and imagination sometimes overpowering but a careful study of the Cowdray engraving and the contemporary accounts of the sinking suggested that the *Mary Rose* lay in shallow water within sight and sound of Southsea Castle. The King had heard the cries of her drowning sailors and it seemed unlikely that even on a calm day they would have carried very much further than the edge of Spit Sand. In February 1966 a chart compiled by Commander Sheringham in 1841 was found in the Hydrographer's Department of the Royal Navy by John Towse and McKee. The chart was clearly annotated with a red cross to mark the spot where the Deanes had discovered the *Mary Rose* five years earlier and where they had been working up until the previous autumn. The new site lay much closer to Southsea Castle than the site of the *Royal George* where the Deanes had been working when they discovered the *Mary Rose* in 1836. It lay on the extreme edge of Spit Sand in six fathoms of water at low tide. We could hardly wait to put divers down to explore the site but first we had to transfer the position on the Sheringham chart onto an up-to-date Admiralty chart. When this was done it was found to correspond with the edge of a scour or depression in the seabed.

In May McKee swam across the site with John Towse and noted that his compass behaved erratically and so in June we attempted to tow McKee across the area on a known compass course which should have taken him across the site marked on the chart and over the shallow depression. McKee swam down below with a compass and instructions to note if and where his compass began to behave erratically and to mark the site with a weighted marker. The operation was not very thorough because we had to change course several times as ferries and other boats came far too close for comfort, an all-too-common occurrence in the middle of the Solent. We needed more sophisticated gadgetry than a pair of eyes and a pocket compass if we were ever going to find the *Mary Rose*. After abortive prospecting with an underwater magnetometer which did reveal an uncharted buried cable but failed to locate the

Professor Harold Edgerton of Massachusetts Institute of Technology reading the chart of sub-bottom and side scan sonar readings as we passed over the site of the Mary Rose *in July 1968.*

Photograph of a sonar trace over the site of the Mary Rose *using sub-bottom sonar operating at 5k/c. The profiler revealed a W-shaped anomaly beneath the surface of the seabed and above the anomaly, a slight mound. On the basis of this evidence the Mary Rose (1967) Committee obtained a lease to the seabed from the Crown Estate Commissioners in order to protect the site from trespassers. Three years later the timbers of the hull were seen for the first time as a result of a tidal scour which removed some of the soft modern silts from the port side of the ship.*

totally buried hull, the real breakthrough came in 1967 when Professor Harold Edgerton's company E G & G International were demonstrating a dual channel side-scanner with a range of up to 1000ft (300m) and combined with a sonar 'pinger' capable of recording the sub-mud sediments. He was demonstrating this gear and equipment to potential customers but through the good offices of Joan du Plat Taylor, then the Honorary Secretary of the Council for Nautical Archaeology, McKee was invited to witness the trials and on the fourth and last day he persuaded John Mills, the English agent for E G & G International, to run the equipment over the supposed site of the *Mary Rose*.

The two sonar systems were complementary to each other; the side scan sent acoustic signals horizontally from each side of the mother vessel and those signals were reflected back to the transducer by disturbances in the seabed like mounds, depressions or obstructions. The 'pinger' or sub-bottom profiler sent acoustic signals vertically down from the mother vessel and they were reflected back from sub-mud clays, rock and even from buried ships! McKee recorded an anomaly 200ft (60m) long by 75ft (23m) wide buried 20ft (6m) below a mound which was 4–5ft (1.20–1.55m) high. The anomaly was on the right alignment and in the area where we believed the *Mary Rose* to lie but was it the *Mary Rose*? At the time we believed it was – indeed we even applied for a seabed lease from the Crown Estate Commissioners to protect our buried anomaly in civil law – but now I am not so sure. When the *Mary Rose* was finally seen in 1971 the slight mounds of the bow and the stern did not exceed 1 metre above the overall seabed level and a solid mass of wreckage and coherent ship's structure lay between the seabed and the lowest part of the keel at a depth of 15ft (4m) below that level. Is it possible that the sub-mud 'pinger' would have penetrated through the hull without reflecting back off these timbers and only reflected back off the compressed sediments below? The overall size of the wreck site including scourpits is 130ft × 65ft (40m × 20m) so the buried anomaly was larger than the ship itself. What could it have been?

It may simply have been a disturbance of the sub-mud sediments either caused by the ship or by some totally separate agency. Whatever it was it gave us the encouragement that we needed to continue the search and the following year we went back again to the site with Professor (Doc) Edgerton, John Mills and the latest generation of sub-bottom profilers. There were two systems: a 12 k/c (kilocycle) instrument which did not send signals very deeply into the sediments but which gave fine resolution and recorded great detail; and a 5 k/c instrument which sent deeply penetrating signals with some loss of

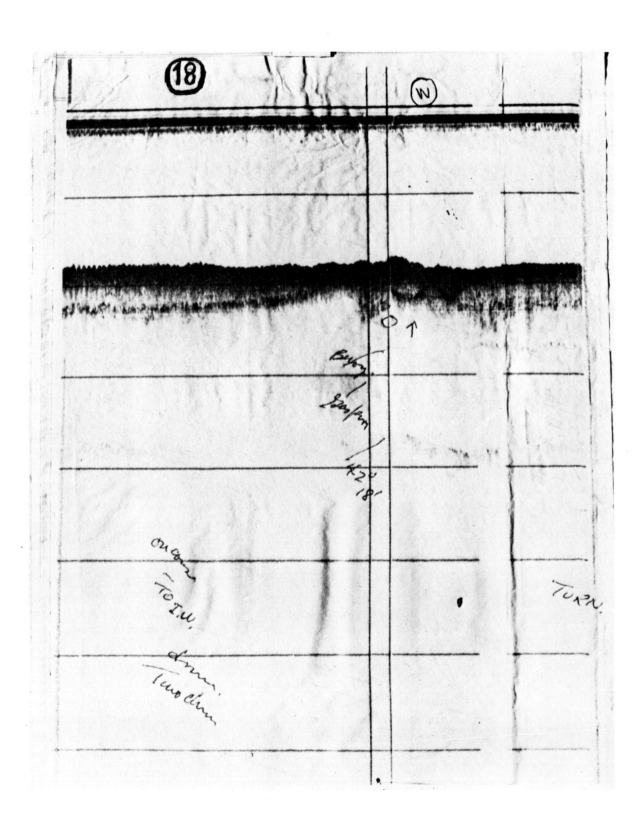

W O B Majer, Alexander McKee, Commander Alan Bax and Margaret Rule, the four original members of the Mary Rose (1967) Committee, signing a lease to the seabed where the wreck was believed to lie in 1967.

detail. Again we recorded the sub-bottom anomaly in the right place and even if it was not the right size it was at least too small to be dismissed simply as a geological feature.

The Mary Rose (1967) Committee was formed as a direct result of this sonar prospection with the aims 'to find, excavate, raise and preserve for all time such remains of the ship *Mary Rose* as may be of historical or archaeological interest.' Now with the seabed anomaly we became increasingly concerned lest pirate divers should jump our claim and even more concerned that their methods might not be as restrained as an archaeologist would wish. At that time, in 1967, there was no way we could protect the ship as a monument in the same way that sites are protected on land. The usual 'contract to salvage' was meaningless and was rejected by the Mary Rose (1967) Committee which at that time consisted of four members: Alexander McKee, the initiator of the project; Lieutenant Commander Alan Bax RN, then a serving officer who delighted in marine archaeology, now the Director of Fort Bovisand Underwater Centre and godfather to most underwater projects in the United Kingdom; W O B (Bill) Majer, who had spent most of his early childhood on a clipper ship, an ardent and scholarly modelmaker and a trustee of the Society for Nautical Research; and myself, a land archaeologist and a member of the Council for Nautical Archaeology. After some deliberation we applied to the Crown Estate Commissioners for a lease to the seabed area where our buried anomaly lay and the lease was duly granted on 1 April 1968 for an annual rental of £1. From 1968 until the Historic Wreck Act was passed through Parliament in 1973 the only legal protection of the *Mary Rose* site was the Crown Estate Commissioners' lease and the normal civil rights of lessees and salvors in possession.

Clearly litigation had to be avoided at all costs if we were to remain solvent and we relied heavily on the best protection of all: secrecy. The site was never marked by buoys until the passing of the Historic Wreck Act and occasional off-site markers were misleading to the uninformed. Relocation on site at the beginning of each diving day was done by means of line-of-sight transects to shore marks 1 to 3 miles away and, as McKee usually observed one set of marks and I observed the other, most people on board had no idea why we stopped when we did!

This was adequate protection until 1971, when the ship was exposed for the first time, because until then even if anyone had bothered to take a fix on our small fishing boat they would have had an unrewarding dive as a result. Even when the ship was found in 1971 the limited excavations to reveal the tops of the ribs at a mean seabed level would not have encouraged an entrepreneur to continue.

During 1969 and 1970 the volunteer divers used water jets to cut a trench through the seabed in the area where the anomaly had been recorded with the sub-mud profiler. The work was unrewarding and heavy going. Water jets operated in soft silts reduced the already poor visibility to zero and one section of black mud looked much like another. In the late autumn of 1970 when funds and enthusiasm were running low the barrel of a wrought iron gun was recovered by McKee using a mechanical excavator. Although it is clear now that it was recovered from an area of wreckage spill more than 150ft (45m) away from the wreck itself it caused a great deal of excitement at the time. An associated oak plank was also recovered and sampled and found to be mechanically strong, yielding both sawdust and shavings when cut into sample sections. It was however badly bored by gribble and a species of shipworm (*Nototeredo norvagica*) which showed that it had remained as wreckage on the surface of the seabed for some considerable time before becoming buried. The wood samples were used for conservation experiments in anticipation of conservation problems to come and the gun was removed to Southsea Castle to be conserved using electrolysis by the City Museum Keeper of Conservation, Chris O'Shea. See p169. After removal of the concreted shell of carbonate, silicate, shells and sand it was found to be the barrel of a wrought iron gun and, superficially at least, very similar to the ones recovered by the Deanes 130

In the early years of work on site many pleasure boats came too close to the diving area and a sharp watch had to be kept to prevent divers being 'run down' on the surface.

years before – but examination by gamma radiography showed it to be a very different gun indeed.

The barrel was formed from a single plate of wrought iron which had been formed into a cylindrical tube with a single seam along its length. The gun caused excitement, as guns always do, and the resulting publicity brought the committee a great deal of material help, in the form of boats, compressors, diving equipment and transport. Offers of help poured into the committee. Even more importantly the diving team were reinspired – it had been a long hard road with little to show for their efforts until the recovery of the gun. Now they hoped to find not isolated bits and pieces but the ship herself.

CONTACT AT LAST

Saturday 1 May 1971 was a bright sunny day with a fresh south-easterly breeze and a forecast of force five winds to come in the afternoon. Thirteen members of the team arrived at Flathouse Quay two miles north of the harbour entrance for the formal presentation of an Atlas Copco 'Silencair' compressor which we planned to use to power new air-lifts and underwater lights. The publicity of the gun recovery eight

THE SEARCH FOR THE SHIP

months previously had opened new doors and at last we had the necessary equipment to do a controlled excavation. A second timely gift, from Douglas Sharp on behalf of United Services Garages in Portsmouth, was a van to carry divers and portable gear to the quay each weekend.

An inevitable delay caused by publicity interviews and photographs for the local press meant a late start and we finally left the quay at 10.50 am. We were on site by 11.30 with a fresh south-easterly wind veering to the east whipping up white seahorses on the surface. This is the worst direction for winds on our site, which is sheltered from the north and the south but totally open to any winds from the east; but we decided to anchor on the Gosport marks and drop divers down the southern end of the last year's 'trench'.

The first diver was kitted up and in the water by twenty to twelve, and was charged with buoying the end of last year's trench. For this important job we chose our underwater bloodhound Percy Ackland, one of our most experienced divers and a man with an uncanny sense of location underwater. Following a brisk 'OK' signal, he went down the anchor rope to the bottom 40ft (12m) below and then, towing a multi-coloured buoy, he headed off towards Southsea. Fifteen minutes later, Percy, back on board, reported 'low visibility and strong currents – no sign of last year's trench'.

Alexander McKee suggested that he should try to pick up the old trench by doing a swim search in a north-westerly arc from the anchor. By my reckoning we seemed to be anchored well to the south of the old trench and by searching in a semi-circular arc from the anchor it should be possible to pick up the steel poles which had been used to mark the trench last year. I only hoped that they had not been dragged away by the heavy otter boards of an inshore trawler!

At noon Ackland was back in the water to return only six minutes later fizzing with controlled excitement. 'There's wreckage, including planking, sticking up from the mud', he muttered. We had found the *Mary Rose*!

The wreckage lay some 60ft (18m) south of the anchor and well to the south of the old JM3 trench excavated last year. Our task was now to buoy the wreckage so that we could fix its position with transects from the land and survey the exposed structure. Andy Gallagher, a fireman from Chichester, now had the task of fixing the position of the wreck, laying secure ground lines to the site from the anchor and delimiting the area of the wreckage. Curiously muddled reports followed as diver after diver examined the site: 'New site 40–60ft south of old trench'; 'Old trench 50ft NW of anchor'; 'Old trench has collapsed at one place and undercut an area of wreckage'. As reports flowed in, it became clear that a desire to relate the new discovery to the old JM3 trench was influencing reports and that a proper measured survey would have to be made as soon as possible. There was no time to waste – if this was a temporary exposure of the hull caused by winter tidal scour, it could be filled in on the next big spring tide.

Alan Baldwin, the Chairman and driving force of the Naval Air Command Sub-Aqua Club based at Fort Daedalus near Lee-on-Solent, dived with Barry Ballard and they reported 'large numbers of ends of timbers seen in a straight row, each one approximately 12in × 18in (0.30m × 0.45m) and protruding only 2–3in (0.05–0.08m) from the seabed. To the left of them is timber planking.'

Baldwin and I had a hurried discussion on deck and we agreed that the first task was to measure the size of each frame and the distance between each frame. As each timber was eroded to a pyramid by marine boring organisms, we agreed to clear the silt away to reveal an unweathered surface, then measure each timber from centreline to centreline. In the absence of anything more sophisticated, we used a 10ft (3m) tape discovered loitering in the bottom of my handbag and a polythene squash bottle as an underwater drawing board. Red nail varnish – also in the bottom of my handbag – was used to paint numbers on the hastily-cut plastic labels.

A compass bearing of 195 degrees seemed to confirm McKee's belief that the *Mary Rose* lay on a southerly heading, but there was no evidence to suggest whether the hull of the ship lay east or west of the line of timbers. In limited visibility of 4ft (1.2m), an overview was impossible and an anxiety to interpret the timbers in terms of hull structure coloured nearly every report. However, Ballard and Baldwin soldiered on and by ten past three in the afternoon, they had seen a continuous line of frame heads running at 195 degrees for 66ft (20m). A line of planking on edge was exposed at intervals on the eastern side of the frames and east of the planking the ends of three large timbers protruded from the mud. ·

McKee was as anxious as I was to lay a ground line from the new site to the old JM3 trench, but although Peter Powell and Reg Cloudesdale laid a line to the north-east and tied it to a 56lb weight and a stake in the old trench, it was never properly surveyed in 1971 as the desire to expose the tops of frames and understand the alignment of wreckage overwhelmed all other considerations.

In 1973 and 1979 a survey carried out on the bottom and with surface markers showed that the old JM3 trench lay 120ft (36.5m) NE of the wreck, but in 1971 we had to concentrate on recording the exposure of the wreck so unexpectedly offered to us. This survey continued throughout the day and at twenty to six we raised anchor and headed home – the *Mary Rose* had been found at last!

But what were the timbers we had seen? Were they the ribs of the main hull below the waterline, or, as we wanted to believe, the frames of the bowcastle? Was the line of planking inboard or outboard – was it ceiling planking or outer hull planking? In a total dive time of 6 hours 58 minutes, we had recorded 66ft (20m) of coherent structure, but it would be many weeks before we began to understand it. How I wished I could dive to see the hull for myself, but my training with Southampton Branch of the British Sub-Aqua Club was only just finished and I had to wait until 15 May to get my first glimpse of the seabed and the timbers of a Tudor carrack.

My first dive was a memorable three-minute dash to the seabed and back. After fumbling and fiddling with my new 'off-the-peg' 5mm neoprene wet suit, I struggled into harness, cylinder, weight belts and all the other paraphernalia that goes with SCUBA diving. Too many hands reached out to help and good cheer and advice poured out from everyone. With relief I held on to my mask, sat on the gunwale and fell backwards into the sea. Accompanied by Morrie Young who had spent so much time with Percy Ackland putting me through my pool

The 40ft catamaran Roger Grenville *from which the team worked between June 1971 and the advent of the* Sleipner *in 1979.*

training, I swam down the shot-line to timber 48. The gloomy layer of suspended sediment and plankton which floated like a curtain 9ft (3m) above the seabed gave way to 3ft (1m) visibility as we hit the bottom. A few rectangular timbers stood out 2–3in (0.05–0.08m) from the seabed – a seabed which fumed and smoked as I fanned the silts with my hand. What a perfect preservative is fine mud – could there really be a whole Tudor ship buried beneath me?

Morrie picked up a whelk and hand-in-hand we returned to the surface. I could not wait to get back and see more but there was a great deal of work to do. We had to rationalise the work programme so that excavation and survey could progress side by side, or at least nose to tail.

The answer at first seemed to be to work from two boats. McKee controlled a group of divers from Southsea and Southampton Branches of the British Sub-Aqua Club in the main boat. They used 4in airlifts and a large low power air compressor to remove the over-burden of silts which concealed the inter-relationship of the timbers. Meanwhile, Alan Baldwin and I huddled damply with Artie Shaw and others from NACSAC and the Chichester Branch of the BSAC in the Avon inflatable or on *High and Dry*, a 20ft (6m) cabin cruiser. Even this surface division of tasks failed to solve the basic problem of working underwater on the *Mary Rose* site. Visibility was bad – 3ft (1m) usually, sometimes 9ft (3m) and very rarely 20ft (6m).

This was our cross and at this early stage of operations, the presence of light seabed sediments all over the site added further complications as divers 'walking to work' carrying heavy gear across the seabed could, and often did, churn up a cloud of sediments which completely wiped out visibility for anyone trying to survey down-tide. McKee and I tried hard to ensure that the two teams did not interfere with each other, but by June, the survey team was basically working midweek to survey any timbers revealed by the excavation team the previous weekend.

As the summer progressed, the survey grew and it became clear that 'inboard' lay to the east of the line of frames – but were these frames part of the port or the starboard side of the ship? Only time and further excavation would tell.

By early June the last essential piece of equipment was in action. A 40ft (12m) catamaran *Roger Grenville* donated by Chichester businessman John Barber was christened by Mrs Gwen Holder, a descendant of Roger Grenville, the Captain of the *Mary Rose*, and launched at Flathouse Quay. Now we had room to work and a home for our Atlas Copco Compressor and other heavy equipment. *Roger Grenville* had one cabin with a calor gas burner for hot drinks, a bucket lavatory in a cupboard and a clear after-deck for excavation equipment and diver control. But it did not have any power – no engines and no sails – so we had to be towed to the site each day by our faithful fisherman friend Tony Glover. Tony would secure us to our moorings and then go about his business, picking us up as he returned to harbour in the early evening. Occasionally we would work the two boats together, but limited funds meant that we could not ask Tony too many favours. After all he had a living to earn whereas we were working in our spare time.

As work progressed throughout the summer of 1971, it became clear that our ability to excavate non-destructively underwater was limited by funds, resources and experience and we decided to concentrate our efforts on clearing away the silts from the edges of each timber to expose a 'fair face' and then draw it in plan and fix its relationship to adjacent and connecting timbers by trilateration or by measuring short distance offsets from an arbitrary straight datum pole secured to the heads of the frames.

As the alignment of the frames curved gently to the north-east, it was necessary to realign the tube as the survey line extended. Clearly any errors would accumulate along the line of frames and there was an artificial 'flattening' of the curvature of the tops of the frames seen in plan. However, long distance check measurements indicated that the survey was acceptable for the present purpose, which was to demonstrate how much hull remained intact buried in the seabed. It would have been easier and more accurate to erect a series of 'stations' to the east and the west of the timbers and then to measure the distances to each timber from at least three stations with a fibron tape. However, in the soft upper sediments heavy weights sank down into the mud with alarming rapidity while to use stakes ran the risk of damage to underlying structure or objects. Stakes had an additional disadvantage as they collected weed and toppled over in the strong westerly tide-runs.

Our primitive survey system in 1971 used only rudimentary survey equipment: 6m lengths of 0.05m diameter steel tubing, a 2m folding rule and a 10m length of fibron tape. The steel tubing was fixed over the heads of the frames with 2in (0.05m) nails and short distance measurements were taken centreline to centreline on each frame, and to the edges of the frames and the planks.

On 29 June our first major *in situ* artifact was found. Alan Baldwin's team exposed a wrought iron muzzle-loading gun lying 1ft (0.30m) below the seabed only 8ft (2.44m) from the first frame seen on the seabed. When I dived on the following Saturday, the light sediments had been removed by Baldwin at the southerly end of the line of frames to expose a heavily concreted iron gun 7ft 8in (2.33m) long lying on a layer of hard sediments. I remembered the guns recovered by the

Revealed by winter scour 1971

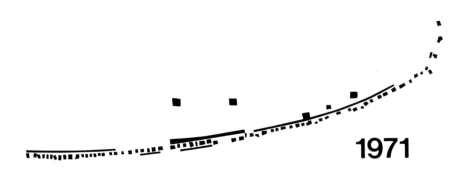

1971

Deanes in the 1830s: had they seen them like this, disassociated from the hull, dropped down from a gunport higher up the ship as the upper timbers of the hull disintegrated and collapsed? The hard sediment was puzzling. A compacted layer of clay with finely crushed oyster shell, it appeared to be impenetrable. Some members of the team argued that no ship could have sunk through such a hard sediment and that this was the Tudor seabed. Removal of the lighter sediments, usually 2ft 6in–3ft (0.7–1.0m) thick, revealed this hard grey shelly clay everywhere and if it *was* the Tudor seabed, then very little of the hull had survived.

The objects recovered from the upper silts also posed a problem. It was easy to understand the assemblage of nineteenth and twentieth century objects: clay pipes, wine bottles and Coke cans were easily explained – after all, we were excavating at No 3 Naval Anchorage in Spithead, one of the busiest anchorages in the world – but if we were working through the collapsed debris from a 700-ton Tudor carrack, why were we not finding more Tudor objects? A few eroded loose timbers, one gun and a couple of dubious sherds of pottery did not seem very much material for a ship which had eroded down almost to the level

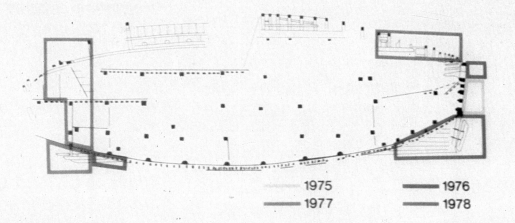

TRENCH GRIDS 1975-8

1975   1976
1977   1978

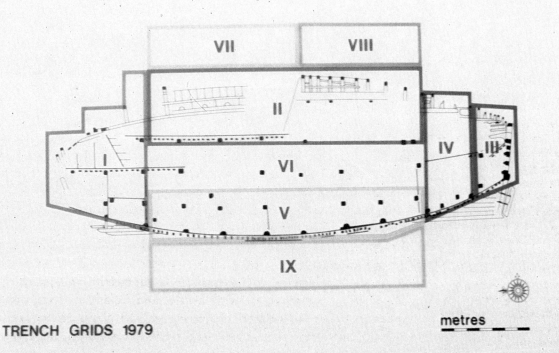

TRENCH GRIDS 1979

metres

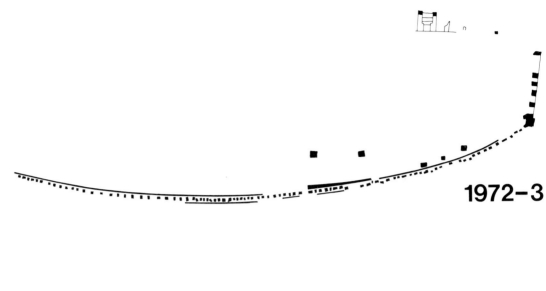

1972–3

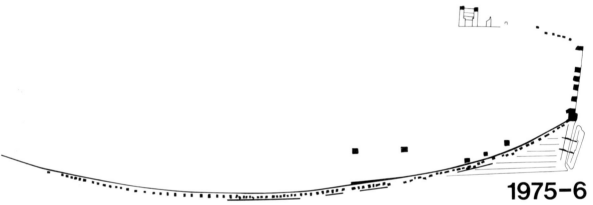

1975–6

of the seabed on which she rested. We decided to excavate a trench around timber 48, one of the large timbers found east of the main line of frames and planking. The timber had rebates in the north and south face and it appeared to be collapsed at an angle of 30 degrees from the horizontal and opinions varied about its function.

McKee and Young (a shipwright by trade) thought that the ship was on a southerly heading and that the planking east of the frames was outer hull planking. If this was so, then timber 48 had to be some sort of supporting brace for the chain-wales or the bowcastle. Young had reservations however, because it looked remarkably like a deck beam. In the absence of any other deck structure, it was difficult to be sure. Bill Majer, who had researched ships since his youth, agreed with the 'external brace' theory. I had an open mind and determined to cut a section across the frames and timber 48 to show their relationship (if any) to each other. The excavation was inconclusive: no coherent structure emerged; just frame, planking and an oblique detached timber with rebates for fore-and-aft timbers.

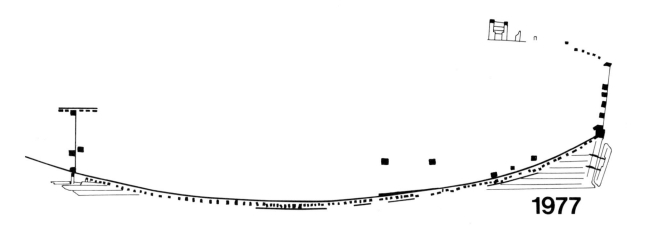

1977

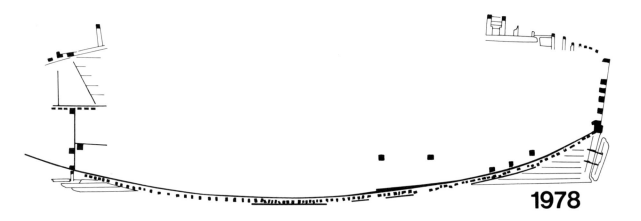

1978

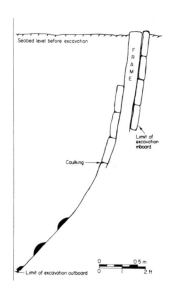

The next attempt to excavate a trench took place late in the season. A profile of frames, ceiling planking and outer hull planking, complete with semi-circular seam ribbands or chafing pieces, was revealed and surveyed to a depth of 3m (10ft) below the tops of the frames.[5] The removal of the hard shelly layer, previously thought to be impenetrable, revealed soft lenses of silts and muds with eroded hull planking aligned north and south in line with the hull. Fortunately by now I had inspected the 'impenetrable' hard shelly clay. Whatever it was, it was not Tudor seabed! The trench had to be abandoned without reaching any conclusive structure in November as underwater visibility was by then reduced to zero and water temperatures dropped to 10 degrees centigrade: too low for amateur divers in thin neoprene suits!

It was clear by now that west of the frames was 'outboard' and east was 'inboard'. The inboard collapsed timbers now looked more like deck beams than braces, but so far we had no coherent deck structure. The external carvel planking was well-preserved and the oak shone a warm brownish red in the light of a torch. The trenails which fastened the planks to the frames were tight and sound and often they could only be distinguished by a change in line of the grain of the wood. The profile outboard of frames 5 and 8 led Young to conclude that the hull was 'probably preserved to a height of 9.1m (35ft 8in) above the keel at this point.'

Our hopes rose: if he was right, we had a British *Wasa,* intact to the upper deck. As an archaeologist, I hoped he was right. What a unique opportunity to examine a sample of Tudor society, and if we could bring the hull into the sheltered waters of Portsmouth harbour to conduct the excavation in shallow water, we would be able to take our time unhindered by the constraints of decompression and no-stop dive tables! In 1972 we needed to examine the 'bow' at the southern end of the ship and determine the angle of heel.

1972–1978

During 1971 the discovery of timbers at seabed level had been a major step forward which lifted the *Mary Rose* project away from the casual charm of picnic-party archaeology. From a 'season' of 19 operational days on site in 1970 we went forward to accomplish 70 operational days in 1971 and the volunteer divers spent a total of 644 hours defining the shape of the timbers exposed on the seabed and measuring them.

During 1972 it was planned to spend 68 days on site and our main task was to determine the 'heading' of the ship and her angle of heel. A 33m (108ft) run of timbers was exposed on the west of the site and at the southern end of the ship a composite fashionpiece and the frames and planking of the transom were identified. It was obvious that the ship lay on a northerly heading with her bow pointed towards the 'swashway' and the entrance to Portsmouth harbour. It may be that a badly executed turn intended to bring her starboard battery of guns to bear on the enemy was the sole cause of her sinking, but even today after 11 years of excavation and survey the question of why the ship sank is still open.

On the starboard quarter a small section of frames and clinker planking was identified as the sterncastle. The light, overlapping planks, and the frames and standards which supported them, were eroded and fragile and with our limited resources it was agreed to back-fill the area with silt and leave further investigation until we could fund a major programme of work on site.

1973 was disastrous: bad weather, insufficient funds and, finally, after a late start, the loss of our diving platform during a gale in August, meant that only 12 days were spent excavating the site. During the following winter months spirits were low and we needed the enthusiasm

The Archaeological Director, Margaret Rule, and HRH Prince Charles, planning a proposed dive. From 1979 the project received the active and enthusiastic support of the Prince of Wales, who became the President of the Mary Rose Trust.

of the newly-formed support committee which had been established by the Lord Mayor of Portsmouth in September 1973 to inject new initiative into the project.

For the first time the Mary Rose (1967)Committee had a representative group of authoritative people to assist them and the four meetings held in 1973–74 were attended by City and County officers and members of the Council, representatives of major national and local companies, The National Maritime Museum, The Maritime Trust, the British Sub-Aqua Club, BBC (Chronicle) and the Commander in Chief Naval Home Command. During the year, the Committee had become a registered charity, which helped with raising funds, and the *Mary Rose* had become one of the first wrecks to be protected by law in the United Kingdom. No longer did we have to rely on a seabed lease to protect the site; the new Historic Wreck Act which received parliamentary approval in July 1973 empowered the Secretary of State for Trade to designate and protect wrecks of historic, archaeological or artistic importance.

The Committee had applied for designation and for a licence to survey, excavate and salvage the *Mary Rose* and the Advisory Committee established to advise the Minister had endorsed the application. Now at last we could carry our an archaeological programme without fear of trespass or obstruction and for the first time the site was marked with permanent markers.

In 1975 the transom and the port quarter were examined and the angle of the sternpost, rudder and deck beams showed conclusively that the ship lay on her starboard side at an angle of 60 degrees from the vertical. The stratified layers of silts, muds, and decomposed organic material in the scourpit outside the stern gave the first clear indication of how the upper portions of the wreck had broken up in the seventeenth century.

Working in almost impossible conditions with near-zero visibility, Keith Muckelroy (then a young archaeology graduate at Cambridge) and I cut clean sections through the silt and took samples of the silts and the 'seaweed' lenses home in ice cream cartons to re-excavate them in the controlled conditions of the kitchen sink! The seaweed lenses were mainly eel grass, which had compacted to form a series of dense organic layers, rather like turf lines in the infill of an ancient ditch on landsites. The lower levels of finely levigated, light-coloured silts were clean and contained no artifacts but the upper levels contained stone shot moulds, shot and other heavy objects, together with eroded portions of the rudder and wing-shaped pieces of eroded timber which had once been secured to the hull with an iron bolt. Countless small holes in the 'wings' bore witness to infestation by gribble (*Limnoria lignorum*), but the bolt hole itself was usually smooth and clean without any trace of the bolt. The migration of iron from the bolt in the wood was obvious from the colour change and the petrified appearance of the wood around the hole and it would seem that the high iron content had inhibited biological degradation.

In 1975 His Royal Highness Prince Charles, Prince of Wales, dived to inspect the wreck for the first time. It was a calm, sunny July day and the turbid underwater visibility, which had persisted for several days, cleared miraculously just before the Prince dived. He inspected the timbers on the port quarter by the light of a small hand torch and the red-brown wood glowed gently in the gloom. After a second dive to confirm his first impressions and a long chat with all the diving team His Royal Highness left to play polo at Cowdray Park near Midhurst.

The visit had been completely informal and a total success. Our small amateur group of dedicated 'Mary Rosers' felt new enthusiasm and our humble 40ft long catamaran no longer seemed so crowded and inadequate.

At the end of the first 'full season' of 74 days on site we had established an angle of heel and the intact junction of the sternpost and the starboard transom — all on a budget of £1200. With only our hard-working Hon Treasurer Jack Barrett to assist with on-shore management, it was quite some task to undertake in our spare time. In 1976 the budget rocketed, but it was still less than £5000 per annum and we excavated on site for 55 days between June and September. At the end of the season we had excavated what was then the world's

The lower planking of the 'Woolwich Ship' above, shows clearly the seam battens of the type found on the Mary Rose.

deepest archaeological excavation underwater, and exposed a length of the keel on the port quarter at a depth of 4m (13ft). The carvel planks of the port quarter were uneroded with the strakes still firmly attached to the frames by wedged trenails. All the lower seams were covered with rounded battens which had been fastened to the strakes with iron nails after caulking had been placed between the seams. Similar seam battens were found on the late medieval ship discovered on land at Woolwich in 1912 and thought to be the *Sovereign*. Two port lids were recovered from the portside scourpit and they had both been constructed from a 'sandwich' of horizontal outer planks and vertical inner planks banded together with tar and secured by a regular pattern of wrought iron spikes which had been turned over roves on the inside of the lid.[6] The inner face of the lid had been severely eroded but the outer face was fresh and uneroded. Clearly the lids had been bolted back against the side of the hull when the ship sank and they had remained in this position with the outer face protected from the scouring effect of current-borne sediment until the upper hull had collapsed and deposited the lids in the scourpit.

In 1977 a similar deep excavation outside the hull of the bow exposed the keel at a depth of 2m (6½ft) but this time the pattern of scour and erosion told a different story.

All of the strakes and seam ribbands were eroded and worn and forward of the keel/stem scarf there was no coherent structure at all on the port side! This was the worst news of all – we had an open-ended ship See p44-45. with no bow. Careful examination and survey revealed the sequence of events which had led to this catastrophe. As the ship lay on her side there had been considerable current vortexing beneath the overhang of the forward-projecting bowcastle. Over a period of years the outer faces of planks, keel and stern had eroded and thinned until, unable to bear the weight of the bowcastle and its contents any longer, the timbers collapsed forwards and downwards into the great moat that the currents

had excavated in the seabed beneath the bowsprit. The edge of the butt joints between planks and the inner faces of the scarfs on the keel remained clean and fresh with no trace of degradation – clearly once the projecting bowcastle had collapsed the seabed had levelled and stabilised. Now that the scourpit was full of collapsed timber and the superstructure was gone there were no longer any violent currents vortexing around the hull, and below a level of 0.7m (2¼ft) we find levels of collapsed structure and artifacts just as they fell into the scourpits in the seventeenth century.

A perspective view of the Mary Rose *lying on the seabed, based on the excavation and survey up to 1978. The London bus is included to give an idea of the scale of the operation.*

In 1978, for the first time, we excavated a major trench across the hull from the port to the starboard side at the bow. The remains of the orlop and maindeck were identified beneath the bowcastle and an intact section of the bulkhead dividing the forepeak from the main storage areas was recorded. The starboard junction of the bowcastle and the bulwark rail were examined and it became clear that we had a coherent structure with personal possessions and ship's stores *in situ* exactly as they fell across the decks 433 years earlier.

As a result of these discoveries two important meetings were convened in Portsmouth by the Mary Rose (1967) Committee. The first meeting, attended by archaeologists, ship historians, naval architects and museologists, considered the archaeological evidence and the historical importance of the ship and her contents in cultural, social and military terms, and after due consideration and discussion they recommended that the *Mary Rose* should be excavated *in situ* and that all the objects should be recovered from inside the ship as she lay on the seabed. Only after removal of the contents and the fullest possible survey of the hull would it be possible to recommend salvage and recovery. However, it was agreed that it was desirable to recover the hull to be the centrepiece of a Tudor Ship Museum, if this was considered practical after completing the excavation and survey. The second meeting was attended by salvage consultants, salvage contractors, structural engineers, and naval architects, and they agreed that on the evidence available it should be feasible to reinforce the empty hull and recover it for conservation and display in Portsmouth.

At both meetings it was recognised that 'if 'twere done, 'twere best done quickly'! The hull and its contents were only preserved because a benign blanket of silt had covered it for more than 400 years. Excavating meant removing that blanket and immediately the process of decay and corruption would begin. A major operation was needed – to excavate the hull quickly and non-destructively – and this meant a large full-time team of totally committed workers with a support base ashore and adequate conservation facilities. We were moving away from the 'kitchen sink' phase in 1978 just as we moved away from the 'picnic party' in 1971.

CHAPTER 3

The Work of the Mary Rose Trust 1979-1982

ONCE THE DECISION TO GO ahead with a major programme of total excavation and survey had been taken by the Mary Rose (1967) Committee in 1978, certain conditions had to be fulfilled very quickly. The formation of a charitable trust with a trustee board that would include representatives of all the major interested bodies was needed urgently to manage the operation and raise the required funds. Since early in 1977 Richard Harrison, Chairman of the Mary Rose (1967) Committee, had chaired a small sub-committee convened to study the composition and status of the new body which we knew would be required to take over operations when and if the decision to go ahead with total excavation was made. Most of the legal research and drafting was done by Edward (Ted) Mason who had advised the committee so often in the past, and in July 1978 John Reid was seconded from IBM to prepare a plan for the management structure. I had made it clear in my report at the two seminars in Portsmouth in 1978 that unless the excavation could be completed within a reasonable time-scale of two to three years it should not proceed, as it was considered that the timbers of the wreck would deteriorate unacceptably if the site were left open for a longer period.

This meant that finance had to be obtained to purchase a diving vessel that would allow us to work all the hours of daylight from spring until late autumn and to staff the project with a hand-picked team of divers and diving archaeologists. A series of cut-off points was identified whereupon it would be possible to back-fill the site with sand and fine shingle in order to preserve the remains of the hull if it became impossible to complete the excavation because of lack of funds. The programme broke down into four phases: 1) to remove the over-burden of secondary silts which overlay the Tudor levels within and around the hull; 2) to remove all the contents from between the decks and the collapsed timbers lying in the scourpit around the ship; 3) to reinforce the hull, replace the lost iron fastenings if necessary and prepare the hull for recovery; and 4) to lift the remains of the hull from the seabed into air

The salvage vessel Sleipner *was in position for the 1979 season, offering vastly improved facilities as a diving platform and floating headquarters. She is located permanently over the excavation site during the diving season on a four-point mooring.*

and bring it ashore for conservation and display to the public in Portsmouth, the town where she had been built.

On 19 January 1979 the Mary Rose Trust was formally inaugurated. Sir Eric Drake CBE, a former Chairman of the BP group of companies was elected Chairman and HRH Prince Charles, Prince of Wales agreed to become President. The trustees included: Dr Basil Greenhill and Dame Margaret Weston, representing the National Maritime Museum and the Science Museum in London respectively; Vice-Admiral Sir Patrick Bayly, Chairman of the Maritime Trust; the Flag Officer of Portsmouth; and representatives of Portsmouth City Council, Hampshire City Council, major industrial sponsors and the British Sub-Aqua Club. An Executive Committee was appointed to manage the work of the trust and Richard Harrison was seconded from Portsmouth City Council to act as Executive Director for the first six months. In order to complete the programme within the tight time schedule it was necessary to recruit a full-time staff of diving

archaeologists, finds assistants, conservators and illustrators in addition to the shore-based administration, secretarial and fund-raising staff. I was lured from a rather pleasant post as curator of the Roman Palace at Fishbourne to become Archaeological Director for the Mary Rose Trust with responsibility for recruiting and directing the archaeological team that was so urgently required.

A safe diving vessel was also required – one that could be moored on station above the wreck from March until the end of November and one that would be safe and stable throughout the south-westerlies and the easterlies that occasionally turn the sheltered waters of the Solent into a maelstrom. Only one suitable vessel could be identified in time to start work on site in March 1979, the salvage vessel *Sleipner* which had been used as the mother ship during the recovery of the Swedish galleon *Wasa* in 1961. *Sleipner* was built as a salvage vessel for the Royal Navy in 1943. With a keel length of 43m (170ft) and eight buoyancy tanks throughout the length of her hull, she was considered the most suitable

View of the deck of Sleipner *in 1980. Divers entered the sea from an ancillary platform supported on the starboard side of the ship and from here they followed a rope to the bow of the* Mary Rose *12m below. Two airlifts can be seen in action above the port side of the wreck, ejecting an emulsion of water, air and silt down-tide to the west.*

vessel available by the Trust's marine salvage consultant, Alan Crothall. Acting on his advice Portsmouth City Council purchased *Sleipner* from the Neptune Salvage Company on behalf of the embryonic Mary Rose Trust. Later, ownership was transferred to the Trust who accomplished the miracle of raising her purchase price in two months from scratch.

After a storm-tossed voyage across the North Sea from Gothenburg *Sleipner* arrived at Husband's Shipyard in Marchwood, Southampton, in February to be fitted out as a diving platform. The space below decks at the bow was stripped out and the peeling, flaking paint was scraped down by a band of enthusiastic volunteers. Separate compartments were installed for log-keeping, finds recording and examination, storage and maintenance of equipment and a special room was fitted out with video recording equipment which enabled us to control and monitor the underwater operations. Plumbing and electrical wiring had to be replaced and a wide steel companionway was built to connect the loading hatch in the forward deck with the finds bay in the hull. Money was in short supply and most of the carpentry and painting was done by volunteers but the essential cutting, welding, plumbing and electrical work was done by the tradesmen at Husband's yard at Marchwood. New winches were installed on deck to ease the task of mooring and enable the Master to reposition the ship above any part of the wreck in the shortest possible time. A Portacabin was inserted below the boom at the bow to provide extra sleeping accommodation for volunteers and a diving platform was fabricated to hang over the starboard side of the hull and provide a roomy staging post for divers, objects and equipment on their way through the water–air interface. Very little work was required below decks at the stern.

After her work on the *Wasa* she had been used as an anchor-laying vessel in Norwegian fjords so the living accommodation for 14 people was up to Swedish merchant shipping standards, with constant hot water, comfortable cabins and a neat galley. Later the demands for large numbers on board overnight pushed these domestic resources to the limit and hot bunking and shared cabins strained everyone's good humour! Sam Dooley was appointed Ship's Master at an early stage and he acted as clerk of the works for the refit and appointed a crew of watchkeepers and engineers ready to work on a rota basis throughout the season. Sam's background was marine salvage and he had been schooled in the tough world of commercial scrapping, since the end of the Second World War. Now he was lured away from a dull but safe shore job to join a very different type of salvage team. Initially Sam had very little respect for 'scooby doos' and professional women divers were a contradiction in terms as far as he was concerned. However his natural good manners made it all possible and on site a working relationship based on mutual respect was slowly established. Sam also shared with Henry VIII's Venetian salvage divers a firm conviction that a few strops fastened in the right place would soon have the *Mary Rose* dragged from the seabed. After watching the excavation on video and seeing the unique but fragile objects recovered from inside the hull his ideas slowly changed and he saw the need for continuous painstaking excavation. However, sceptical or convinced, Sam was a good ally and a helpful colleague throughout the excavation.

By 12 April, two weeks later than planned, the ship was ready to go to sea. Volunteer divers and archaeological staff stood by ready to go but centuries of seagoing superstition were stronger than the need to get the show on the road and departure was delayed by fear of Friday the 13th. Normally I am as superstitious as the next man but clear skies and threats of storms to come later in the week urged me to plead for sailing as soon as possible. I was also afraid that the Friday delay might be extended to include the whole of the Easter Bank Holiday and that we might not get on station until the following Tuesday. Eventually I had to give way and we compromised by staying ashore on a calm sunny Friday the 13th and eventually mooring on site in force five to six south-westerly winds the following day.

On Saturday 14 April at 9.55 am *Sleipner* slipped her ropes at Camber Dock and was towed out through the harbour entrance by two sturdy tugs; $4\frac{1}{2}$ hours later the mooring task was completed and the ship lay on station. Sam and I went ashore with a second crew leaving a watchkeeper and an engineer in charge. During the remaining 229 days of the 1979 season diving occurred on 146 days and 6858 dives were made from the decks of *Sleipner*. During that time approximately 600 cubic metres of silt were removed from the site. Work concentrated on removing the secondary post-Tudor silts from the bow, stern and along the starboard side of the ship. We were still committed to the old philosophy of examining the least well-preserved areas of the hull first. It would have been possible to sink shafts into the centre of the main deck in an attempt to recover a few fund-raising 'goodies' but as our main task was to evaluate the structure it seemed better to keep to the old routine of excavating from the known to the unknown and to remove the layers of silt in reverse order to their deposition. The excavation was done with the usual grid of steel pipes supported on the deck beams and on the seabed around the ship. The sediments were peeled away layer by layer and unwanted spoil was fed to a 4in (0.10m) diameter airlift supported some 18–20in (0.45–0.60m) above the bottom of the trench.

The full-time staff worked 48 hours on board and 24 hours ashore

See p82.

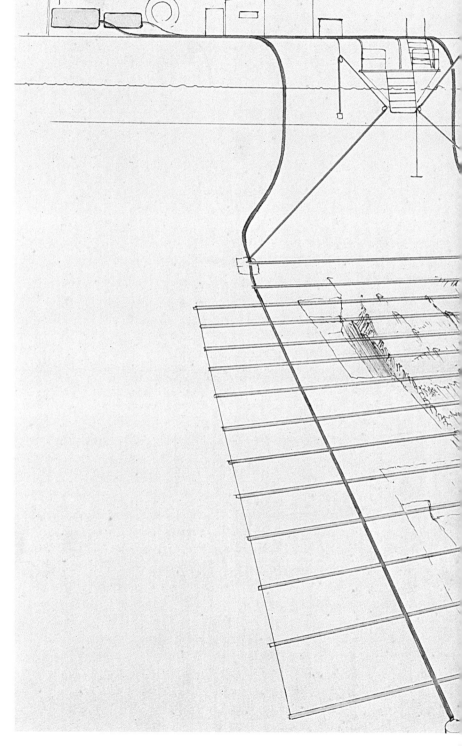

Drawing of the Mary Rose *lying on her starboard side in the seabed by Jon Adams. A grid 3m square was erected above the site to divide it into a series of trenches which were excavated layer by layer using hand tools and an airlift to take away the unwanted 'spoil'. All objects were surveyed in relation to the hull and the grid was never used as a datum for survey — it simply served as a trench location aid in the poor underwater visibility which was usual on this site.*

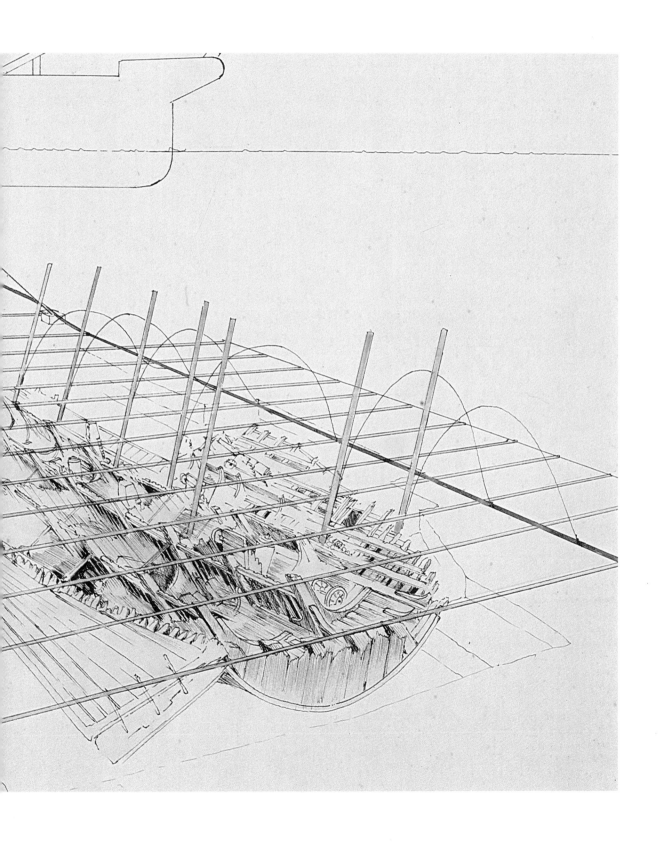

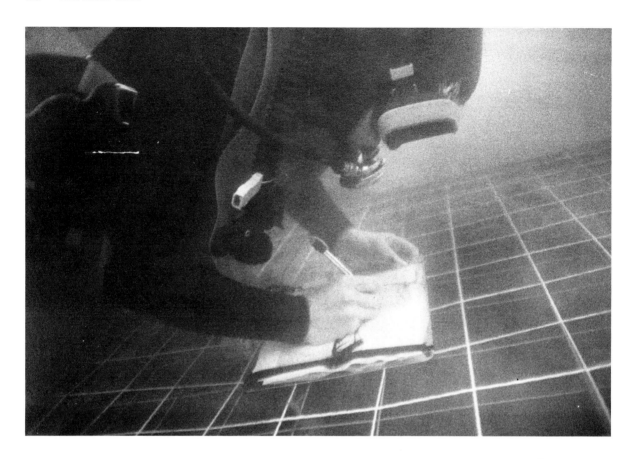

In 1979 groups of objects were surveyed in situ *using a drawing frame.*

and, although in principle 'ashore' meant a day off, this never really happened for the senior archaeologists. Ashore meant endless committee meetings, fund-raising, publicity and management – and all demanded an input from the Archaeological Director. Other members of the diving team had to rush around on days off, begging and borrowing equipment and purchasing essential supplies. No diving was done during periods of the big spring tides when fast currents militated against controlled archaeological excavation. During these periods the diving team tried to catch up on lost sleep and the essential paperwork.

During the season 180 volunteers helped the excavation, most of them coming from the United Kingdom. They had been trained as sports divers by the British Sub-Aqua Club or the Sub-Aqua Association. Others came from Holland, Scandinavia, Canada, USA, Australia and Hawaii. Only their enthusiasm and commitment to the project made the programme feasible and prevented disaster: working from dawn until dusk, diving in cold soupy water, faced with a thankless task of removing an unpromising silt over-burden from areas around the wreck and coming back again and again to put on a never-dry wet suit to continue the process. This regimen demanded something special from the volunteers, and we got it – dedication. A new diver coming to join the team complete with his personal scuba gear and an accredited diving club logbook had to undergo two days of briefing and 'Cook's Tours' of the site before at last he was allowed into a trench. First came the 'aunty' talk usually from me or my deputy, Andrew Fielding. The point of this talk was to give an outline of the whole project, the ship and the excavation, the management and the day-to-day routine; Do's and Dont's of living as a team on a relatively small boat were spelt out and the philosophy of our diving safety measures was explained. The whole point of this talk was to provide a series of pegs on which subsequent lectures could be hung and also to provide an essential 'back door' for the occasional diver who discovered he did not find diving in lentil soup a happy experience and to allow him to withdraw from the project without feeling chicken. The next briefing on diving safety was carried out by the Diving Officer, Chris Underwood, or one of his assistants. Logbooks, medical certificates and personal diving gear were checked and if necessary diver and/or gear were sent ashore on the very next tender. A video film of the excavation was used as an essential part of the archaeological briefing and was supplemented with slides or drawings.

See p86-87.

Later in the season a video of methods of excavation and techniques of survey used on the site was made specifically for introducing the site to new divers. The Blue Ball video camera supplied by Marconi Avionics of Basildon was probably the most important single piece of equipment loaned to the Trust during the excavation. The wide angle 85-degree lens registered 10–12 per cent better than the human eye and, in addition to being used as a briefing tool for new divers and archaeologists, it allowed essential recording of the ship's structure to continue as the excavation proceeded.

Only after these briefing lectures was the new diving volunteer taken on a conducted tour of the site. Guide and volunteer 'keeny' each carried a plan of the trenches on a drawing board and the route was carefully pre-planned to introduce the whole site to the new divers and ensure that the rationale of the grid and shot-line system was fully understood. At the end of the dive there was a debriefing session to ensure that the diver really understood what he had seen on the seabed. On the second or third day a diver was taken down to the seabed by a member of staff or experienced volunteer and set upon a relatively simple task. If it involved use of an airlift then the dive was preceded by another lecture with an airlift on deck and the first practical airlifting session always took place on the seabed away from the ship, where little damage could be done if the diver lost control and dropped the nozzle to the seabed. Only after a diver was completely happy about the route into and out of the trench system and back to the shot-line was he allowed to enter and leave the site alone. There was no free diving from the surface to the seabed. The shot-line from *Sleipner* to the grid was always used and divers were instructed to leave the seabed with 50 atmospheres in their

OPPOSITE
14 April 1979, the Sleipner *takes up her mooring.*

LEFT
Fragile items were excavated by removing the soft silts with a paint brush which were then carried away by an airlift. The diver's right hand partially seals the orifice of the airlift, thus controlling its power.

air cylinders – enough to get them up and down five times if necessary. All dives were done to the 'no-stop' diving tables, which eliminated any need for recompression stops on the shot-line, and divers were recalled to the surface well within their 'no-stop' time by a series of pre-arranged 'bells' tapped out on the diving ladder and easily heard underwater. During the normal working day the teams of volunteers were split into groups and each group worked under the leadership and control of experienced archaeological supervisors. Adrian Barak who had come to work full time for the Trust after eight years as a volunteer was assisted by Berit Mortlock, a Norwegian by birth and startlingly pretty, with experience of working on the underwater site of a sixteenth century ship sunk in the Cattewater at Plymouth. They controlled the difficult excavation at the bow in Trench 1 where marine erosion and anchor damage had left a confusing jumble of collapsed and redeposited structure buried in the secondary silts. Jon Adams returned to the team to

See p63.

OPPOSITE

Nic Rule preparing to photograph the sterncastle using a calibrated three-dimensional scale.

LEFT

A diver surveying the maindeck planking using a plastic measuring tape.

supervise the excavation of Trench 2 along the starboard side of the ship. His task was to define the limit of the starboard side in the waist of the ship and show its relationship to the starboard side of the sterncastle.

Two trenches across the ship at the stern forward of the transom were excavated under the supervision of Andrew Fielding, who had worked with me on the site since 1977. Bob Stewart, another recruit who returned to work for the Trust after experience on the Cattewater wreck, was joined by Chris Dobbs, a new graduate with only limited experience but a great deal of enthusiasm and an enquiring mind. Together they worked amidships supervising the removal of over-burden in Trenches 5 and 6.

The key to the whole operation was the pre-dive briefing session. Most of the supervisors were natural teachers and when the briefing session went well the operation went ahead with few difficulties. Sometimes in mid-season the continual influx of new divers and over-tiredness led to poor briefing and wasted dives but the spring tides provided much-needed breaks and no serious mistakes were made. After each dive the diver wrote out a detailed log on a printed form which was filed away as a basic site record. Any objects were given to the finds supervisor immediately after the completion of the dive and each object

PAGE 86 TOP

Christopher Dobbs, one of the archaeologists, discussing the dive rota with Jon Adams. All the dive times were strictly monitored by the Chief Divers and it was possible to tell by glancing at the control board who was in the water and where they were working.

PAGE 86 BOTTOM

Jon Adams briefing volunteers 1981. All volunteers were given briefing talks using video recordings made from time to time as the excavation progressed.

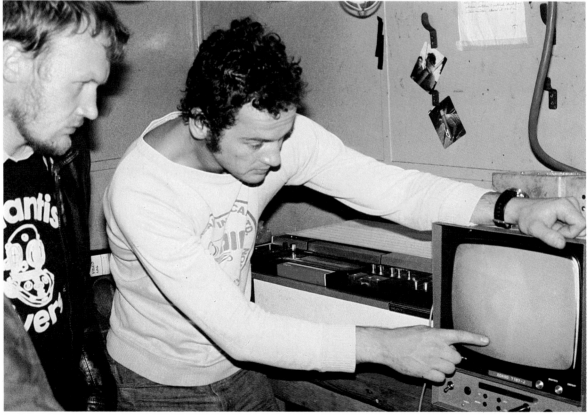

ABOVE
New divers receiving a detailed briefing on the site geography and diving safety from the Deputy Director, Jon Adams.

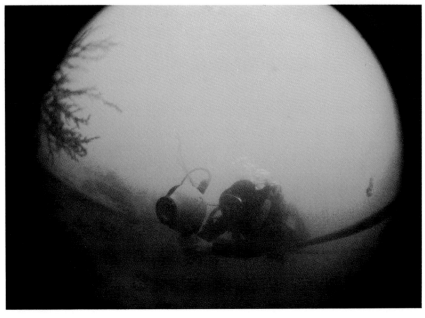

LEFT
The Marconi Blue Ball camera was an invaluable tool for recording details of the structure of the ship.

was allocated a unique number. This number and the associated survey measurements were also noted in the diver's log. The supervisors maintained a daily trench journal which synthesised the information recorded in the diver's logs and they also drew up-to-date trench plans and sections as the excavation progressed. Later in the season a programme was initiated to examine whether environmental material was preserved within the sediments and soon an assemblage of beetles, seeds and small vertebrates began to emerge from the silts and clays. Bob Stewart took charge of this section of the work and developed a programme of sampling and sieving in 1980 which led to the appointment of a full-time non-diving environmental archaeologist in 1981. Finds were cleaned when possible immediately after recovery. They were recorded in a sequential journal with a unique number for each individual find and basic details of association, context and position within the ship. This information was also entered on a finds card and the card accompanied the object ashore. Tie-on plastic number tags and double bagging in polythene bags were sufficient for the majority of objects but others required the support of polyurethane foam, polystyrene or wooden splints, and countless hundreds of scrounged empty margarine tubs and ice cream boxes have been pressed into service as finds containers during the excavation. Arrows soft as cream cheese cannot support their own weight and each arrow needs its own furrow to lie in on a sheet of corrugated perspex.

See p90.

Once ashore information on the record card was expanded to include the identification of the material from which the object is made and any essential measurements and the object was usually drawn and photographed before being passed to the laboratory for conservation. Most objects were drawn at full scale but timbers, furniture and guns were drawn at one to five.

CONSERVATION

The majority of objects recovered from the *Mary Rose* are of wood or leather and right from the beginning it was recognised that large numbers of waterlogged organic objects would present a major problem for the conservators. It was decided to tackle the task in close alliance with Portsmouth City Museum where material from the *Mary Rose* had been conserved since 1971. A small laboratory was built within the disused bonded warehouse leased by the Trust from Whitbreads in the late summer of 1979. Half the laboratory was allocated for use by a small team of three scientists led by Dr John Harvey, a chemist from Bristol, and funded by a grant from the Leverhulme Trust. This research team was charged with the task of evaluating the existing methods of conserving wood and leather objects

OPPOSITE
HRH Prince Charles and Sir Eric Drake, Chairman of the Mary Rose Trust, inspect a velvet coif after restoration by a volunteer worker Pat Edge.

ABOVE

*'Archaeology is fun' but it also
produces a mass of paperwork. The
'Bow Trench Teams' of
Supervisors, Finds Assistants and
Chief Divers with their on-site
records.*

OPPOSITE, TOP

*Loading finds aboard the diving
tender* Sea Lance. *All finds were
indexed and packed in airtight
bags and boxes before transport
ashore.*

OPPOSITE, BOTTOM

*View inside the vacuum chamber.
Most of the organic materials are
conserved by freeze-drying in this
chamber.*

from the sea. It had long been suspected that arbitrary application of impregnation techniques to material from varying underwater environments and from different sources was little more than 'kitchen sink' conservation. It was hoped that examination of the chemistry and the biochemistry of the objects, and the environment from which they came, might lead to a more realistic evaluation of the problems of shrinkage and distortion and non-penetration of consolidants. John Harvey began a systematic study of the problems of monitoring the penetration of polyethylene glycols into waterlogged wood and Ian Panter initiated a programme of semi-scale trials designed to evaluate the efficacy of current conservation methods on leather from the Solent, including the use of polyethylene glycols (PEG), freeze-drying and the Bavon process. Sue Green carried out identification of wood types and she is continuing work on the problems of conserving rope.

At the sharp end, the routine conservators, led by Chris O'Shea, Keeper of Conservation in Portsmouth City Museum, tackled the task of conserving iron, wood, bronze, leather, ceramics, textiles, lead and pewter. As early as 1974 a large hydrogen reduction furnace had been built with the aid of grants from Portsmouth City Council and the Area

Museums Service, in order to treat wrought iron from the *Mary Rose* and an evaluation of this method had been made by a postgraduate student at Portsmouth Polytechnic in 1978.

The wrought iron and the cast iron guns from the *Mary Rose* have all been stabilised by heating them in this furnace in an atmosphere of hydrogen and converting the oxidised iron to metallic iron during the reduction process.[1] Although the method has been criticised by conservators on the grounds that the metallographic structure of the iron is irreversibly changed, it has proved to be the only reliable method for preserving wrought iron from the site and it is now Trust policy to preserve pre-conservation samples of the iron for future analysis should they ever be required by metallurgists and to use the hydrogen reduction furnace for routine conservation.

Early experiments to conserve waterlogged wooden objects using the acetone rosin process gave very variable results and since 1979 most objects have been treated by freeze-drying after soaking in a tank of polyethylene glycol to bulk the cells of the wood. All wooden objects are pre-treated before conservation begins by washing them in a cascade washer to remove soluble marine salts and then they are soaked in a 5 per cent bath of the disodium salt of ethylene diamene tetracetic acid for 24 hours to remove the insoluble salts of iron which have migrated into the wooden objects from the lost iron fittings of the ship.

After these initial treatments the wood is then rewashed and placed in a series of baths of polyethylene glycol with a molecular weight of 3400. By early 1981 Howard Murray, the conservator responsible for conserving organic materials, had established a routine pre-treatment of

The 1979 survey of the site.

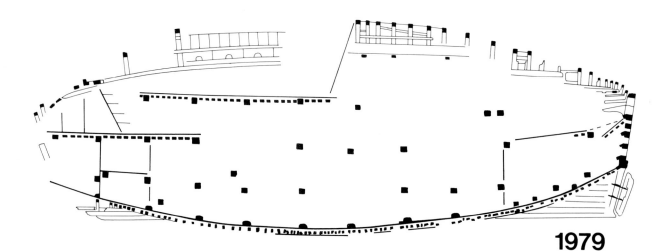

1979

soaking in twelve baths containing different strengths of PEG 3400 solution. Wooden objects were kept for one week in each bath in turn and the concentration is stepped up from an initial 5 per cent (two baths each for one week) through to 25 per cent in increments of 5 per cent. After the first six weeks the wooden object is removed to a series of baths heated to 35–40 degrees centigrade and increasing the strength from 25 to 50 per cent, and again the wood is soaked in each bath for one week in turn. The wood is finally removed from the 50 per cent PEG tank, washed free of surface PEG and then frozen in a deep freeze at −20 degrees centigrade. Howard Murray believes that the wood can be stored for long periods in a deep freeze without further degradation. Finally the water remaining in the wood is removed by sublimation under vacuum in a vacuum chamber. The chamber is pre-cooled to −20 degrees centigrade and the frozen PEG-bulked objects are placed in the chamber. As the chambers are evacuated, and the temperature is brought up to −10 degrees centigrade, the water vapour is removed under vacuum. After treatment, excess PEG is removed and the object is stored at 50–60 per cent relative humidity.

The demands of fund-raising and the public relations activities which are so essential to the success of the *Mary Rose* project sometimes necessitate the urgent conservation of individual objects, but whenever possible the conservators try to treat batches of similar material at any one time. Rigging blocks of similar woods and similar weights and mass may form one group, barrel staves another and components of wooden chests a third. Leather is treated in a similar fashion but following recommendations by Ian Panter in 1981 the leather is soaked for one hour in 5 per cent oxalic acid to remove iron corrosion products and it is then washed before soaking it for two weeks in a 10 per cent ASAK 520S Bavon solution. The Bavon solution acts as a lubricant and it combines with the collagen in the leather to give a more more satisfactory appearance and pliability than the old method which used PEG 400.

1980 SEASON

At the beginning of the 1980 season it was all systems go. We had a well co-ordinated team of volunteers, finds assistants and illustrators, with abundant help from volunteers of all ages to assist with the never-ending task of fund-raising, cleaning finds, drawing and recording objects, and, of course, diving. As in the past, a large team of volunteer divers gave up their holidays to work on the *Mary Rose*; some, like Eric Sivyer, had years of experience with our team, others came fresh from university, full of new ideas and injecting new enthusiasm into the project.

The over-burden of secondary silts had been removed in 1979 and it was now necessary to excavate between decks to remove the objects and the silts from within the hull. In an attempt to 'probe' the silts non-destructively, Jim Clark, the honorary technical advisor to the archaeological team, invited Bill Andrews of EMI to test his underwater acoustic camera on the site. It was hoped that the ultrasonic soundwaves would be reflected off buried objects lying in the silts and be reflected back and recorded through the acoustic camera (see Appendix).

The images produced were highly encouraging and once one had learned to differentiate between the known objects in the foreground and the unknown objects beneath the silts, it was possible to isolate and interpret a buried mass 50–80mm (2–3in) beneath the surface of the silts. Unfortunately the signals were displayed through a modified television cathode ray display unit which had to work at the frequencies required by the ultrasonic image converter tube. The result was a picture with only 200 scanning lines instead of the more usual TV

ABOVE

Jenny Woodgate, a finds assistant, cleaning a leather shoe.

OPPOSITE

Howard Murray, Senior Conservation Officer, restoring a barrel from the ship's stores.

system of 625 lines. While it was possible to photograph specific images as they were displayed on the screen, it was difficult to monitor an excavation using this equipment. The system undoubtedly has great potential for future excavators working in turbid conditions with light sediments, but wherever sufficient light is present, it would aid interpretation to link the sonic camera with a conventional video system, thus enabling the archaeologist to view the 'known' structure in the foreground and the unknown sub-mud object simultaneously.

See p86-87.

We have been using conventional underwater video on the *Mary Rose* since 1978 and we were fortunate enough to have a Marconi Blue Ball camera on site each season to record and monitor the excavation as it proceeded. During 1979 a stereo television camera was used on site with illuminating results, particularly for the non-diving crew of the *Sleipner*, who for the first time realised the massiveness and depth of the structure being revealed on the seabed. The system consisted of two camera assemblies (V328) driven from a common synchronising generator. The two video signals were taken to the surface display unit which consisted of two television monitors mounted at 90 degrees to each other with a semi-silvered mirror mounted at 45 degrees between them. Each monitor was covered by a plain polarised filter mounted to produce cross-polarisation at 90 degrees and the three-dimensional image was seen by viewing the monitors through 'Mickey Mouse' goggles fitted with similar cross-polarised filters. The three-dimensional pictures of a shoal of fish swimming in and out of the upper frames was enthralling, but more illuminating was the 3-D view of frames, stringers and beam shelves in the sterncastle, and the archaeologists took great delight inspecting the site at close quarters in three dimensions without ever having to get wet!

In 1976 the BP group of companies, who had assisted the 1967 Committee with gifts of fuel and lubricants since the earliest days, agreed to provide much-needed technical assistance with our survey problems. The primitive survey system established in 1971 had been adequate as long as the measurements were limited to short distances, but errors had been cumulative and as the excavation continued across the transom and along the starboard side it became more and more necessary to establish firm datum points and relate them to the National Grid. An old friend of mine, Nigel Kelland, was asked by his company, Sonar Marine, a BP subsidiary, to evaluate an acoustic rangemeter developed by John Partridge, on the *Mary Rose* site. In November 1976 he had worked for five days in deplorably cold, storm-tossed conditions but managed to establish a series of datum points on the wreck which could be used as a reference point for all future surveys (see Appendix).

In 1979 Nigel Kelland added further points to this rangemeter survey and these fixed reference points provided the basis for a system of direct trilateration which was introduced by Nic Rule in 1980. Using direct measurements from any four fixed points, it was possible to survey structure and objects as soon as they were exposed and fix their position within the ship with an accuracy of ±0.5m (20in) over the length of the ship.

1981 SEASON

In 1981, it was decided to record and dismantle all the internal structure before attempting to salvage the empty hull. This decision imposed an enormous new workload on the archaeological team and the finds assistants. Every single element of the internal structure had to be recorded *in situ* before it was removed. It then had to be recovered from the seabed and stored ashore to await reinstatement inside the hull in 1983. The decision was unavoidable because excavation in 1980 had shown that many of the supporting knees on the starboard side of the deck had moved, either when the ship hit the seabed or during the centuries of entombment in the silts. The deck planks, which had once been fastened to the deck beams and ledges with iron nails were now held in place by the weight of the sediments alone, and once these were cleared, the planks began to shuffle down the slope of the deck like a collapsing house of cards. The whole of the internal structure was unstable and inherently dangerous. We had to remove it to ensure our safety as we worked between the decks.

Christopher Underwood, a professional diver who worked with us as Diving Officer in 1979 and Chief Diver in 1980, took charge of dismantling operations and he recruited a small team to assist him with this task. The archaeologist's job was to record the structure in plan and section and then Chris and his team removed the individual timbers to a 'timber park' 50m (160ft) to the north-east of the site. There he constructed a rectangular container from timber boards and scaffold poles and the dismantled timbers were stored there until the end of the season. Volunteer divers were actively discouraged from visiting the new 'timber park', which stood 3m (10ft) proud of the seabed and was a hazard to unwary divers in bad visibility, but as the season progressed it became the biggest fish-farm in the Solent and in good visibility it was a wonderland of brightly-coloured pout, bass and lobsters.

At the end of the season the timbers were manhandled into large steel lorry bodies which were lifted by crane onto a barge and towed ashore. Ultimately these timbers will be stored in the dock alongside the ship, but at present there is hardly a reservoir or tank in Portsmouth that has not been called into service to store *Mary Rose* timbers.

RECORDING

A conventional data bank has been established using a micro-processor to record all the timbers, objects and scientific samples recovered from the ship and document their relationships, locations, conservation, publication and display. It is planned to publish simple catalogues of this material as soon as possible, to be supplemented by *catalogues raisonnés* when the necessary research is completed.

Between 1979 and the end of 1981 the register of finds included 2958 timbers, 11,362 objects and 662 samples. It was an enormous task to document and record these finds after recovery, and Debbie Fulford, the Senior Illustrator, and Adele Wilkes, the Keeper of Collections, had their work cut out to keep a flow of material passing on to the conservation laboratory. Both girls had a small dedicated staff and as always the volunteers had an essential part to play in washing, repacking and drawing the objects. It does not take much effort to stimulate someone to make a good job of washing a unique Tudor jerkin but 2000 look-alike bricks are a different problem. However, if we are ever to reconstruct the brick galley excavated in the hold forward of the mainmast, then each brick must be washed, cleaned and stored with its unique identification number to await the day when the structure is reassembled in the museum for visitors to enjoy and understand.

FUNDING

Commitment and dedication are fine but they do not pay the mortgage, and in addition to funding capital purchases and paying professional fees to architects, engineers and other consultants, the Trust has a salaried staff of some thirty people. In 1979 when the Trust was formed it was admirably supported by the local city and county authorities, but it became clear that if the project was to be properly financed it would be necessary to seek funds from national and international donors. On the advice of the Wells organisation, a firm of professional fund-raisers, the Mary Rose Trust established a separate fund-raising organisation to be known as the Court of the *Mary Rose*. Court members were prominent leaders of industry or influential private donors who had supported the project in the past. Their task was to seek gifts from new sponsors and donors and to arrange major fund-raising events. Eventually the Court became the Mary Rose Development Trust, a limited liability company with charitable status, and it still flourishes as a major fund-raising trust, under the enthusiastic and able chairmanship of Charles Tidbury, the Chairman of Whitbread and Co Ltd.

In 1980 Ian Dahl was appointed Director, with the task of co-ordinating the fund-raising campaign which had already been initiated

to raise £4 million in cash, or its equivalent in supporting equipment and technical services. A local fund-raising committee was established in Portsmouth and in late 1979 the Mary Rose Trading Company was formed to market souvenirs, brochures, prints, and other fund-raising paraphernalia for the benefit of the Trust funds. Although this company has always been run on a shoestring, there is clearly enormous potential for the sale of souvenirs and replicas, once the *Mary Rose* is ashore and the exciting original objects can be displayed in close proximity to the ship.

SAFETY

Throughout the years of excavation, diving safety has always been uppermost in our minds. For this reason one-day visitors and inexperienced divers have always been discouraged. During the early amateur days a code of practice was established which has been improved many times as conditions changed on the site and the task became more demanding. By 1980 there were often as many as eight divers working on the seabed at any one time and each diver had to enter and leave his work area by a route which disturbed other divers as little as possible. Good briefing was essential so that in poor visibility one diver did not swim too closely to another and cause a total blackout by stirring up the sediments with his fins. The supervisors maintained a sequence of work which enabled divers to work 3m (10ft) apart in safety and with the least possible aggravation. Our divers were logged by a Chief Diver and a log-keeper and no-one was ever alone in the water but in spite of all our precautions a young scientist, Louise Mulford, drowned before she reached the surface in July 1980.

Louise was an able diver with experience of underwater biological surveys with her university diving club. On 2 July, after coming on board *Sleipner* and kitting up, she dived to do a fairly routine job. Neighbouring divers saw her working happily on the bottom, but Louise failed to return to the surface alive. The day was calm and sunny and diving conditions were superb. Why Louise left the trench where she should have been working, we will never know, but as soon as she was seen floating on the surface above the diving area the two Chief Divers, Chris Underwood and Peter Dobbs, recovered her and began to apply mouth-to-mouth resuscitation. Later a mechanical resuscitator was used and resuscitation continued until she was winched on board a helicopter and taken to Haslar Naval Hospital, a mile away, where she was found to be dead.

The whole diving team was shattered. What had gone wrong? How had we failed? Certainly all the recovery equipment had been effective and the personnel involved had worked with passionate professionalism in the attempt to save Louise. At the Coroner's Court in September a verdict of death by misadventure was recorded and it was agreed in evidence that nothing could have been done to save Louise and that her death was caused by vomiting underwater and then choking.

Although we are all aware that such accidents happen and that a glottal spasm is almost impossible to deal with, even if a buddy diver observes it happening, we still wracked our brains to see if diving techniques could be improved and made safer. During the winter, Jim Clark, John Walliker and I searched through industry to see if any monitoring equipment was suitable for use on our site.

First we investigated a sonic 'panic' button which could be installed on the diver's wrist to emit a constant signal which could be interrogated on deck by the diving supervisor. Such a system would need at least ten different frequencies to be efficient on our busy site and a diver working in the shadows of the ship's structure would be effectively out of range and out of sight. The difficulties appeared to be insoluble and eventually the idea was abandoned.

The next idea was to scan the area of the wreck by a system of sector scanning sonar developed for monitoring the presence of intruders in military harbours and anchorages. This sonar scanner is very useful for recording bulky mid-water objects which are tracked on a monitor on the surface vessel. On our site the most easily recognisable signal came from a rising stream of air bubbles, but unfortunately we had too many bubbles on site to determine which were caused by stationary divers breathing underwater and which were leaks from airlift hoses or manifolds. In fact we had so many multi-path reflections of the signals and so many areas of shadow in the lee of the structure that the system had to be abandoned as impractical on our site, although once again it may well be the answer for a more open site with less underwater 'noise'.

1982 SEASON

By the end of 1981 the excavation was almost complete. The ship lay revealed beneath a 3m (10ft) grid of steel poles and two separate steel manifolds carried low pressure air to take-off points on the port and starboard side of the wreck to power a system of sixteen airlifts. See p78-79. Hydraulic power hammers and explosives had been used successfully to remove areas of accreted iron shot from the angle between the maindeck and the starboard side of the hull and revealed the coherent strength of the structure. The tasks remaining for the archaeologists were still formidable. We had to record and dismantle the brick-built galley, and remove all the ballast and stores from within the hold amidships, but this work was completed during May and early June 1982 by a specially invited team of volunteers working together on day and night shifts under the supervision of Barrie Burden, Alex Hildred and Adrian Barak. As usual Andrew Fielding and I split the shifts between us but the demands of management kept me ashore rather more than I liked and I usually ended up diving at weekends and overnight so that I could attend vital meetings during the working day. The publicity machine really began to take over in late 1981 when the press and TV teams began to realise that the *Mary Rose* was finally going to be recovered.

On my first visit to the US in January 1981 the only person I mēt who had ever heard of the *Mary Rose* was a taxi driver who had seen an advert for Damart thermal underwear and who recognised me as 'The Damart Thermal Underwear Lady'! However, a series of lectures, newspaper and television interviews soon altered that and in November I flew to New York with Sir Eric Drake, Chairman of the Mary Rose Trust, to attend the inaugural meeting of the Society for the Archaeological Study of the Mary Rose, held at the New York Yacht Club. This lively and prestigious fund-raising organisation is registered with the tax authorities; any US citizen making a donation to the Trust is assured that it is tax-deductible, and the Society has already donated significant funds to the *Mary Rose* project.

Since 1971 the BBC Chronicle film unit has been recording work on the surface and underwater, and in 1979 the Trust entered into a joint marketing contract with BBC Enterprises to film all aspects of the project. The result is that we now have access to a great deal of archival film which will be invaluable in the future and that we have had the benefit of working with an experienced crew who know the site and understand the difficulties. John Gilbert, who produced the *Mary Rose* programme for Chronicle arrived on site in 1980 as a non-diver and he went through the same frustration as I had ten years before. Sending a diving cameraman out of his control – and worse than that, out of his sight – did not suit John and by the end of the summer he had learned to dive. Now neither the cameraman, Tim Johnson, nor I can escape; John is right behind us, above and below the water, observing, recording and interpreting.

By the middle of June 1982 the ship lay empty of objects – only a few deck beams needed to be removed and the hull was ready for bracing and recovery. Hopefully she would be ashore within four months and as always speed was essential. Biological and mechanical damage would soon reach unacceptable proportions and the *Mary Rose* would not survive another winter.

CHAPTER 4

The Hull

'A SHIP IS A CONCAVE body framed of timber, plank, and iron work, and contrived into several decks and rooms fitted for the use of men, munitions and victuals.'[1] Slightly less than half of the 'concave body' which is the *Mary Rose* was discovered as a coherent structure beneath the seabed. Excavation and survey was concerned with recording the structure as it was found and interpretation and reconstruction will take many years. It was essential that the survey was totally objective and that any errors inherent in the methods were recognised and quantified (see Appendix).

If there had been any movement of the timber framework either at the moment of impact with the seabed or during the 430 years entombment we needed to understand and quantify the resulting

Terri Palmer processing survey data using a Sintrom microprocessor.

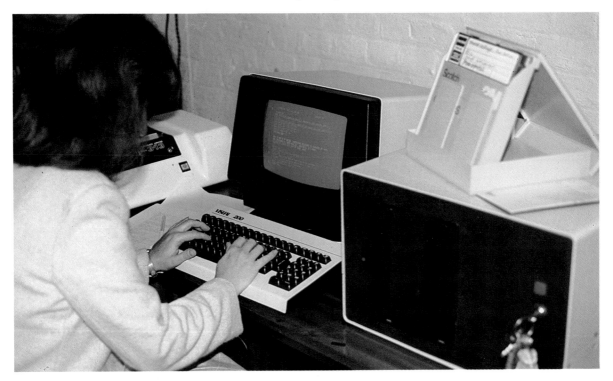

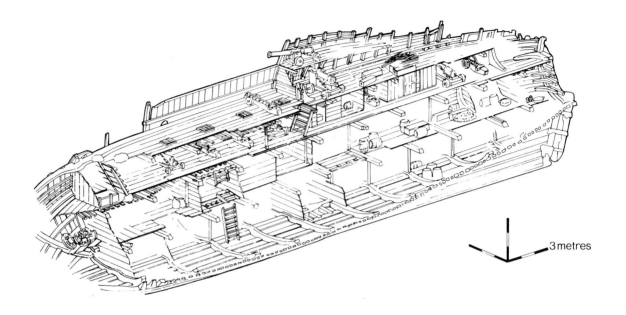

3 metres

Interpretation of the remaining structure of the Mary Rose *by Debbie Fulford, based on archaeological survey of the structure* in situ *in the seabed. The remains of four decks have been recorded on the starboard side of the ship, but most of the port side has been destroyed by tidal action. Ten guns were found on their carriages and run forward through open gunports and several other guns were found which had fallen from the port side and from high in the sterncastle. The hold and the orlop deck were below the waterline and they were used mainly for storage of supplies, spare rigging and personal equipment. Aft of the four guns on the main gundeck there were four small cabins and the one immediately aft of the companionway was used by the barber-surgeon as a surgery and dispensary. Four hatches cut through the weather deck allowed fresh air to circulate down to the gundeck below.*

weakness in the hull. Accurate external hull profiles were only possible on the port side at the bow and the stern and we had to rely on internal sections across the hull and a detailed examination of the junctions between hanging knees and the deck beams they supported. Andrew Fielding was responsible for this work in 1980 and 1981 and he was aided by Nic Rule who rationalised the system of survey and introduced a method of direct measurement from a series of established datum points on the ship in order to fix the x y z coordinates of features and thus achieve a three-dimensional plan of the objects and of the ship within which they were located. This method not only speeded-up routine surveys of objects and hull detail but it enabled us to quantify the error and reject anomalous results. Missing points on the resulting sections were then interpolated using a computer programme and a perspective view of the hull was obtained. Using these internal sections Colin Mudie was kind enough to draw sketch lines for the hulls and to date these are the best lines we have for the ship. All comments on the hull conformation are based on these lines and on the underwater survey. Undoubtedly fresh evidence will be found when the hull is examined in air after the vessel is salvaged but the establishment of hull lines within a known degree of error was essential to enable John Grace, the consultant structural engineer, to calculate the weight of the structure to be recovered (see Chapter 9) and design a cradle to support the hull as it was lifted from the sea.

The main hull is carvel-planked externally with oak planks placed edge to edge and securely fastened to the frames with wooden trenails. Many of the trenails were expanded with wooden wedges to ensure a tight fit and in some cases the presence of trenail fastenings can only be determined by a change in the line of grain of the wood.

The butt ends of the planks were fastened to the frames with iron bolts and in most cases these have corroded away, but in spite of this, the adjacent wooden trenails still hold the planks firmly in place.

Examination of the hood ends of the hull planks where they fitted into the rebate on the sternpost at the port quarter showed that these joints were still tight and sound, although the end of each plank was secured by an iron bolt of doubtful residual strength. The butt joints of the planks were secured to the frames and iron bolts in a similar manner and most of these bolts had corroded away completely to leave a void. However the planks were still *in situ*, secured by the trenails.

The sterncastle above the level of the bulwark rail was lightly planked with overlapping clinker planking and there was some evidence to suggest that a light internal planking had been used to give added strength without seriously increasing the weight of the superstructure. The clinker planks were secured to the frames and supported externally by a series of standards or braces which were fashioned to fit over the wales and were secured by bolts and trenails to the frames. The resulting structure was strong and lightweight and it would have been an effective shield against most contemporary low-velocity missiles as the outer planking would have slowed down the missile allowing the inner planking to stop its flight. Internal examination of the superstructure shows no damage which can be attributed to battle, although clearly it has undergone a series of modifications during the career of the ship.

Parts of four decks remain above the hold and each deck had a different function. The hold lay well below the waterline with a low headroom of 5ft 9in (1.75m) amidships and its main function was to contain ballast and for storage of barrels of wood tar and spare cables. A series of planks and 'thick stuff', or footwales, completely sealed the floor of the holds on either side of the keelson except in the area immediately adjacent to the mainmast-step. At intervals of approximately 10ft (3m) a series of compass-grown riders was fitted over the keelson and the footwales ending at the rungheads where the futtocks begin to bend to the lines of the bilge.

A series of diagonal braces ran obliquely from the first stringer above the head of the rider and passed upwards through the orlop deck to a point immediately below the maindeck beams. Both riders and

See p118.

The sterncastle was built of overlapping clinker planking and was of much lighter construction than the main hull, which was planked with smooth-skinned carvel planking, 0.09m thick.

braces were securely fastened to the keelson, footwales and the frames with iron bolts and trenails. At the bow and towards the stern vertical braces or 'futtock riders' were fastened to the stringers abaft the lower end of the diagonal braces, then rose through the orlop deck forward of deck beams and were secured to the rising knees above the deck level.

See p118.

The futtock rider SR-10 terminated forward of the maindeck beam M-10 and served to strengthen and to brace the hull at this point. There is some evidence to suggest that these diagonal and vertical braces, and possibly even the riders, were secondary insertions put in to strengthen the hull athwartships as the futtock scarves and plank seams opened up with the weight of the heavy guns on the main deck. Careful examination in air after the ship is salvaged may show that the chamfered seam ribbands which covered the seams in the outer plank-ing below the waterline were also part of this secondary strengthening necessary to reinforce a weakened and deteriorating hull. The political and military exigencies of 1536 may have left little time for a full rebuild and the work may have been limited to adding internal hull stiffening and replanking the hull with carvel planks. The riders fitted over the keel bolts, and the rather casual alignment and fit of the braces over the footwales and stringers, plus the slipshod carpentry to allow the passage of the brace through the deck of the orlop to the maindeck beam, all suggest that this hull stiffening was not part of the initial design.

See p69.

Light bulkheads of lapped planks ½in (0.02m) thick divided the hold area into a series of compartments and access was via a companionway which led up to the orlop deck and then to the main gundeck. Other hatches were covered and were only accessible by rope ladder. The main use of the hold was for stowage of ballast and clearly the light bulkheads with their reinforcing battens were sufficient to keep the ballast isolated within the separate compartments. The ballast material was flint, well-rounded but broken black flints which originally derived from the chalk hills but had been washed downstream and redeposited in one of the gravel beds around Southampton Water. The pebbles were contaminated with cockle, winkle and oyster shells suggesting that they had been obtained from beach deposits and several fresh leaves were found preserved among the ballast.

This type of ballast would stay permanently in the hold with only minor additions and subtractions when major changes in guns or numbers of crew were made. A large number of carefully cut logs were found in the hold immediately forward of the galley, and elsewhere barrels of wood tar and coils of spare cable were stowed. Most of the bay immediately forward of the mainmast-step was taken up by the brick-built foundations of the galley.

THE GALLEY

The whole of the brick galley foundation had slumped towards the starboard side when the ship hit the seabed, displacing all deck planks and partitions. Lying on the keelson and viewing the tumble of more than 2500 bricks, one began to realise the impact which had caused so much damage, not only to the galley, but also to the starboard side of the structure and to boxes and barrels stored within the ship. No

A few of the 2500 bricks of the collapsed galley.

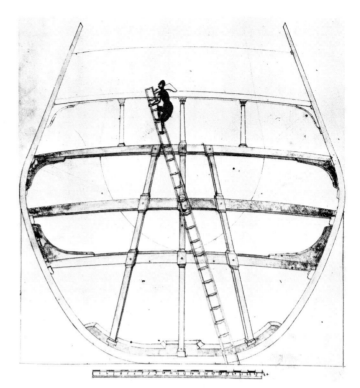

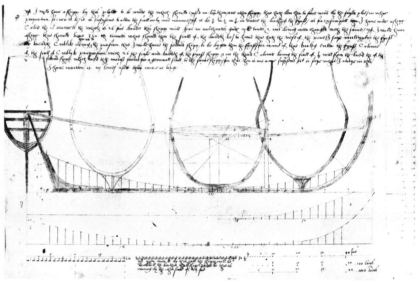

The earliest English ship plans are those of Matthew Baker, dating from around 1586 and there is no direct evidence of how ships of the Mary Rose type were designed. It was for this reason that the decision to totally excavate the Mary Rose was taken in 1979 and the detailed survey of her structure after recovery will throw new light on the construction methods used and the proportions of early sixteenth century ships.

wonder so few people had survived the sinking – they would have been knocked off their feet by the impact and probably many of them were already dazed or senseless when they drowned.

The foundations of the galley were laid athwartships across the keelson and the footwales and a large firebox with fire-bars and ash-pits was built within the rectangular brick mass. Four large copper cauldrons with wide lead rims were found in the galley and at least three were used for cooking the meals of the crew. The fourth was full of pitch and as it was found forward of the galley in area H-4 it may have been used on some subsidiary hearth. Fragments of the brick and mortar support for each cauldron have been recovered and an enormous three-dimensional jigsaw puzzle awaits the archaeologists as soon as all the material is cleaned and recorded. Above the galley a large beam was rebated for ledges to support the deck on the starboard side only, but it would appear that a lead-lined hood above the galley continued up through the orlop deck in the middle of the ship. No trace of a chimney has been found, but this may well have been damaged when the mainmast was removed immediately aft of the galley.

The orlop deck above the galley was divided into three bays athwartships by sawn-off partitioning and this may have been to leave a free space around the galley hood and the chimney. Sheet lead sheathed the orlop deck beams immediately fore and aft of the galley area and flat sheets of lead probably lined the hood above the galley. Once again, reconstructing the jigsaw puzzle is necessary to be sure, but it would seem that smoke and heat from the galley passed upwards through a timber hood lined with lead sheathing and then up through an open hatch in the maindeck and a hatch or a chimney in the weather deck above.

No records have been found to indicate where the materials came from to build the ovens on the *Mary Rose* but the accounts of Robert Brygandyne, Clerk of the Ships, contain details of similar ovens built on board Henry VII's great ship the *Regent* in 1497. The materials included 6500 bricks brought from 'the brickhill of our Sovereign Lord the King at Portsmouth', and a load of tile brought from John Keyte in Petersfield.

Lime, tiles, and bricks were manufactured from the fifteenth century up to the 1960s, and even today a few bricks are still made by the Pyecroft family on Hayling Island using brick-earth dug from their own fields.

MAINMAST-STEP

The mainmast-step lay immediately aft of the brick-built galley foundation and was separated from this area by a well-made partition of lapped planks which were supported by light battens rebated into the footwales and nailed to the after face of the orlop deck beam O-50. This structure added little if anything to the strength of the hull; it simply served to delineate the area round the mast-step. The mast-step appears as a well-fitted, thickened section of the keelson and effectively the keelson swells athwartships from 0.4m to 0.76m (16in to 30in) and diminishes to 0.48m (19in) aft of rider 6. Unlike all the other riders, rider 6 stopped and fayed into the keelson but the junction was so tight that the nature of the carpentered joint could not be ascertained.

AREA OF MAST STEP

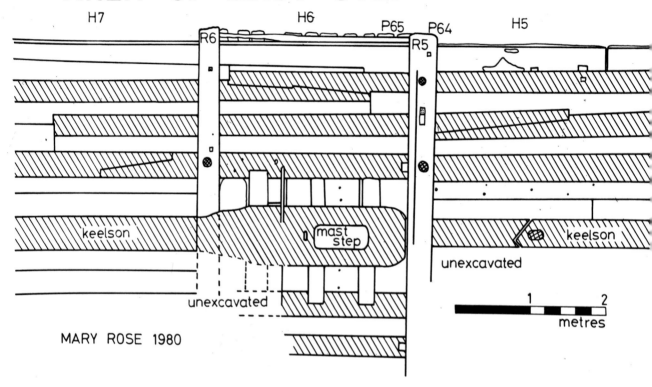

MARY ROSE 1980

Plan of structure of port side of hull and the step for the mainmast.

Within the bed of the mast-step a shallow rebate 0.3m by 0.7m (12in by 27½in) carried the heel of the mast and a smaller rebate 0.1m by 0.02m (4in by ¾in) aft of this may have held the locking piece. There was no trace of the mast in the step or indeed anywhere else within the ship and the sediments immediately over the step in the hold on the orlop deck suggest that the mast was removed from the step soon after the ship sank and before she filled with the primary silts. There were no recent intrusions as one would expect if the removal of the mast from its step had occurred during the nineteenth century when the Deanes were active on the site and the whole area was sealed by the hard grey shelly clay which built up over the remains of the hull in the eighteenth century. It is much more likely that the mast was removed immediately after the ship sank, when the 'two hulkes the *Jesus* and the *Samson*' were 'brought unto the *Mary Rose* because they must weight her up'.[3] Any attempt to lift the ship using the buoyancy of empty hulks and the force of the rising tide would necessitate securing ropes to the hull. If in addition ropes had been secured to a mast in an attempt to drag the hull upright on a rising tide the result may well have been to drag the mast out of the step through the mast partners on the orlop and the maindeck and out through the open weather deck. Certainly the Duke of Suffolk in his letter to Sir William Paget on 5 August 1545 records that the sails and sailyards 'be laid on land and to her masts there is tied three cables with other ingens to weigh her up and on every side of her a hulk to set her upright.' Although we have no mainmast, the dimensions of the step suggest a mast which conforms well with the approved dimension

A view looking upwards from the chain-wales to the clinker planking above the gunport on the castle deck.

given by Captain John Smith in his *Sea Grammar* published in 1627. He recommended that the length of the mainmast should be four-fifths the breadth of the ship measured in feet multiplied by three to give the height of the mast in feet, and that the diameter of the mast in inches should equal the height of the mast in yards.

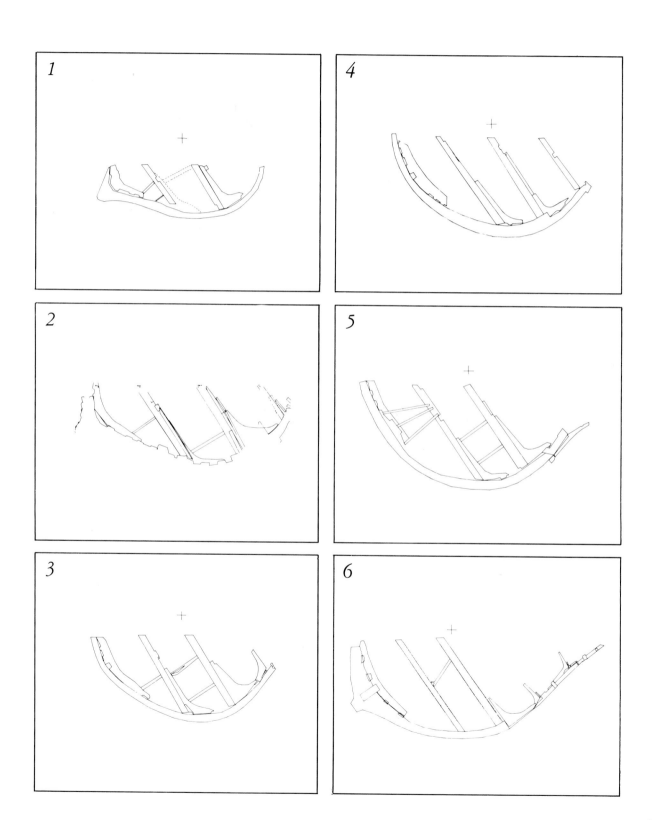

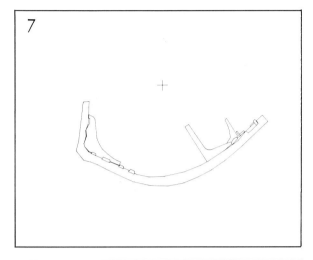

7

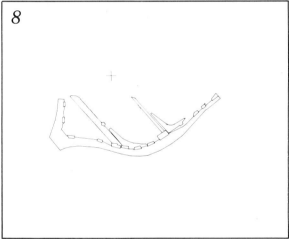

8

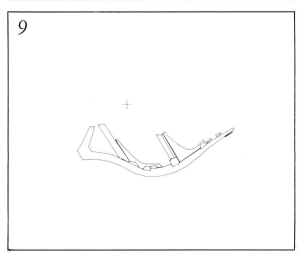

9

1
Section through rider 1. A section through the ship at nine stations was made so that the support cradle, designed by John Grace of R J Crocker Ltd to support the hull when it was lifted into the air, would be based as closely as possible on the lines of the hull.

2
Section through rider 2 showing relationship of deck beams, knees and stanchions to each other and the starboard side of the ship.

3
Section through rider 3. Note that one of the stanchions has been splintered by the movement of heavy objects across the orlop deck when the ship sank.

4
Section through rider 4.

5
Section through rider 5.

6
Section through rider 7.

7
Section through rider 9.

8
Section through orlop deck beam 0-100. Note, there is no rider as far aft as this section.

9
Section through orlop deck beam 0-110.

View across the wing transoms at the stern of the ship looking upwards from the keelson.

LEFT
Underwater view of orlop deck beam 0-10 supported on a stanchion from rider 1. In the righthand foreground a diagonal brace runs forward and upwards towards the stem of the ship.

View beneath the sterncastle looking at the sill of a gunport on the upper deck (in the lefthand corner) above the first of the carvel planks of the main hull.

ABOVE
A timber plate securely braced against the starboard side of the hull immediately aft of the companionway leading up from the maindeck to the bowcastle. Its use is as yet uncertain, but it may have functioned as a chesstree.

View of one of the grown lodging knees and a rising knee which brace the starboard side of the hull.

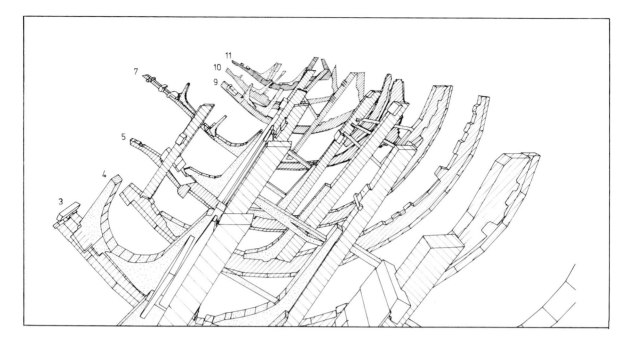

A perspective view through sections 3-11 looking aft from the bow. Based on archaeological survey, but interpolated using a computer programme.

The mast-step was braced on each side by three short timbers, which butted onto the first footwales on the port and starboard side of the step. The spaces between these braces were filled with a limber board with two holes for a rope lifting loop which enabled the board to be removed with ease for cleaning or draining the well around the mast-step. Light boards running athwartships aft of the mast-step were part of a box-like structure around the well, and a pump may have been fitted in this position. If it was ever there it had been removed with the mast as no trace of a pump survived in this bay.

Further aft in a storage compartment on the orlop deck a spare section of a pump shaft was found which corresponds remarkably closely with a fragment of a pump found *in situ* on a Basque whaling ship — believed to be the *San Juan*, which sank in 1565 — currently being excavated by Robert Grenier in Red Bay, Labrador.

The only companionway from the hold was constructed of solid wooden steps set into two jambs which housed into the rebates on the main fore-and-aft carling on the port side of the orlop deck. This carling was rebated for ledges or half-beams in the normal way, suggesting that the hatch could be closed with battens and planks whenever necessary. When the ship sank, access to this companionway was open and the damp dark recesses of the hold were being used as a sick bay. The remains of several men were found lying on the gravel ballast, two of them at least were lying on straw- or hay-filled mattresses and in the evil-smelling darkness of the moving ship it must have been a terrifying place to lie and await the outcome of battle.

CHAPTER 5

The Decks

THE ORLOP DECK

The orlop, or overlop, deck functioned as a storage area, and it was divided into a series of compartments by light feather-edge planking which ran athwartships between the deck beams. These bulkheads were held in place by light but well-made battens and stanchions which housed into the rising knees and the main beams of the maindeck.

Access from one bay to the next must have been via a central gangway and traces of light timber planking which divided this central access area from the storage compartments on the port and starboard side were found in Trench 5, on either side of the galley. The access from the maindeck to the orlop and then down to the hold was by a substantial wooden companionway, securely fastened to the deck carlings and, by iron plates, to the floor of the deck. The deck had been badly damaged and displaced when the ship heeled, took in water through her starboard gunports, and sank. The ballast shifted violently across the hold to the starboard side, displacing the deck planking and the ledges and fracturing badly the stanchions on the orlop deck above.

Examination of the structure shows how easily this would have happened, as the almost total absence of either wooden or iron fastenings suggests that the decking was inserted as a tight fit after loading ballast and other heavy stores into the hold.

Above the deck beams, the rising knees which braced the beams to the starboard side of the ship appear to be permanent fixtures, but the decking and the bulkheads were inserted or altered as required from time to time. Amidships in the hold, just forward of the mainmast and the pump, large cauldrons supported on a massive brick-built firebox served as the main galley, and in the next bay forward a stack of neatly-cut pine logs were piled ready for use as galley fuel. In the same area on the orlop deck above, a large wooden tub contained wooden plates and bowls, and nearby pewter plates were stacked ready for the next meal. Several had owners' marks on the upper rim, including 'GC', possibly the Vice Admiral Sir George Carew; and two plates bore the coat-of-arms of the Lord High Admiral, John Dudley, Viscount Lord

The gartered coat-of-arms of the Lord High Admiral, John Dudley, Viscount Lord Lisle, KG, from one of the pewter plates found on board the Mary Rose.

OPPOSITE, TOP

The portrait of The Ambassadors by Holbein (1533) reflects an interest in the arts and a musical appreciation which is echoed among the officers aboard the Mary Rose. *The discovery of three boxed compasses mounted on gimbals in personal chests on board the ship and the common use of carefully calibrated pocket sundials demonstrates that such objects were not limited to the few.*

At the end of 1979 it was possible to rationalise the numbering system used to identify areas within the wreck. Riders and deck beams were numbered sequentially from the bow to the stern and the excavation area was divided into 11 trenches which ran athwartships between the main deck beams. References to Trench H2 (the area of the hold between rider 1 and rider 2, orlop deck beam 10 and orlop deck beam 20) were much more easily understood than the rather arbitrary numbering which had been used in previous years. From 1980 onwards all objects were surveyed in relation to the main deck beams inside the hull.

Lisle, KG. The discovery of these two plates on board the *Mary Rose* underlines one of the pitfalls of archaeology underwater – the difficulty of reliably dating a known wreck from a random selection of surviving wreck material. If the history of the *Henry Grace à Dieu* and the *Mary Rose* were unknown, it might be tempting to suggest that Lord Lisle was on board when the ship sank in 1545. But history is clear. As Lord High Admiral, he was on board his flagship the *Henry Grace à Dieu*, a quarter of a mile away, and he survived the battle to see his daughter-in-law, Lady Jane Grey, proclaimed Queen of England in July 1553, and to be beheaded himself on Tower Green for treason the following month. On the fatal day, 19 July 1545, only his plates were on board the *Mary Rose*.

It is almost impossible to name or date a wreck from individual objects. This can only be achieved by careful examination of all the documentary and archaeological evidence. Easily-dated objects like guns are captured and re-used; valuable personal possessions are stolen and re-used by the thief; and profitable but illegal cargoes are seldom declared in a ship's manifest. Often the humbler objects like belt buckles, cartridge belts and everyday ceramics provide more secure dating evidence, but only time-consuming analysis of the total evidence will give the right answer.

In the forepeak at the bow an important group of spare axles, trucks and spoked wheels for gun carriages lay piled one upon the other, with the 'comander' or gunner's mallet nearby, and further aft the bosun's stores contained spare blocks, deadeyes, thimbles and parrels close to a store of spare rope and cable.

Aft of the mainmast more compartments contained seamen's and officers' chests with their personal possessions, alongside boxes of bows and arrows and a barrel of tallow candles. Wooden 'lanthornes' with a metal spike to secure the tallow candle were also recovered from the storage area at the stern. Unfortunately the horn windows have been completely destroyed by micro-biological decay, but the lanthornes and the candles provide clear evidence of how the officers' quarters were lit at night.

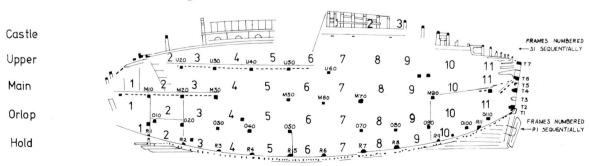

Navigational instruments, including a gimballed ship's compass found in a chest in the small cabin beneath the bowcastle. This is the earliest ship's compass recovered from a wreck but the portrait of Sir Edward Fiennes, the Elizabethan admiral, in the Ashmolean Museum, shows him holding a similar compass.

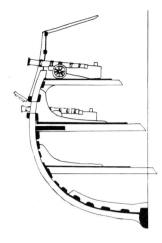

Section through the waist of the ship drawn by Andrew Fielding, showing the orlop deck, main gundeck and upper deck with wrought iron guns in situ *on their wheeled carriages.*

From the orlop deck a series of rising knees, fashioned from grown timber, were securely fastened to the main frames of the ship by iron bolts, and they were carefully rebated to fit over the stringers which strengthened the ship longitudinally. There was no internal planking between the frames, but the gaps between the stringers and the outer planking were filled with flat pieces of wood which effectively provided a shelf, or ledge, between each frame, and prevented small objects from falling down behind the stringers. Many small items – knives, purses, tankards, and so on – were found tucked away on these shelves, and though there is no evidence so far that people ate or slept on this deck, it is clear that personal possessions were stored and hidden away there, and that in the area of the orlop deck below the sterncastle, members of the crew had free access.

THE MAIN GUNDECK

The maindeck was a strongly-built, continuous deck with long lengths of fore-and-aft planking supported on ledges and deck beams. The ledges were supported on the starboard side by a series of lodging knees which functioned as a beam shelf and the inboard ends of the ledges were securely housed in rebates in the deck carlings. Beneath the lodging knee, a robust stringer securely bolted to the starboard frames thickened to provide a supporting buttress beneath each deck beam. The beam was secured in position by large iron bolt fastenings through the lodging knee and the whole structure was strong and sound.

On the maindeck in the waist four guns were positioned with their carriages run forward through the timbers of the open gunports. All the ports were at the same level, and not staggered in a double tier as they are shown in the contemporary picture in the Anthony Anthony inventory. A companionway ran up to the bowcastle from the forward end of the main gundeck, and there were no ports for guns found forward of this companionway. The entrance in the maindeck below the bowcastle must have been on the centreline. Any coaming or decorative wood has been destroyed by anchor damage and erosion.

Immediately forward of the companionway were two small cabins or compartments, and here for the first time we found clear evidence of how the officers lived and slept. The small aftermost cabin was almost intact and measured barely 4 square metres. It was almost completely filled with two bunk beds, supported on timber battens and one of the bunks was still covered by the remnants of a hay-filled mattress. The only other furniture in the cabin was a well-made chest with dovetailed joints at the corners and a large hole where the iron lock had completely corroded away. It was overlain by a wooden gaming-board and con-

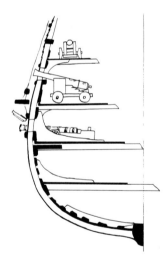

Section through the forward end of the sterncastle showing the disposition of three tiers of guns on the main, upper and upper castle decks. Note that the large bronze gun on the castle deck aimed forward across the waist of the ship, and above the upper deck gunport the external planking changed from carvel to clinker. The chain-wale seen above the maindeck gunport continued from this point to the stern of the ship and carried the chains for the mainmast and the mizzen.

A double bunk bed made by opening up a box seat. Found in the captain's cabin of the Swedish warship Wasa.

tained a fine steering compass and a pair of dividers. The compass bowl was supported on bronze gimbles within a well-made lidded box, and the face of the compass was protected by a glass disc sealed with a putty-like substance which was unfortunately destroyed during the conservation process. No trace of the fly or compass card survived, and only an iron stain remained to indicate the former presence of a magnetic needle. But in most respects the compass is similar to the one held in the left hand of Edward Fiennes, Lord High Admiral of England, in his splendid portrait painted in 1562 in the reign of Elizabeth I and now in the Ashmolean Museum in Oxford.[1]

Fragments of two similar compasses were found at the stern and the occurrence of both of these compasses, together with dividers and a slate protractor, suggests that charts may have been used either for navigation or for planning battle strategy.

The cabin was small and functional with none of the accoutrements of a state cabin. It simply served as a resting-place and storage for an officer's, perhaps even the pilot's, personal possessions. A game of chess, in this cabin, would have been a friendly affair, to be indulged in while curled up on the hay mattress.

The second cabin, forward, was almost completely destroyed by the collapse of the bowcastle but remnants of a mattress suggest that it, too, had been a sleeping compartment. In the primary silts a series of soft lining boards and light, wooden studding were found with traces of white paint still adhering to the under surface. These may have been used to line the walls of the compartment at the bow, to give some semblance of hygiene and privacy.

Aft of the main gundeck in the waist a second companionway led up to the open weather deck in the waist and thence to the sterncastle. Behind the companionway a series of cabins, alternating with gun stations, opened off a central gangway. The first two cabins in M-7 were used by the barber-surgeon and his assistant as a dispensary and surgery, and the furniture was limited to the essential items needed for this purpose — a large chest and a small bench. There was no evidence of any bunk or couch in either cabin.

Two cabins in M-9 were used as sleeping compartments for at least four men who also stored their tools and personal possessions under the bunks. The friendly double-bunking on board was clearly nothing unusual. References to accommodation for shipwrights in Portsmouth when the *Mary Rose* was built in 1509 record that they were provided with mattresses, sheets, blankets, bolsters and coverlets for beds which held two or three men, and double box beds were found in the captain's cabin in the Swedish warship *Wasa* which sank 83 years after the *Mary Rose*.

All the cabins on the starboard side of the maindeck were lined with ceiling planking and the M-9 cabins were closed off from the central gangway by a sliding door with strips of battening to simulate panelling.

Neither the M-9 cabins nor the barber-surgeon's cabin in M-7 had gunports. The single port in M-8 provided an opening for a wrought iron breech-loading gun, and a large bronze gun and a wrought iron gun completed the main gundeck battery aft of the M-9 cabins. The absence of ports for more than seven guns on the starboard side on this deck suggests that some of the guns were located on the main and upper decks above the transom stern. But if this was so, it is surprising that they were not found in the scourpit outside the stern when this area was excavated in 1976. The guns recovered by the Deanes in the 1830s almost certainly came from seabed level above the hard grey shelly clay which seals these Tudor levels.

The absence of rebates for ledges in the western or port side of the maindeck carling between M-50 and M-70 suggests that there may have been an open hatch in the centre of the ship aft of the mainmast, and it will be necessary to examine all the collapsed structure recovered from this area before we can be sure, because most of the internal timbers were displaced when the mainmast was removed and the resulting evidence is confused.

OPPOSITE

Blindages, in use in a land battle in the fifteenth century.

Model by Roger Trise of the blindage found above the gunwale on the weather deck. The upper rail supported the joists for the anti-boarding netting and the upper tier of boards could be lifted out to provide ports for archers and gunners to defend the deck. The lower boards were fixed in position and there were semi-circular ports cut for larger carriage-mounted guns.

Lower gundeck of the Swedish warship Wasa.

THE UPPER OR WEATHER DECK

The upper deck was a strong continuous structure with a slight break in level of 21cm (8¼in) at the forward end of the sterncastle. At this point, a wooden trough-shaped 'daile' ran athwartships and carried water pumped up from the bilges to run across the deck and through a chute below the chain-wale on the starboard side of the ship. Unfortunately this important timber (U-55) was partially displaced at its western end by anchors dragging through the site, but the companionway from the maindeck came up its forward face and the brace for the forward end of the sterncastle housed snugly into its after face. The weather deck between the fore end of the sterncastle and the bowcastle was pierced with four small ventilation hatches which allowed air to circulate down to the maindeck below but which could not have been used for access as they were partially sealed by the ledges or half-beams. The hatches were surrounded by well-made coamings and presumably covers would have been dropped in to seal the hatches in bad weather; there was no trace of scuppers to drain away water from either the weather deck or the maindeck below and great care must have been taken to prevent a sudden ingress of water through either the hatches or the ports.

A series of blinds or lightweight boards existed above the gunwale to protect the gunner or the archer from heavy seas or the enemy. There was no trace at all of the gaily painted 'pavises' with their flamboyant heraldic devices so often seen in illustrations of contemporary ships and in the Anthony Roll illustration of the *Mary Rose*. It is possible that the pavises were only used for ceremonial occasions and that they were replaced by the more adaptable blinds when the ship was at sea or engaged in battle.

The blindage was constructed between the gunwale, the waist rail and the head rail in two tiers and the resulting screen effectively shielded the whole length of the weather deck from the bowcastle to the forward end of the sterncastle. The lower boards ran fore and aft and were fixed permanently in position between the gunwale and the waist rail. These boards were pierced with semi-circular openings for broadside-firing guns and the structure was supported by external braces or standards which continued vertically downwards to the level of the wale immediately above the gunports on the maindeck. Above the waist rail a series of moveable blinds could be dropped into matching grooves in the waist rail and the lower face of the head rail. Alternate blinds were cut with hand-sized notches so that they could be easily lifted upwards into the deep upper groove and then as their lower edge cleared the top of the lower groove, they could be lifted out and stacked amidships. A similar system is often used to enable staff to remove the glass from modern museum display cases!

It is clear from contemporary references that blinds were often used to shield soldiers in small boats and there is reference to rails around the deck. In 1511 Sir Howard Echyngham wrote: 'Because I had no rails upon my deck, I coiled the cable about the deck breast-high and likewise in the waist and so hanged upon the cable mattresses, bed and table covers and such bedding as I had within board'. This tradition of rolling up bedding and using it to provide cover on the open deck continued up to the time of Trafalgar; HMS *Victory* is still fitted with netting in which seamen stowed their hammocks above the bulwark rail to provide protection from small-arms fire. It probably also served to give the bedding an airing.

The head rail was rebated on its upper edge to support a series of joists which ran from the central purlin to each side of the ship and supported the anti-boarding netting. This central purlin was supported on a bracket 1.95m (6½ft) tall and most of the people found on the weather deck had been trapped there as a result of the collapse of this structure and the netting it supported. The discovery of a large coil of cable immediately aft of the bowcastle companionway seemed at first to

See p128.

Looking aft along the starboard side of the ship with the frames of the sterncastle and outer clinker planking of the upper castle deck.

OPPOSITE, TOP
Double block lying in secondary sediment at an early stage of the excavation. Note the collapsed deck planking, ledges and carling in the background.

Looking aft along the orlop deck with the ledges and deck carling exposed in the background after the deck planks have been surveyed and removed.

OPPOSITE, BOTTOM
Looking forward along the upper deck in the sterncastle after removing the deck planking. The photographer is using a calibrated cube to produce a scaled survey of the structure photographically.

One of the compartments which divided the orlop deck into a series of storage areas with the ledges and carling in the background.

The Mary Rose *was among the last English vessels to carry high superstructure above the bulwark rail and by the end of the century the sterncastle was much reduced in height as can be seen in this smaller vessel, from the* Fragments of Ancient English Shipwrightry.

Diamond mesh of anti-boarding netting found collapsed over the weather deck in the waist of the ship.

suggest Sir Howard Echyngham's screen of 'coiled cable', but further excavation revealed that the cable was attached to the ring of one of the spare anchors which had fallen across from the centre of the deck as the ship heeled and sank. The stem of the anchor lay across the only gun found on the weather deck, with its rings to the north and the flukes immediately forward of the sterncastle; above it lay the spare blinds and the collapsed anti-boarding netting. The recovery of this anchor in 1981 was a triumph for the dismantling team, led by Chris Underwood, who had to break the accreted corrosion products which sealed the anchor to the gun and recover each item separately without damaging either the deck or the blinds.

The anchor was found without a stock but the two elements of the spare wooden stock lay amidships outside the entrance to the barber-surgeon's cabin.

THE UPPER DECK AT THE STERNCASTLE

Immediately aft of the forward end of the sterncastle a large bronze culverin (A-80/976) was supported on a truck carriage above light deck planking barely 5cm (2in) thick. This planking was supported on a series of deck beams fitted into beam shelves which ran fore and aft along the starboard side of the ship. Severe anchor damage had occurred in this

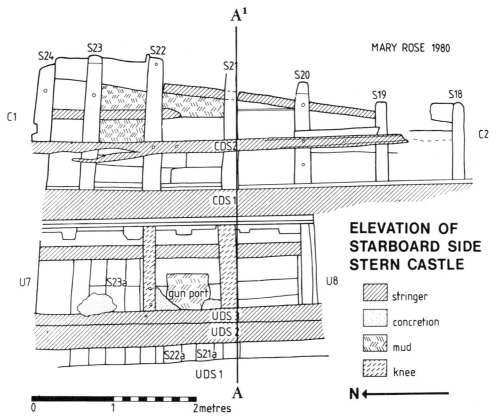

MARY ROSE 1980

ELEVATION OF STARBOARD SIDE STERN CASTLE

- stringer
- concretion
- mud
- knee

N ←

0   1   2 metres

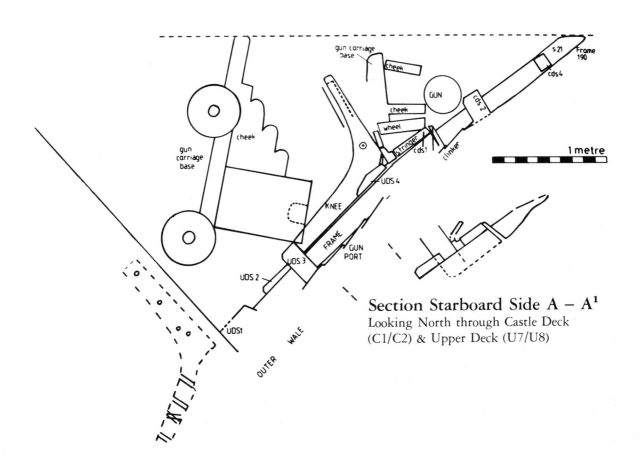

Section Starboard Side A – A¹
Looking North through Castle Deck (C1/C2) & Upper Deck (U7/U8)

1 metre

PREVIOUS PAGE, TOP

Elevation of the starboard side of the sterncastle between frames 18 and 24 showing the beam shelf for the upper and castle decks and their relationship to the internal stringers and the starboard frames.

PREVIOUS PAGE, BOTTOM

Section through starboard frame S-21 showing the relationship between the deck beams, hanging knees and framing. There has been some movement of the structure caused by heavy objects such as gun carriages and shot falling against the side of the hull.

A peaceful evening in the Solent in 1979, with the diving salvage vessel Sleipner *safely moored on site.*

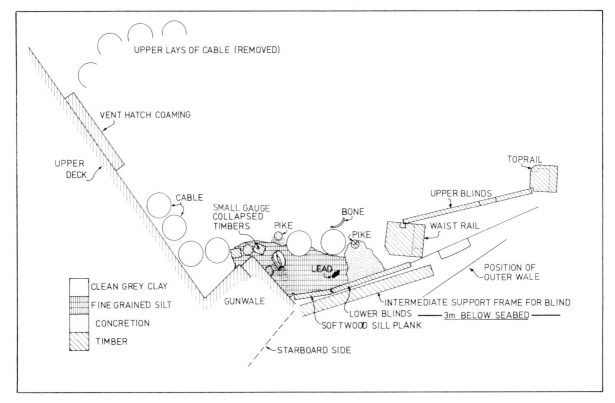

UPPER LAYS OF CABLE (REMOVED)

VENT HATCH COAMING

UPPER DECK

CABLE

SMALL GAUGE COLLAPSED TIMBERS

PIKE

BONE

PIKE

LEAD

GUNWALE

TOPRAIL

UPPER BLINDS

WAIST RAIL

POSITION OF OUTER WALE

INTERMEDIATE SUPPORT FRAME FOR BLIND

LOWER BLINDS ── 3m BELOW SEABED ──

SOFTWOOD SILL PLANK

STARBOARD SIDE

CLEAN GREY CLAY
FINE GRAINED SILT
CONCRETION
TIMBER

Section through starboard side of the ship to show relationship of the bulwark rail and the rails which support the blinds. The bulwark rail is a composite structure and both the capping piece and the standards which support the blinds have been displaced outwards. This movement can be seen elsewhere at upper deck level and it was probably caused by the impact as the ship hit the seabed and heavy objects moved across the ship.

Rider 1 and deadwood viewed from the north (bow) in situ. The first futtock on the starboard side can be seen forward of the floor timber which has a rectangular limber hole cut through its base. Ceiling planking and a thickened plank or footwale lie between the rider and the floor. In the foreground can be seen an eroded scarf in the keelson and the second strake on the port side. Visibility as good as this is extremely rare on the Mary Rose site.

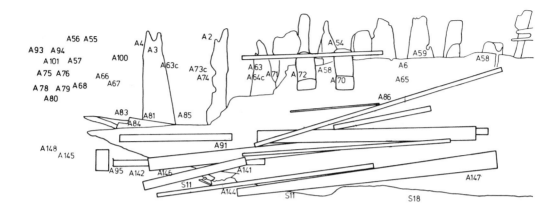

area and several of the deck beams were badly displaced when they were found, but one of them (U-70) passed right through the outer planking and must have been secured by driven wedges or pegs outside the hull in a manner reminiscent of the clinker-built cogs of the previous century. The deck beams had been supported by hanging knees which were bolted to the frames of the hull and the face of each deck beam and were carefully rebated around the stringers which as on other decks stiffened the hull longitudinally. All of the gunports on this deck were simple openings cut between two stringers with no evidence at all of gunport lids.

Planks and frames from the port side of the hull lying in the scourpit after tidal erosion had weakened the section of the ship which was exposed above the level of the seabed and caused it to collapse. The 'A' and 'S' numbers mark the position of finds and samples of sediment.

THE CASTLE DECK

Very little of the castle deck survives but a large bronze gun made by John and Robert Owen was found slumped against the starboard stringer (CD-S2). It was clear that this gun and its carriage had originally been housed in a port above the forward end of the sterncastle and that it had served to bombard enemy ships attempting to come alongside. Little of the supporting deck structure remained and when first examined the light planking, barely 4.5cm (1¾in) thick, appeared to be part of a temporary structure; however, further excavation showed that a continuous beam shelf and a deck clamp (CD-S1) had supported deck beams and planking. Aft of Trench 9 the upper castle deck had

See p165.

been completely destroyed by anchors dragging through the side, but among the scattered debris small swivel guns and hailshot pieces indicated the sort of weapons that had been used to defend the fighting castle at this point. Underneath the sterncastle a deep scourpit was formed soon after the ship sank but it had only been open to the currents for a relatively short period of time and the structure had clearly never been exposed to the violent scouring tides which degraded and destroyed the bow and the port side of the hull. Small oysters had settled on the outside of the hull in the calm water in the lee of the ship and then had smothered and died within 20 months as both the ship and the scourpits filled with fine silts. Most surprisingly of all, the pool-like calm of the sea beneath the sterncastle had left untangled and undamaged the blocks, ropes, deadeyes and lanyards of the running and standing rigging.

All of this delicate area had to be strengthened and reinforced before the ship could be recovered. The timber was immaculate, undamaged by tidal scour or biological degradation, but it needed special support by airbags to prevent it chafing on the steel support cradle when it was lifted into air.

The rigging elements consisted of two groups: single blocks attached by ropes to the chain-rail and deadeyes with five and seven holes for lanyards. The deadeyes were rigged in pairs and together they served to tighten and brace the standing rigging of the mainmast. The chain-rail was heavily buttressed by wooden braces bolted through the standards to the frames of the sterncastle in order to take the upward strain of the rigging. Below the chain-rail, the chains — a large slab of wood 60cm (2ft) broad — were also braced with robust brackets secured to the standards and to the main hull. These served to spread the shrouds as they passed outside to the chains on the side of the hull just above the level of the maindeck. Both the chain-rail and the chains bear a striking resemblance to those on the English galleon depicted in Matthew Baker's *Fragments of Ancient English Shipwrightry* (dated to *c*1586).

OPPOSITE
Recovering the spare anchor from the weather deck. The wooden stock for this anchor was stored aft in two sections which would have bolted together over the shank.

See p146.

CHAPTER 6

The Running and Standing Rigging

EVIDENCE FOR THE USE of blocks and deadeyes in running and standing rigging on sixteenth century warships in Northern Europe is confined to a limited number of contemporary but often confusing references, a few paintings and one or two loosely-dated rigging blocks in museum collections. The only contemporary picture of the *Mary Rose* sheds very little light on how the ship was rigged and how the standing and running rigging was used. The artist has depicted lifts, stays, halyards, shrouds and ratlines, but the lines are blurred and the detail fades out and disappears against the detailed drawing of the hull and the superstructure.

See p26-27. In the Anthony Roll the ship is seen with furled sails and four masts and a small furled spritsail protrudes forward below the bowsprit. The sails and the fore yards of the mizzen and bonaventure mizzen masts were triangular lateen sails with single lifts similar to those listed in the inventory of the *Henry Grace à Dieu* when she was launched in 1514.[1] A similar carrack depicted in the contemporary engraving of a naval battle in the Solent in 1545 has a lateen sail set on the mizzen mast and the *Henry Grace à Dieu*, the Admiral's flagship, attempts to beat off the challenge of the French galleys in the same picture with course and topsails set on her foremast and the lateen sail set on her bonaventure mizzen mast. Sails of this type were in use in the Mediterranean from the ninth century onwards where they were particularly useful for sailing close-hauled in coastal waters. By the sixteenth century their use on larger ships was usually confined to the mizzen mast and they were probably more efficient than square sails in light winds. Their use continued until nearly the end of the eighteenth century by which time the lateen sail was largely replaced by a gaff sail.

The *Mary Rose* carries three yards on her mainmast. The mainyard with furled square sail is suspended below the lower fighting top and the lifts or tackle to raise the yard can be clearly seen attached to blocks on the yardarms. The topsail yard has similar lifts securing it to a point on the topmast below the upper fighting top and a small top-

gallant yard carries a furled sail above the upper fighting top. The
original manuscript has been mutilated at this point but presumably
the topgallant mast carried a standard on a flagpole above the topgallant
yard. The foremast carries a lower yard and a topsail yard each with a
furled square sail and the rigging of the foresail lift with blocks and
lines is clearly depicted.

The artist has done little to illustrate the standing rigging other
than show a confusing assemblage of shrouds, ratlines and stays. The
chain-wales and chain-plates which served to spread the shrouds securing the mast athwartships are not shown, and their absence on the
Anthony Anthony picture has led some scholars to doubt if they were

A close-up of the Henry Grace à
Dieu, *depicted in the Cowdray
engraving on the day that the*
Mary Rose *sank, with topsails set
on her foremast and a lateen set on
her bonaventure mizzen.*

Henry Grace à Dieu, *the largest ship in the Anthony Roll, was built in 1512 and listed as 1000 tons. The illustration from this Roll contains a complete inventory of the 'ordnance, artillary, municions and habilliments for the warre' carried aboard the ship, including 21 bronze guns, 39 iron guns, 40 hailshot pieces, 90 handguns and 500 yew longbows. She carried 329 soldiers and 50 gunners, in addition to 301 mariners. The munitions include comanders, or heavy mallets, used to hammer the wedges behind the breech chambers, and tompions which must have been similar to those found in the* Mary Rose.

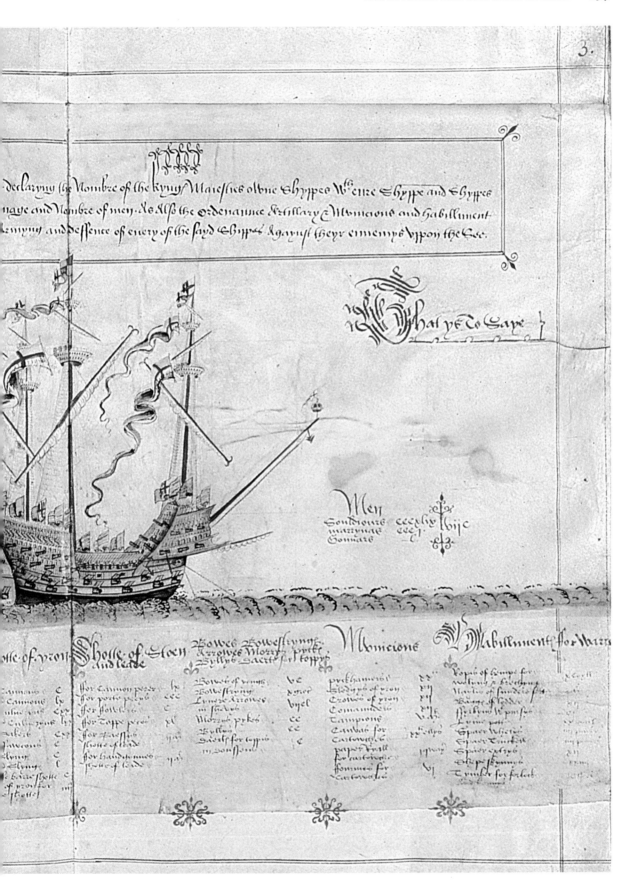

A large set of parrels folded and tied with rope in situ. When recovered, these were found to be suitable for a mast 0.50m in diameter. The parrels allowed the yard to be hoisted on the mast with comparative ease as the trucks, or wooden balls, acted as roller bearings.

A sister block with two sheaves set at right angles to each other.

necessary on a ship thought to have excessive tumblehome above the maindeck. However the Flemish carrack drawn by the artist 'W A' in the late fifteenth century clearly had channels for deadeyes and lanyards for securing and tensioning the shrouds from the mainmast and in 1981 excavation beneath the sterncastle revealed a similar assemblage of standing and running rigging lying close to the chains on the starboard side of the *Mary Rose*.

When the excavation of the *Mary Rose* began in 1971 it was considered unlikely that any elements of standing or running rigging would have survived the concerted salvage attempts in the sixteenth century and the combined effects of tides and storms over four centuries. Eroded blocks and sheaves were found in secondary deposits from 1976 onwards but it was always possible that these were anchorage contaminants abandoned by the salvors in the sixteenth century or lost from later ships.

During 1979, 1980 and 1981 an important group of blocks, deadeyes, thimbles and parrels were excavated in Trench 3, just forward of the main companionway. Most of these items were found in a compartment on the orlop deck, but some were found in the hold immediately below. It seems likely that originally they were all stored together in a compartment on the orlop deck, but as the ship sank movement of heavy ballast in the hold displaced some of the orlop deck planks and the heavier items fell through into the hold. The collapsed and fragmentary remains of a box or locker lay around the items in the hold. Sixteenth century items of ship's rigging are rare and as it rather begs the question to apply later terminology with definitive implications of usage and function, we have decided to construct an objective typology for *Mary Rose* rigging elements. The

The set of parrels discovered in the rigging locker being examined after cleaning by Adele Wilkes and Peter Whitlock, the Trust's Public Relations Officer.

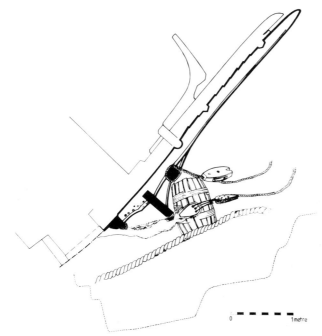

Section through chain-wale showing blocks and deadeyes found attached to the chains, and a barrel which may have contained joints of salted meat.

Excavation beneath the sterncastle showing the chain-rail and one of the standards which brace the chain-wale. One of a series of blocks can be seen attached to the rail by 1in diameter rope.

Two bronze sheaves from large blocks found in secondary levels and probably derived from collapsed rigging.

Spare parrel ribs and trucks from the rigging locker on the orlop deck.

Archaeological Supervisor Christopher Dobbs inspecting a large double block found in secondary sediments at the bow of the ship.

typology at present consists of five types: Type A – single blocks, consisting of a single sheave set in a roughly rectangular, rounded or pear-shaped shell; Type B – double blocks with two sheaves set into the shell, either parallel to each other, one above each other in series or at right-angles to each other; Type C – deadeyes, pear-shaped blocks of solid wood with a concave outer groove for a rope and holes for lanyards; Type D – thimbles, pear-shaped with a concave outer groove for a rope or iron hook to connect them, usually with one major hole and one or more smaller holes; Type E – parrels, composed of two elements: 1) the ribs with either three, four or five holes, sometimes with small secondary holes; 2) the trucks, solid wooden beads set alternately with the ribs to get a spaced 'necklace' of roller bearings which enabled a yard to be raised and lowered on a mast with friction-free ease.

BLOCKS, DEADEYES AND THIMBLES

These single blocks or pulleys consisted of a shell carved out of a single piece of wood with an ash or elm sheave wheel or pulley set within the shell and secured in place by a pin or choke which served as a spindle around which the sheave could rotate. Usually a sheave was of ash or elm but occasionally they were bronze and while most of the pins were of wood some of the larger sheaves, particularly the bronze ones, were secured with iron pins. Many of the blocks were still bound with a rope ring or block strop which passed over both ends of the pin, over a score in the tail of the block and through two concealed channels or scores in the head of the block. The same system of concealed scores for the head ropes of the block strop also occurred on double blocks. A single-sheaved block, Type A3.2, with a pronounced shoulder at the head and tail may have been used as a clew line block to hoist the clew or lowest corner of the sail to the middle of the yard.

Most of the double-sheave blocks found in the rigging store had two wooden sheaves set side by side in the shell and rotated around the same wooden pin. These general-purpose blocks were used singly or in pairs to set up the rigging, tension stays or secure restraining tackle and the heavier guns.

The second type of double block had two sheaves set in series, one above the other but turning in the same plane. These may have been used as part of a system of halyards and tyes used to raise and lower the yard.

The deadeyes found in the rigging stores were generally more crudely made than blocks which were well finished with chamfered and smoothed edges and they varied in size from 0.08m by 0.16m (3in by

$6\frac{1}{4}$in) to 0.23m by 0.36m (9in by 14in). The holes were crudely cut and the pear-shaped flat-sectioned block of the deadeye had deep concave grooves for a rope or iron strop around its outer edge. Thimbles were similar in shape and size to some of the smaller deadeyes but they were distinguished by having one large hole placed more or less centrally. Some thimbles had one, two or three smaller holes above the large hole and a group of thimbles have been found still attached to rope.

PARRELS

Individual parrel ribs and trucks were found in the storage area in O-3. See p140-141. Most of these were simple ribs with three or four holes for rope 1in (0.02m) in diameter and they were associated with trucks with holes of similar diameter. When in use the ribs were spaced alternately with the trucks on a length of rope to form a triple or quadruple necklace of roller bearings. This was secured to the yard by the rope ends which passed round the yard on either side of the mast and then passed back over the notches in the ribs to be secured by marling the ends of the rope together.

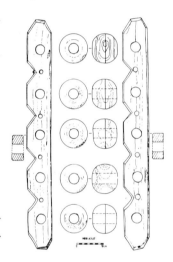

A set of parrels from the Mary Rose.

A breast rope, similar to one recorded in an inventory of the *Regent* in 1497, may have been used as a preventer to ensure complete security. Some of the ribs had additional holes of smaller diameter at the base of the V-shaped notches which were cut back into the face of each rib. These may have been used to nip the rope with a small length of line and secure its position in the base of the notch. In 1981 a group of 7 ribs and 29 trucks were found in the storage area complete with their cordage. This complete set of parrels had been carefully folded for storage and when extended they measured 0.8m by 0.9m ($31\frac{1}{2}$in by $35\frac{1}{2}$in).

The edges and outer face of the ribs had been painted with a flat cream paint but the flat faces of the ribs where they passed against the mast were unpainted. Four ribs had been folded over onto three ribs with the trucks and the ropes still *in situ* and the carefully folded strands of rope leading from one row to the next had been sandwiched between the two layers; the ends of the rope had been used to secure the bundle. As rigged the parrels would fit a mast 0.5m (20in) in diameter and they were almost certainly used on the main lower yard. Ten strands of line still *in situ* in the small holes at the base of the notches would have served to secure the rope as it passed over the ribs.

THE CHAIN-WALES

The chain-wale (or channel) for the mainmast remains *in situ* above the gunports on the maindeck. Although it has been eroded just forward of the transom on the starboard side, it seems to have run the complete length of the sterncastle. The chain-wale itself is a sturdy timber 0.6m (2ft) wide and 70mm (2¾in) thick, and a series of stout wooden braces support it against the upward thrust of the rigging. Above the chain-wale a rail ran fore and aft rebated into the vertical standards and supported by the braces, which rise from the chain-wales. One-inch diameter ropes still lay wrapped around the rail and attached to a series of blocks, lying in the silts above the chain-wale. Most astonishing of all was to find the chain still *in situ* passing up from the wale immediately above the maindeck gunports over the edge of the chain-wale to a heavily concreted deadeye. The chain consisted of seven well-preserved links of iron bar approximately 25mm (1in) in diameter and each link is about 175mm (7in) long. A corroded base-plate or a large ringbolt attached the chain to the wale above the gunports and there was no protective edge to the chain-wale to prevent abrasions when the chains moved with the movement of the masts. This arrangement of rail, chain-wale and standards is almost identical to that depicted in Baker's *Fragments of Ancient English Shipwrightry*, and its occurrence in the *Mary Rose* shows that its history and tradition goes back a long way. Brygandine's accounts of payments made on behalf of the King to merchants

Detail from Matthew Baker's Fragments of Ancient English Shipwrightry *showing chain-rail above chain-wale, similar to the chain-rail and standards seen beneath the* Mary Rose *(see p141 bottom and p142 top).*

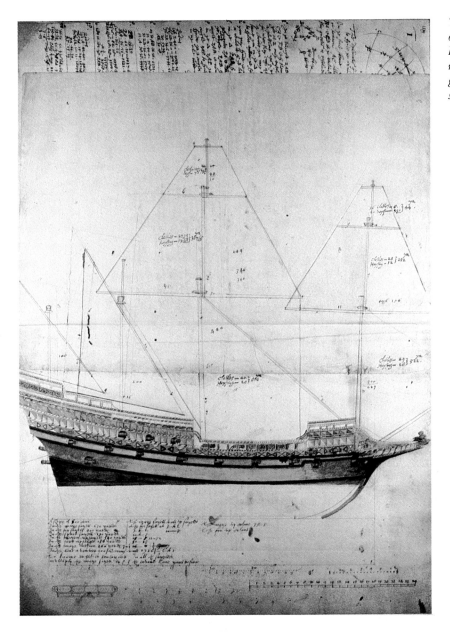

The earliest English representation of a sail plan, from Matthew Baker's Fragments. *Although representing the practice of a generation later, it shows many similarities with the* Mary Rose.

equipping the *Mary Fortune* and the *Regent* in 1497 include references to payments for fourteen chains 'which fastened with bolts of iron to the sides of the said ship (the *Mary Fortune*) for to serve to the shrowds'.

The *Regent* inventory lists chains, halliards and 'dedemessen' (deadeyes) for the mainmast, main mizzen, bonaventure mast and foremast. In the case of the *Mary Rose* it seems that a single chain-wale served to spread the chains and standing rigging for each of the three masts aft of amidships. An eroded chain-wale and deadeyes found above the maindeck beneath the bowcastle suggest that a similar wale served to spread the shrouds from the foremast.

See p 141. Above the chain-wale a series of barrels contained a quantity of animal bone and one is reminded of the Dutch practice of de-salting meat on board East Indiamen by placing it in barrels of fresh water, secured in the chains for coolness. This long-standing practice may well have been in use on that hot day in July 1545. Certainly barrels do not float downwards and the ones excavated beneath the sterncastle are difficult to explain unless they were there when the ship sank.

A group of wooden thimbles recovered from the stores in the hold complete with two strand ropes.

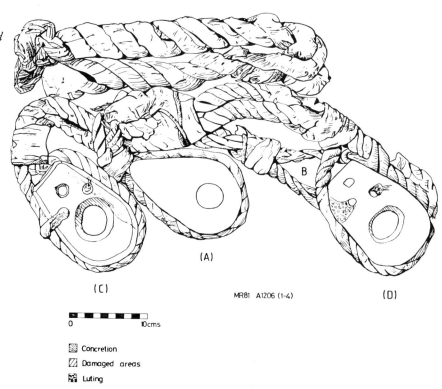

(A)

(C)

MR81 A1206 (1–4)

(D)

0   10cms

▓ Concretion

▨ Damaged areas

▨ Luting

CHAPTER 7

Ordnance

GUNS

THE ASSEMBLAGE OF BRONZE and iron guns used on board the *Mary Rose* mirrors the great technological changes taking place in warfare on land and at sea during the first half of the sixteenth century. The first use of guns by an English army had been nearly two centuries earlier, in 1346, when Edward III used bombards to demoralise and scatter the serried ranks of Genoese mercenaries ranged against his longbowmen at Crecy.

The royal wardrobe accounts list guns, barrels of powder, shot of lead and pieces of lead purchased for the King's use in France, and these stores went ahead of the King when he sailed to Normandy. The contemporary historian, Froissart, in the *Chronique Abrigées* written towards the end of his life, recorded: 'The English had with them two of the bombards and they made two or three discharges upon the Genoese who fell into a state of disorder when they heard them roar.' This confusion opened up the way to victory, and the supremacy of the English archer with his longbow over the French crossbowman confirmed that victory.

Edward III continued to demonstrate his faith in the new guns at the siege of Calais the following year and although contemporary accounts make it clear that these new guns were more effective in breaking enemy morale than breaking down town walls, the era of the gun was here to stay. During the fifteenth century merchant ships were often armed with light guns in the tops and in the waist, but the range of these early guns was small and the field of fire so limited that guns of this type can have been of little use except at close quarters.

An illustration of a Flemish carrack of 1490 shows five small guns on the quarterdeck and a swivel gun mounted on the mizzen top, and the great Portuguese carrack, *Santa Caterina do Monte Sinai*, carried more than 160 light guns on the open weather deck in the waist and in the bow- and sterncastles. All of these guns appear to be small calibre, and the fire-power of these early ships was limited by the weight of guns they could carry without seriously affecting the ship's stability.

One of the earliest pictures (fourteenth century) showing a city being attacked by a gunner. The weapon appears to be a small stave-built gun mounted on a wooden rest, and the holes in the timber support at the rear suggests that its elevation could be adjusted by a locking pin. A similar arrangement of holes in the 'tiller' which passed through the bed of the carriages for the iron guns on the Mary Rose enabled the gunner to elevate the gun as required.

Until a way could be found to bring guns down into the hull, it was impossible to use many heavy guns on board ship.

Loading hatches cut into the sides of the hull, high above the waterline, can be seen in fourteenth and fifteenth century illustrations and there is a large open hatch cut low down on the port quarter of the Flemish carrack of 1490. At first glance this hatch appears to be ridiculously low and there is no evidence of an external lid to prevent water pouring into the ship. However, it would have been perfectly feasible to batten down this hatch with an internal lid after the ship was loaded and before she left port. It would have been quite a different problem in a clinker-built ship to devise a way of cutting a series of

ports which could be swiftly opened to run guns forward to battle stations and to ensure equally swift closure when it became necessary to disengage the enemy and go about.

Heavy cast bronze guns recovered from the starboard side of the Mary Rose.

The problem of how to cut ports low down in the hull and provide them with a lid which could be secured rapidly and effectively apparently remained unsolved until the change from clinker to carvel hull planking occurred some time at the beginning of the sixteenth century. For example, the remains of an early ship discovered and surveyed in 1912 at the site of Woolwich Power Station in London, show evidence of her hull having been rebuilt from clinker to carvel some time in her life. The ship has been tentatively identified as the *Sovereign*, a ship which was built in 1488 and rebuilt in Portsmouth in

1509. A comparison of her armament in 1495 and 1514 shows that she carried 141 comparatively lightweight guns in the waist, stern- and bowcastles in 1495 and 84 heavier guns after her rebuild in 1514. The Woolwich ship had undoubtedly been rebuilt because, although her main hull was carvel-built with smooth edge-to-edge planking fastened to the frames with oak trenails, the frames had lands (or notches) cut into them where overlapping clinker planking had once been fitted. This change may well have occurred when she was rebuilt and the change from clinker to carvel planking made feasible the installation of watertight gunport lids and a purpose-built gundeck between the weather deck and the waterline.

As soon as the rebuild of the *Sovereign* was complete, Henry VIII ordered the construction of two new ships in Portsmouth, the *Mary Rose* of 600 tons and the *Peter Pomegranite*. There is some evidence that the hull of the *Mary Rose* may have been clinker-planked originally — certainly some of her frames which now carry carvel planking on the starboard quarter have lands cut in them to receive overlapping plank- ing — but until the ship has been carefully examined, it is difficult to be sure; the adzed notches and inserted filler strips may simply be evidence of frugal re-use of secondhand timbers from other ships when the ship was rebuilt in 1536.

The earliest published inventory of guns on board the *Mary Rose* dates from 1514 when she was put into reserve after the war with France. This inventory lists 7 heavy bronze guns and 34 heavy iron guns as well as lighter guns. It may be that even at this early date she carried the heavy guns on a purpose-built gundeck. This important change to heavier armament and a defined weapons strategy at sea meant more than just cutting a few ports in the side of the ship and fitting them with efficient lids: in order to counter the challenge of bow-chasers — long-range culverins firing from the bow of oared gal- leys — it was necessary to place efficient long-range weapons in the stern of the great carracks.

To meet this need the rounded stern of the fifteenth century ship was replaced by a square transom stern with lidded ports on each side of the rudder and tiers of lighter guns high in the after end of the sterncastle above the transom. This change is well illustrated in the *Mary Rose* and the artist who illustrated the Anthony Roll has done his best to suggest, by subtle use of colour and shading, how bronze and wrought iron guns were disposed about the King's ships. However, if we really want to understand exactly how these guns were used, we must take *all* the evidence — the documentary, the circumstantial and the results of the archaeological excavation — and consider it together.

When the *Mary Rose* sailed out of Portsmouth harbour to meet the French fleet, she seems to have carried fewer guns than were listed in the Anthony Roll. Although it is possible that some of her guns were recovered during the sixteenth century by Peter Paul, to whom King Henry VIII paid £57 11s 5d in 1547 and £50 in 1547 for recovering guns from the wreck, it seems clear that the number of gunports in the starboard side of the hull were fewer than can be seen in the contemporary illustration and it is difficult to see how the full armament listed in the inventory could have been sensibly disposed around the ship. Perhaps the ship was ill-prepared for action when she left harbour; certainly the rot found in her keelson and deadwood suggests that she was ready for a refit! As we examine the archaeological evidence there are intriguing signs of hurried and makeshift alterations to the disposition of heavy ordnance on board the ship when she sank.

One of the gunports cut into the blindages (or screens) above the gunwale on the weather deck is empty. The surrounding timbers are undamaged and where a gun should be, there lay a coil of anchor cable fallen from amidships and tumbled across the deck as the ship hit the seabed.

See p104.

Aft of this empty port, a heavy wrought iron gun, supported on a two-wheeled gun carriage, protruded through an unlidded semi-circular port. This gun was overlain by the spare anchor, still connected to the coil of cable, and the whole complex was covered by fragments of netting and the supporting joists and purlins which were intended to provide a protective anti-boarding screen above the open weather deck and which, at the moment of disaster, proved to be a death trap for the men on the deck below. It would have been impossible for either Tudor salvors or the Deanes to remove a gun from this deck without disturbing either the collapsed superstructure or the anchor and cable, so we must assume that the vessel went to sea with only a single wrought iron gun in position in the waist of the starboard side of the ship. This is surprising, as there was room for three guns on each side of the weather deck.

On the same deck in the sterncastle, a large bronze muzzle-loading gun was found in position, still on its carriage and run forward through an unlidded gunport. After removing the gun, we found a socket cut in the sill of the port to take the pintle of a swivel gun and a lighter gun of this type would have been much more suitable in this position high above the centre of gravity on a lightly-built deck. Was the heavier gun placed on board in a hurry because the ship was sailing to engage an enemy in sheltered waters close to her home port?

On the main gundeck only six guns have been found *in situ*, and

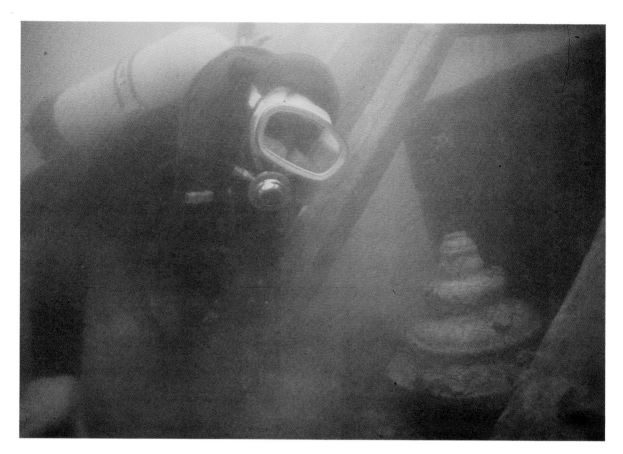

Margaret Rule looking through the ledges of the weather deck at a bronze gun made by Peter Baude in 1543 which had fallen against the upper deck beams when the ship heeled onto her starboard side.

One of the quoins or wooden wedges used to secure the breech chamber of a wrought iron gun in position.

Recovering a wrought iron gun complete with the bed of its carriage. All of the wrought iron guns found in situ *had carriages with a single axle and a pair of wheels.*

See p161.

their positions do not correspond to the picture in the Anthony Roll. Gun carriages with large diameter spoked wheels, normally associated with field carriages, were found *in situ* on the main gundeck supporting a wrought iron breech-loading gun, and similar carriages were found on the upper deck at the stern as well as in the stores on the orlop deck at the bow. Were these carriages really intended for use at sea or is this further evidence of 'making do' in an emergency? What we have to do is piece together the evidence – from the contemporary documents, from the Deanes' salvage in the nineteenth century and from our own excavations – and see if we can come to any conclusions.

THE DEANES' GUNS

On 16 June 1836, Charles and John Deane recovered a superb demi-cannon made by Arcanus of Cesene in 1542 for King Henry VIII from the long-lost site of the *Mary Rose* wreck. The following August, two more bronze muzzle-loading guns and two wrought iron guns were recovered from the site, brought ashore to Portsmouth and handed over to the Board of Ordnance. With commendable speed, a committee of the Board of Ordnance issued a 13-page report on 30 September 1838 in which they concluded, 'It appears quite certain that the *Mary Rose* was lost at Spithead, that the ship was never weighted up and from the description of the guns lately discovered, there is every reason to believe that they formed part of her armament.' There the matter rested until 1840 when the Deane brothers recovered further guns from the site including six wrought iron culverins nearly 12ft long and once again made by Arcanus of Cesene in 1542.

Guns recovered by the Deane brothers 1836 and 1840

Bronze (4)   Cannon Royal, 8ft 6in (2.60m)
              Demi-Cannon, 11ft 10in (3.40m)
              Culverin, 10ft (3.00m)
              Culverin Bastard, 8ft 6in (2.60m)
Iron   11 large
              9 small guns or chambers

Although most of these guns have lain in museums for the last 140 years they have confused rather than illuminated scholars and ship historians. The list of ordnance and ammunition on the Anthony Roll tells us little of how the various guns were disposed around the ship and although the Deanes took pains to record the guns with immaculate watercolour sketches immediately after recovery there is no record of how the guns related to each other or to the wreck from which they were recovered.

See p42-43.

The random mixture of Henry VIII's newest weapons of cast bronze with antique stave-built wrought iron guns was difficult for some scholars to accept and although all the guns recovered by the Deanes were loaded and primed ready for action, it was easier to believe that the 'old-fashioned' inefficient breech-loading guns were ballast from the hold, than that the gunners, guns and ship, were welded together as one co-ordinated strategic weapon of war. I hoped that if we could record the guns *in situ* as we excavated, we might be able to understand and analyse this Tudor strategy.

Andrew Fielding and Ted Clamp with one of the wrought iron guns recovered from the main gundeck.

RECENTLY RECOVERED GUNS

The recovery of a barrel of a wrought iron gun from an area north-west of the wreck site in 1970 was fortuitous. It was not associated with the hull and a double layer of concretion products suggests that it may well have been dropped or jettisoned by early salvors. The barrel had been part of a breech-loading gun and although the chamber was missing when the gun was recovered, a cast iron shot and traces of carbon and sulphur from the charge were found in the breech. Gamma radiography revealed that the barrel had been made from a single plate of wrought iron which had been forge-welded into a cylinder with a single seam along its length. The gunsmith had then hot-shrunk a series of collars and hoops onto the barrel to reinforce it and the result was a strong, gas-tight cylinder. This was a narrow bore, high-velocity

See p 169.

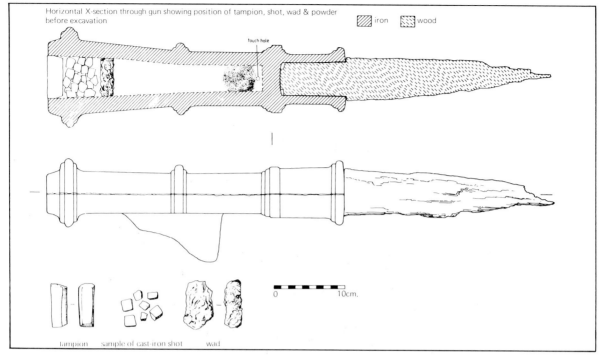

Horizontal X-section through gun showing position of tampion, shot, wad & powder before excavation

iron   wood

touch hole

tampion   sample of cast-iron shot   wad

0   10cm.

A Hailshot piece made of cast iron recovered in 1979. This short range weapon had a rectangular bore and was loaded with iron dice. A tompion sealed the muzzle and the triangular lug beneath the barrel was hooked over a rail or the sill of a port to absorb the recoil. The gun was also fitted with a short wooden tiller.

Base, forward axle and two elements of the starboard cheek of the carriage for the Owen gun.

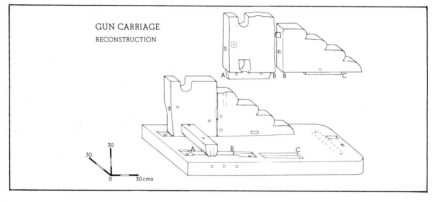

GUN CARRIAGE
RECONSTRUCTION

30

30

0   30cms

gun capable of damaging the light superstructure of an enemy ship at a distance, but unfortunately because it was found some distance away from the site we will never know how or where it was mounted on board the ship. It was not until 1971 that a gun was excavated and recorded in relation to the hull of the *Mary Rose* and this was in a secondary position where it had fallen into the scourpit on the port quarter from its original position in the stern.

Since 1971, six bronze guns have been recovered, five of them with their carriages, as well as six large chambered wrought iron guns, six wrought iron swivel guns and three cast iron hailshot pieces. The disposition of the guns on the decks is completely rational: long range anti-ship cast bronze guns firing cast iron shot interspersed with anti-personnel wrought iron guns which fired either stone shot that shattered on impact with devastating effect or cast iron or lead shot.

The relative inefficiency of the crudely-built iron guns did not matter — they were meant to function at short range with maximum

HRH Prince Charles and Margaret Rule inspect a bronze demi cannon made by Robert and John Owen in 1542 and found on its carriage on the main deck beneath the sterncastle in 1981. The makers' inscription reads 'ROBERT AND JHON OWYN BRETHERYN MADE THYS DEMI CANON ANNO DN 1542'

effect. Made of staves or bars of iron formed into cylinders around mandrels and forge-welded along each seam by a blacksmith, each barrel had a series of iron collars or sleeves hot-shrunk along their length to give extra strength. The ill-fitting stone shot and the uneven inner surface of the barrel meant that windage, or loss of gas, was inevitable and close range must have been the order of the day.

CARRIAGES FOR WROUGHT IRON GUNS

Several iron guns were recovered by the Deanes with solid wooden carriages and although no evidence of axles or wheels survived, iron staining on the under surface suggested that bolts had been used to secure the carriages to some form of mounting. All the iron guns found *in situ* in 1980 and 1981 were supported on a wooden bed with a single axle and a pair of wheels enabling the gunner to run the guns back whenever necessary to close and secure the gunport lids. The guns are chambered breech-loading guns and the chambers are held in position by a T-shaped wedge. Aft of the wedge, a rebate through the carriages housed a wooden tiller. The undersides of the carriages were grooved longitudinally, although whether this is simply to lower the ratio of mass to volume or to allow air to circulate beneath the barrel for cooling purposes, is uncertain. The guns were tied to the carriages with tightly wound cordage which was laid securely into purpose-cut chamfers in the sides of the carriage.

On the main gundeck a row of four large guns has been found, each one run forward on a wooden carriage with the muzzle protruding through an open, lidded gunport. The double-axled carriages with solid wheels which support the bronze guns vary only in detail from the carriages used on Nelson's flagship, HMS *Victory* but a close examination reveals subtle differences: the cheeks are made of two elements secured with simple mortice and tenon joints. The foremost element supports the trunnions of the gun which are held in place by a flat capsquare which passes across the top of the fully recessed trunnion. This iron capsquare continues down the forward and trailing edge of the fore cheek and is bolted to the bed of the carriage.

No trace of a hinge or gudgeon pin has been found, but without such a device, it would have been impossible to insert or remove a gun without removing the stepped trailing element of the cheek to unbolt the iron strap. The foremost cheeks are connected by two transverse iron bolts and the cheeks slope towards each other to match the

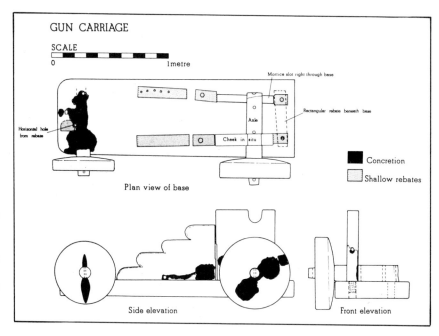

Plan view and elevation of the gun carriage found in the upper castle deck. Note that both axles were above the base of the carriage. This may have been done to lower the centre of gravity when this gun was placed at such a high position in the ship.

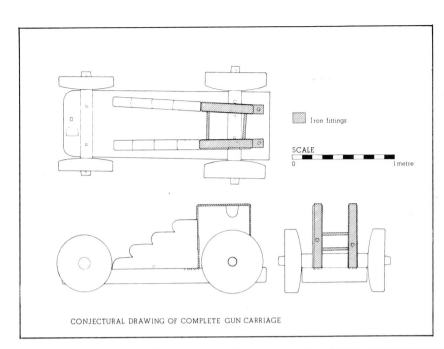

CONJECTURAL DRAWING OF COMPLETE GUN CARRIAGE

A reconstruction drawing of the complete gun carriage used to support the gun made by John and Robert Owen in 1537 recovered from the upper castle deck of the Mary Rose.

Chief Diver David Burden with a wheel from the carriage of a wrought iron gun.

Plastic ice cream containers used to support a wooden wheel as it is recovered from the sea.

narrowing diameter of the gun. Each carriage seems to be purpose-built for a particular gun and the one which supported the heavy gun made by John and Robert Owen high in the castle deck above the waist of the ship had axles above the bed of the carriage to lower the centre of gravity.

AMMUNITION

Guns and munitions of war (Anthony Inventory 1546)

Gonnes of Brasse		*Gonnes of Yron*	
Cannons	2	Port pecys	12
Demi Cannons	2	Slynges	2
Culveryns	2	Demi slynges	3
Demi Culveryns	6	Quarter slynges	1
Sakers	2	Fowlers	6
Fawcons	1	Basses	30
Total	15	Toppe pecys	2
		Hayleshott	20
		Hand gonnes	50
		Complete total	126

Shotle of Yron, Shotle of Stoen and Leade

Shot of Iron		*Shot of Stone and Lead*	
For cannon	50	For port pieces	200
For demi-cannon	60	For fowlers	170
For culverin	60	For toppe pieces	20
For demi-culverin	140	For basses	400
For sakers	80	(shot of lead)	
For falcon	60	For hand guns	1000
For sling	40	(shot of lead)	
For demi-sling	40		
For quarter sling	50		
Dice of iron			

All of the guns recovered by the Deanes and in the excavations of the 1970s and early 1980s were loaded and primed ready to fire, and in some cases rams, reamers and powder shovels lay nearby, ready for reloading when necessary. The large bronze guns were certainly loaded with cast iron shot as in the inventory and the active chemical attack generated by the corrosion products of iron acting on the cast bronze has provided severe headaches for the conservators charged with preserving these fine guns.

Some of the wrought iron guns were loaded with cast iron shot, others with stone or lead shot. Each gun had a specified function and was loaded for a particular use. Several types of lead shot had been found on the decks of the ship and among the collapsed superstructure of the sterncastle. Two pairs of finished stone shot-moulds and offcuts of sheet lead were also recovered from the area of the sterncastle and an unfinished stone mould was found in a compartment on the orlop deck. No stores of finished lead shot were found and nothing like the 1400 shot listed in the inventory have been recovered and it seems that the gunners only had the relatively small amount of shot which were

A cast iron hailshot piece with a rectangular bore and a wooden tiller. This was a muzzle-loading weapon and when recovered it was loaded with rectangular iron dice. The muzzle was sealed with a rectangular tampion and at short range it would have been a devastating anti-personnel weapon.

found with them at battle stations. The lead shot falls into several distinct types:

Type 1   Plain shot 10–25mm diameter ($\frac{1}{2}$–1in)
Type 2   Plain shot 25–35mm diameter (1–1$\frac{1}{4}$in)
Type 3   Plain shot 35–45mm diameter (1$\frac{1}{4}$–1$\frac{3}{4}$in)
Type 4   Bar shot 35–45mm diameter (1$\frac{1}{4}$–1$\frac{3}{4}$in)
Type 5   Plain shot 45–55mm diameter (1$\frac{3}{4}$–2in)
Type 6   Bar shot 45–55mm diameter (1$\frac{3}{4}$–2in)
Type 7   Wire-linked shot 50mm diameter (2in)
Type 8   Wire-linked shot 77–80mm diameter (3–3$\frac{1}{4}$in)

The bar shot were usually in poor condition with either a complete void where the iron bar had been set into the lead during the moulding process or considerable distortion of the lead shot caused by a 'growth' of corroded iron. The wire-linked shot were all found on a collapsed wooden basket or fender in the sterncastle below a thick layer of redeposited silt and shell and in an area where there had been considerable damage caused by anchors dragging through the ship. Although these shot may just have been more recent contaminants or naval anchorage rubbish, no other recent material was found in this area and it seems much more likely that they derived from guns used on the upper castle deck. This theory is reinforced by the discovery nearby of a small iron swivel gun, 79.543, with a bore of 50mm (2in).

This weapon could have fired either the smaller wire-linked shot or the numerous single lead shot found in this area. A small bronze powder ladle of similar diameter was found close by. Cross bar shot of iron are mentioned in an inventory of the Tower of London of 1559:[2]

Crossebarred shot for demy cannons	11
Crossebarred shot for culveringes	13
Crossebarred shot for demy culveringes	53
Crossebarred shot for sacres	138
Crossebarred shot for mynions	79
Crossebarred shot for fawcons	109

The term 'fawcon' (or falcon) was used for widely different guns in the early sixteenth century and an inventory listing equipment in the Tower of London in 1523 refers to 'Fawcons of iron with chambers' and 'Fawcons of brasse' in the same list. In general terms it was a small calibre gun with or without a chamber and in spite of the Anthony Roll reference to '1 falcon with 50 iron shot', it seems possible that the small swivel gun found in the stern of the *Mary Rose* is a chambered falcon of the type referred to in the 1523 inventory and that it fired lead shot weighing 2lb of 2in (0.05m) diameter. No iron shot of this diameter have been found on the site.

THE GUN MADE BY JOHN AND ROBERT OWEN IN 1537

In 1511 when the *Mary Rose* was commissioned, a foundry for casting bronze guns and bells was established at Houndsditch in the East End of London in Belle House. By 1529 John and Robert Owen were working there with Peter Baude, a Frenchman, and they cast guns for the King and bells for the church. Only five of their guns survive today and the one found on board the *Mary Rose* may have been specially cast for use on the ship after she was rebuilt in 1536. The guns had a bore of 0.11m (4in) and an overall length of 3.3m (10ft 9in). The button of the cascabel is unusually long (0.25m, 10in), possibly to take a breeching rope, and the gun was loaded with a solid cast iron shot when it was recovered.

The two inscriptions on the gun are particularly interesting. Between the first reinforcing ring and the 'dolphins', a simple inscription records in English 'ROBERT AND JOHN OWYN BRETHERYN BORNE IN THE CYTE OF LONDON THE SONNES OF AN INGLISH MADE THYS BASTARD ANNO DNI 1537'. The term 'bastard' simply refers to the fact that the weapon was non-standard and

Drawing by Debby Fulford of a bronze gun and carriage recovered from the sterncastle.

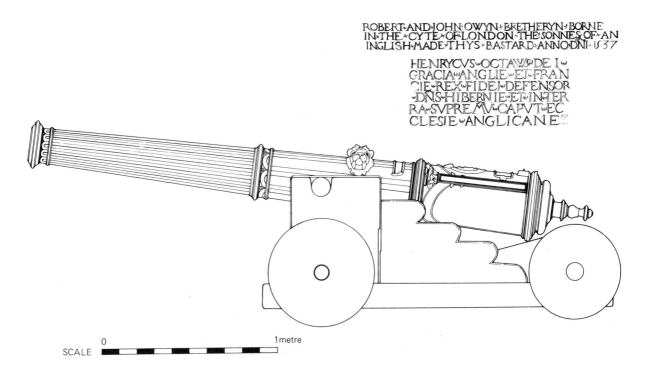

ROBERT·AND·JOHN·OWYN✦BRETHERYN·BORNE
IN·THE✦CYTE✦OF·LONDON·THE·SONNES·OF·AN
INGLISH✦MADE·THYS·BASTARD·ANNO·DNI· 1537

HENRYCVS✦OCTAW✦DE I ✦
GRACIA✦ANGLIE✦ET·FRAN
CIE✦REX✦FIDEI·DEFENSOR
·DNS·HIBERNIE·ET·INTER
RA✦SVPREMV✦CAPVT·EC
CLESIE✦ANGLICANE

SCALE
0   1metre

A selection of stone, iron and lead shot, and a pair of stone moulds used for casting lead shot on board the ship. The two halves of the mould were tied securely together and molten lead poured through the v-shaped orifice. The modern lead shot seen in the mould would have been ready for use after the v-shaped riser had been removed.

BELOW
Stave-built cannister shot seen underwater loaded with sharp broken flints.

Stone shot fallen against a rising knee on the main gundeck. The impact of the ship hitting the seabed when it sank caused most of the heavy objects to break loose and fall against the starboard side.

BELOW
Some of the hundreds of iron shot recovered from the main gundeck being brought on Sleipner *in a steel cube.*

could not be either a culverin or a cannon, but more interesting perhaps is the simple pride and patriotism reflected in the term 'Sons of an English [man]'.

The second inscription lies on the first reinforce below a crowned and gartered Tudor rose. It reads, in Latin, 'Henry the Eighth by grace of God, King of England and France and Lord of Ireland, Defender of the Faith and on earth supreme head of the Church of England'.

Four of the guns made by the Owen brothers survive in public and private collections. In 1543, as a result of the French destruction of villages and homesteads in earlier years, Henry VIII ordered that each parish on the Isle of Wight should provide a falconet of brass or iron for the defence of the island. Two still survive and they were both made by the Owen brothers. The first, on public display in the museum at Carisbrooke Castle, is a cast bronze falcon with a 70mm (2¾in) bore and an inscription recording that 'ROBERT AND JOHN OWINE BRETHERINE MADE THIS FACONE ANNO 1549' This gun, although smaller in bore and length, is similar to the *Mary Rose* gun in that it has a long cascabel button. The second gun on the Isle of Wight is in private ownership in Brading and it was last fired to celebrate the passing of the Reform Bill. Two 'parish' guns from the Channel Islands were also made by members of the Owen family: one in St Peter Parish, Jersey was made by John 'Owin' in 1551 and a falcon cast in 1550 by Thomas 'Owin' for the Island of Guernsey, is now in Plymouth, Massachusetts.

ARCHERY

Henry VIII did all he could to preserve by statute and by example the premier position of the bowmen of England. In 1509 as a young man of 18 'his grace shotte as strong and as great a length as anie of his garde' and in 1520 he again demonstrated his skill with a longbow at the lavish summit meeting with the French King at the Field of the Cloth of Gold where he repeatedly shot into the centre of the white over a range of 240 yards (220m). In 1510 he purchased 40,000 yew bow staves from the Doge of Venice and in 1512 he appointed Henry Southworth and Henry Pikeman Surveyors of the Bowmakers and Keepers of the Bows at the Tower of London.[3] As late as 1534 Henry ordered 30,000 bows to be made and stored at the Tower and the Anthony inventory records that in addition to great guns of brass and iron his ships were equipped with 2940 yew longbows. It is amazing that none of the archery equipment

Alex Hildred, one of the team of archaeological supervisors, examining a bronze gun made by Robert and John Owen soon after recovery from the sea.

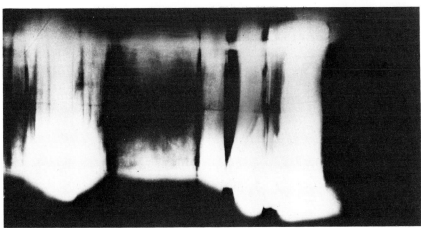

Gamma radiograph of a section of the barrel of the plate-built wrought iron gun recovered in 1970. The dark line of the single seam indicates that the gun was made from a plate of wrought iron formed into a cylinder and forge welded on a mandrel.

Spoked wheel of a gun carriage as first seen on the gundeck in the sterncastle.

OPPOSITE
Recovery of heavy objects such as the large wrought iron gun on its timber bed within the Mary Rose *took place whenever tidal conditions were right, and sometimes the work went on after dark.*

A linstock with its head carved as a man's fist used to apply a slow match to the breech of a gun in order to ignite the charge. Many of the linstocks are carved in the form of a dragon or crocodile's head and similar tools have been found on the wreck sites of an Armada vessel, the Trinidad Valencera, *dating from 1588*

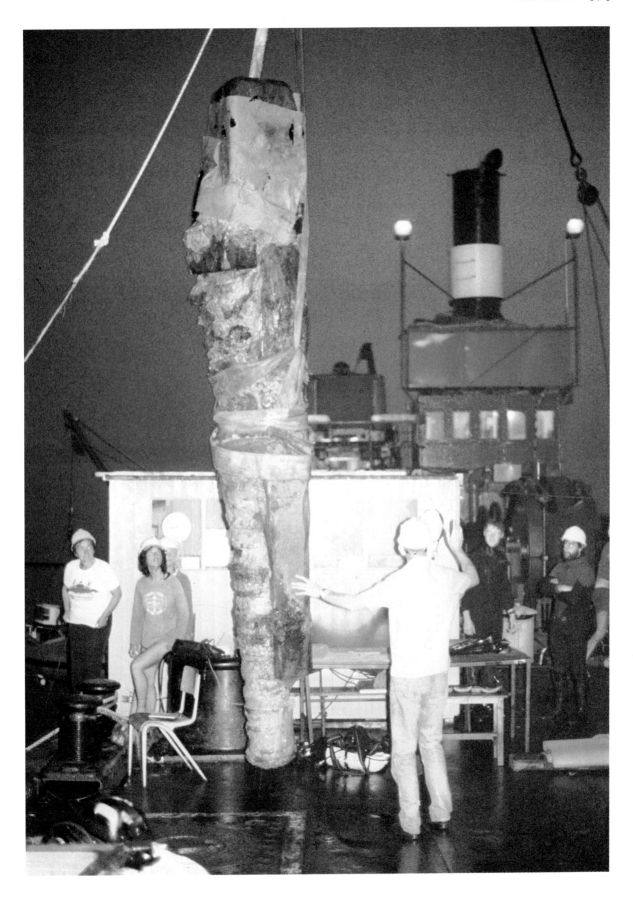

bought and stored for use on land or at sea has survived. The one dubious exception is the arrow belonging to the Dean and Chapter of Westminster and found in Henry V's chapel in Westminster Abbey. However this arrow was only discovered in 1887 and we await confirmation of its medieval origin by scientific examination. Bows recovered from the *Mary Rose* in the nineteenth century were thought to be yew staves from stores in the hold and since their discovery there has been scholarly disagreement about whether they had self-nocks or notches cut at each end to take the strings, or whether they had been fitted with horn nocks to take the strain at each tip.

Since 1979 over 2000 arrows, 138 bows and 12 bracers or wrist guards have been recovered from within the hull. Some of this material comes from battle stations on the main and upper decks but chests of bows and arrows have also been recovered from storage compartments on the orlop deck. The Anthony inventory records 250 yew bows, 6 gross of bow strings and 400 sheaves of arrows on board the ship and the same inventory records archery equipment on board all the King's great ships. Even the *George* of 60 tons carried 30 bows and the *Rose* See p 174. *Slype* a small row-barge of 20 tons carried 10 long bows to back up a bronze saker and hand guns. Whether these long bows were intended to be used as part of a ship's artillery or whether they were for land use when troops were sent ashore has been an open question, but sufficient archery equipment has been found alongside the remains of archers on the fighting deck to suggest that archers were preparing to defend the ship when she sank.

See p 150. Longbows had been used alongside ordnance on land since the early fifteenth century and numerous illuminated manuscripts show longbows and crossbows in action alongside breech-loading ordnance. Henry VIII had ensured a supply of trained bowmen to augment the militia which was recruited as required from the land-holding yeomanry.[4] In 1512 an act was passed to encourage the use of the longbow and this was confirmed by an Act of Parliament in 1541. The act ensured that fully-trained men would be available as required throughout the kingdom. Every man 'being the King's subject, not lame, decrepid or maimed nor having any other legal cause or impediment and being within the age of 60 years' was to exercise regularly with the longbow and every father was to provide his male children between the ages of 7 and 17 years with bows and arrows. At the age of 17 every young man was to have his own bow. A bowman on board the *Mary Rose* would have trained since childhood at the village butts and many an English church in sandstone country shows the marks left by archers who whiled away the time after church by shaping their arrows while waiting for their turn at the target. The skill of the English bowman was legendary in Europe long after the introduction of wrought iron and cast bronze guns. Philip de Commines said in his memoirs in 1580 'the English are the flowers of the archers of the world'[5] and Giovanni Michel reported to the Venetian senate in 1559 on the weapons used by the English:

> But above all, their proper and natural weapons are the bow and arrow, of which so great is the number, owing to the general use made of them by all sorts of persons without distinction of grade, age or profession, that it exceeds all belief . . . They draw the bow with such force and dexterity at the same time, that some are said to pierce corselets and body armour . . .[6]

In 1542 an act was passed to ensure that no man who had reached 24 years of age might shoot at a mark of less than 220 yards (200m).[7] Although an act of Parliament did nothing to ensure accuracy it certainly set the standards, and obligatory practice and open competition at the butts ensured that standards were maintained. It is against this background of a trained band of archers probably selected for service in the King's army and paid an honourable wage of 2d per day, that the equipment on board the *Mary Rose* will be examined. The most personal items are undoubtedly the archer's bracers or wrist guards. Bracers are known from the Bronze Age onwards but in the sixteenth century they were usually a wide strip of leather or a piece of wood, ivory or horn which was tied to the archer's left wrist to enable the bow string to glide swiftly and freely across the inside of the forearm when the string was released. It also served to protect the left sleeve or the wrist from abrasion by the bow string when it was loosed.

Eleven bracers in leather and one in horn have been recovered from the *Mary Rose* so far. The horn bracer was miraculously preserved from destruction by micro-organisms because a coil of tarred tope had fallen across the archer and the protein in the horn had been preserved by the biocidal action of the tar.

The leather bracers are simple rectangular strips of leather with leather straps fastened to each of the longer sides by iron studs or rivets. Three of the bracers are embossed with the royal arms and See p200. garter and in the four corners of the rectangle there are the Tudor Rose and the Fleur-de-Lys of Henry VIII, and the pomegranate and castle, the badges of Catherine of Aragon. It is perhaps surprising to find these badges still in use thirteen years after the annulment of Henry's marriage to Catherine and nine years after her death. Could they have been the cherished possessions of members of a Queen's company of

The Anthony Roll of Henry VIII's ships lists thirteen 'Roo Barges', which were small ships of 20 tons, but even the Rose Slype, *shown here, carried one bronze saker with 70 shot, 11 basses with 160 lead shot, 30 hailshot pieces, 3 handguns and 10 longbows of yew.*

archers or were they just old stock being used up at sea in the King's service? No tabs or leather guards for the fingers of the right hand have been found on board and probably years of practice had given these archers a horny layer of skin which was sufficient protection. If the guards had been used on board it seems unlikely that they were destroyed when leather jerkins and shoes were so well preserved in these silts.

Several boxes of arrows have been excavated and the fragile arrows are providing a severe challenge for the conservators and scientists. One chest found on the upper deck in 1980 contained 1248 arrows which appeared to be tied in bundles of 24 by thin cord. Because this box was originally crudely made, with nailed sides and base and two

simple rope handles, it was in imminent danger of collapsing once the supporting silts had been removed from around the chest. It had to be excavated underwater in extremely difficult conditions by Berit Mort-lock and Adrian Barak and the fragile arrows were removed in batches and brought to the surface supported in sections of plastic rain water guttering. The arrows had been stored tip-to-tip in bundles of 24 but only a soupy black sludge survived to indicate that there had been heads on the arrows when they were placed in the box. The arrows were 0.80m (2ft 6in) long and an average diameter of 0.01m ($\frac{1}{2}$in) and although no flights remained, traces of a green-tinted glue or seating compound and the spiral impression of binding thread indicated that the flights were about 0.15m (6in) long. A nock, or notch, had been

Adele Wilkes, Keeper of Collections, with some of the longbows recovered from the upper decks in the sterncastle.

Drawing of arrows in a leather spacer and single spacers found within the ship.

cut into the base of the arrow shaft and reinforced with a slender V-shaped horn insert. In most cases the insert had been completely destroyed by micro-biological decay but clearly in every case there had once been an insert to protect the head of the shaft when it was placed against the string. Most of the arrows were of poplar, which Roger Ascham, the tutor of Princess Elizabeth and an author of a contemporary treatise on archery, considered inferior for war arrows. Ascham presented his treatise, entitled *Toxophilus: the Schole or Partitions of Shooting,* to Henry VIII in 1545 and was rewarded with a pension of £10 a year. He listed suitable woods for making arrow shafts and commented that some made 'dead, heavy, shafts hobbling'; others,

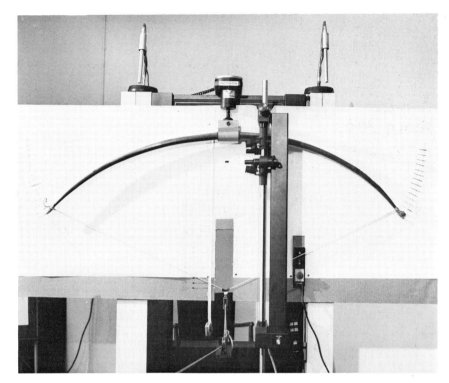

A Mary Rose longbow (A 1648) drawn with a 15in tip deflection during trials using an Instron 1185 Testing Machine to establish draw strengths.

Robert Hardy, Professor Peter Pratt of Imperial College London and George Zahler compare a specimen of wood from a Mary Rose longbow with a modern longbow during the trials at Instron.

such as blackthorn, service tree, beech, elder, aspen and sallow made 'hollow, starting, scudding, gadding shafts . . . But birch, hornbeam, some oak and some ash being both strong enough to stand in a bow but also light enough to fly, are the best for a mean, which is to be sort after in all things.' He continued, 'yet as concerning sheaths of arrows for war it were better to make them out of good ash and not of aspen *as they are nowadays*'; clearly Roger Ascham would have considered most of the *Mary Rose* arrows — which are made of poplar (aspen) — most unsuitable.

Some arrows were found on the upper deck and on the main gundeck in circular leather spacers which appear to have served as ammunition

A *bundle of arrows tied together with a leather thong.*

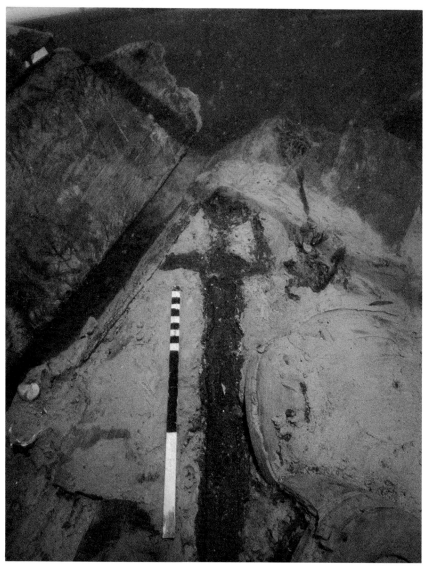

Underwater view of the discoloured stain left in the silts by the blade and hilt of a steel sword. To the right of the sword stain can be seen the inverted wooden bowl of a ship's compass.

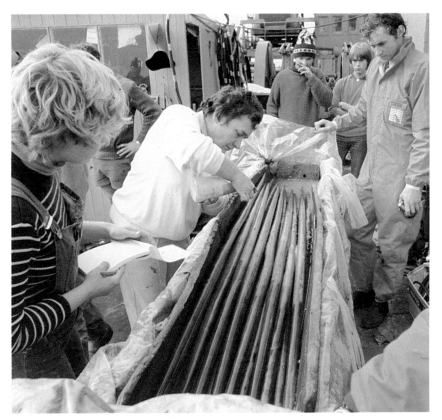

Berit Mortlock removing arrows from a chest in the storage area of the Mary Rose.

Margaret Rule, Alex Hildred and Christopher Dobbs excavating a box of longbows which was recovered intact and excavated in air on the deck of Sleipner.

A piece of leather with 24 holes for a charge of arrows. The disc served as a spacer to prevent the flight feathers crushing and the close fit of the disc to the shafts of the arrows suggest that the arrow heads were of the bodkin type.

Finds assistant Andrew Elkerton recording some of the 2000 arrows recovered from the ship.

A wheel from the carriage of a wrought iron gun incised with a broad arrow to show it had been paid for with money from the Royal accounts.

Wooden carriage for a bronze gun recovered from the upper deck in the sterncastle.

clips. The arrows had been passed through each of the 24 circular holes stamped in the disc (one of which was marked with a broad arrow). The spacer served a dual purpose as it not only standardised the rate of issue from the stores but it also served to space each arrow from its neighbour and prevent the flight feathers from crushing. When the archer removed the arrows from the spacer and tucked them in his belt the spacer could be recharged from the nearby box of arrows. In practice the spacer served in the same way as a .303 rifle clip of ammunition, and groups of ready-to-use charged spacers many have been assembled at battle stations on the upper deck and the fighting tops.

BOWS

To date 138 yew longbows have been recovered from within the ship. They fall into three main types, and one suspects that they served quite different functions: a massive bow with well-made handgrips; a light D-sectioned bow; and a similar bow of heavier section. These last two may simply reflect the needs of individual archers, but the lighter

Diver swimming to the surface with one of the longbows found in a chest on the orlop deck.

The English longbowman on Southsea Common. A detail from the Cowdray engraving which depicts the scene of the sea battle in which the Mary Rose *sank.*

bows may be snipers' or target bows and the heavier ones may have been used for blanketing the enemy with arrows at a rate of 12 or more a minute. Three examples of massive bows are more difficult to explain. The handgrip may well have been whipped with a binding material; but if so, why? There is no trace of binding on the lighter bows and the bowyer has carefully marked the arrow pass with indented toolmarks. One possibility is that the large bows were used to shoot fire arrows. Setting fire to rigging was well recognised as legitimate warfare in the sixteenth century and the cauldrons and barrels of tar found on board would have been ideal for either torches or fire arrows. A pair of left-handed mittens, found in a soldier's sea chest would have been ideal for protecting the left hand of an archer from scorching as he drew the bow.

All the bows are made of fine-grained yew and the bowyer has cleft the wood so that each stave contains a natural section of sapwood and heartwood. The bows were shaped to a D-section with the sapwood on the back of the bow and a thicker section of heartwood on the belly. Modern wood scientists know that sapwood under tension and heart-wood working under compression form an efficient natural laminate and a modern replica of a bow made in this way could be expected to have a range of 200–250m (220–270 yards). A programme of experimental archaeology based on the statistical study of the dimensions of the *Mary Rose*'s bows is just beginning and a study group (comprising Robert Hardy, the actor and an authority on longbows, Professor John Levy, Professor of Wood Science at Imperial College, London, Professor Peter Pratt, Professor of Crystal Physics at Imperial College, and myself) has been established to follow through a programme of practical research. Tests with air-dried longbows have demonstrated that while it is possible to string and draw a bow to 30in (0.8m) considerable degrada-tion within the cell structure of the wood has prevented a realistic assessment of the original load required to drill the bow. In January 1982 bow number A1648 was braced at a bracing height of 7in (0.17m) by Robert Hardy and John Waller, one of the most experienced modern English archers. The braced bow was placed in an Instron machine to enable a draw length to be measured against load in kilo newtons. Gradually over 55 minutes at a temperature of 20 degrees centigrade the load was increased to a maximum draw length of 26in at 21.0 kilo newtons. The bow was then unbraced and rested for 95 minutes and then drawn to 30in (0.8m) draw length at a load of 24.8 kilo newtons. The bow was then unbraced and examined carefully. It was in good condition. The load needed to draw the bow is considerably less than that expected for a bow of this size.

Clearly the scientific evaluation of the longbows will continue but enough is now known to attempt to make a replica *Mary Rose* bow and see how it performs in a series of range and velocity tests. Making a replica is easier said than done, however. The fine-grained yew wood used to make the *Mary Rose* bows in the 1540s is difficult to match today and samples of suitable wood are being examined from the USA and Italy. Only when Professor Levy is satisfied that a suitable wood has been found will Robert Hardy, John Waller and Roy King get together to make the bow we need.

It will take time, but hopefully we will again witness that 'proper and natural weapon', the English longbow, being strung and shot over a range — or even, in time, from the weather deck of the *Mary Rose*.

CHAPTER 8

The Crew, Officers and Life on Board

LESS THAN THREE DOZEN men were saved from the sea when the *Mary Rose* sank. Some of the crew may have drowned trying to swim to the small boats which hurried forward from the surrounding ships to offer assistance but clearly the ship sank so swiftly that many of the men were trapped inside. Skeletal remains of some of the men were found beneath the collapsed anti-boarding netting which covered the open weather deck in the waist of the ship. Others lay on the upper deck and on the main gundeck and it is clear by the positions, clothing and the surrounding weapons that they were still at action stations when the ship sank.

Below in the darkness of the hold more groups of human bones were found and some of them still lay on mattresses or palliasses on the piles of shingle ballast. These pitiful remains would suggest that John Hawkins' description of placing wounded men on the ballast in the hold, so that their cries should not demoralise or hinder soldiers during battle at sea, was general practice in the Tudor period and is reminiscent of the concern of the ship's officers to cover Nelson's medals and uniform before he was hustled down below to die on the orlop deck at Trafalgar. Morale was everything in battle and the wounded had to die where they caused least distress to the men still at battle stations. It is hoped that when the study of the human bones found on board the ship is complete it will provide a sound basis for reassessment of diet, nutrition and the health of the men of Henry VIII's navy and that the remains will then be reburied with full military honours close to the ship on which the men served and died. Even a brief preliminary study by Mrs Anne Stirland, a human skeletal biologist, suggests that generalisations about height and nutrition will go, to be replaced by a statistical study of the remains of a hundred or more healthy people who died together at one specific moment in time.

The bones of two young men, almost certainly both archers, lay alongside the companionway which led from the main gundeck up to the weather deck and thence to the starboard side of the bowcastle.

One was 5ft 7in tall (1.70m) and in his mid-twenties, and the other 6ft tall (1.83m) and about 22 years old. It is clear from their position that they had slipped from the steps of the companionway as the ship listed during their attempt to scramble from the lower decks to the freedom of the upper deck and the older man lay sprawled across the younger man as the water poured in through the open gunports and engulfed them. The older man was sturdily built and he probably suffered from severe halitosis for, although his teeth showed no sign of caries or tooth decay, bad dental hygiene had caused severe pyorr-hoea. He had already lost one tooth and probably would have lost most of his teeth through recession of the alveolar bone of the jaw had he survived the wreck until his middle years. Both his teeth and his lower leg bones exhibited traits which suggested he suffered from either dietary deficiency or recurring bouts of a severe illness as a very young child. Some of his bones clearly showed the effects of many hours spent at the butts or in action with the longbow. The articular surfaces of two of the vertebrae in his central spine had been pulled round and forward to the left indicating that stress had been applied which involved twisting the spine. His lower left arm bone (ulna) was thickened and the lower articulating surface of this bone was flattened and splayed by frequent application of pressure. As Anne Stirland says, 'Persistent use of the longbow might well have produced these results.'

A mass of shapeless iron accretion lay between the two bodies and whether either man was wearing armour or a steel breast plate is

Pat Edge, a volunteer finds assistant, cleaning a wicker basket.

Fragments of a wicker basket and the stones of prunes or small plums.

impossible to tell. Careful excavation of the remains by Adrian Barak yielded no conclusive evidence either way but the bones were stained with calcium phosphate hydrate and iron phosphate hydrate, or vivianite, which may have come from decomposition of steel in close contact with the body. The lower man was tall and fewer of his bones survived *in situ*. He was associated with fragments of a leather undershirt or jerkin and a bundle of arrows contained in a leather spacer and attached to a waist thong were firmly attached to the concretion around the man's spine. Some of his thoracic vertebrae had nodes (Schmorl's nodes) caused by persistently lifting heavy objects or possibly by compression fracturing. It is hoped that the complete study of the remains of the men will, in association with their clothing and their weapons, lead to a better understanding of where gunners, archers and seamen were on the ship as well as yielding evidence for a study of diet, nutrition and hygiene.

The human bones are unavoidable; they were there and they have to be removed and studied with dignity and understanding before their reburial. But the fine silts also contain less emotive and less obvious evidence for life at sea. From the prune mite still attached to a small plum or prune in an officer's chest, to the bones of a rat and a small whippet-like dog which probably chased it across the deck, the evidence is all there, but it will take several years of study by archaeologists and scientists to fit the evidence into a meaningful pattern.

MEDICINE ON BOARD

Four small cabins on the starboard side of the main gundeck contained tools and personal equipment indicating the trades or professions of the occupants and the most important of these was the ship's surgeon. In two small compartments with the headroom of barely 5ft 6in (1.67m) below the deck beams the master surgeon and his mate worked as barbers, surgeons and physicians, healing the wounded and curing the sick. The name of the surgeon on board in 1545 is unknown but in 1513 the accounts of Sir Thomas Wyndham, Treasurer of the Fleet, showed that Robert Symsom, master surgeon on the *Mary Rose*, was paid 13s 4d a month and that his mate or junior surgeon, Henry Yonge, was paid 10s a month. Robert Symsom was a skilled surgeon and in 1526 he became the Second Warden of the Company of Barber-Surgeons. Until the twelfth century the practice of surgery and medicine had been almost wholly confined to the clergy, but in 1163 Pope Alexander III at the Council of Tours forbade the clergy to continue any practice which involved the shedding of blood and after this edict the clergy confined their healing to the art of

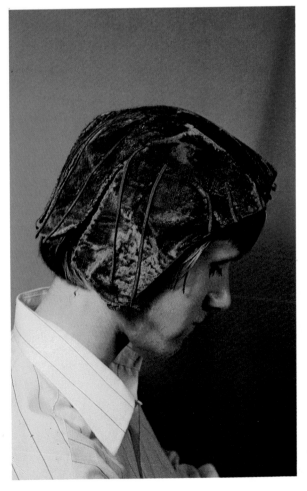

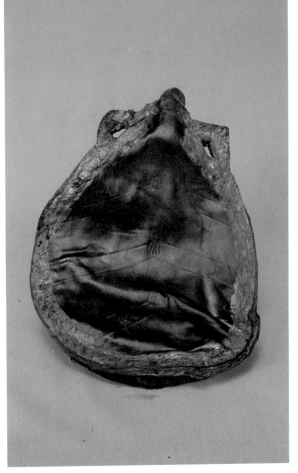

medicine. From this time onwards minor surgical operations such as blood-letting, pulling teeth or cauterising wounds were done by the barbers and by 1308 they were well organised into a guild with some responsibilities for maintaining standards within the trade. On 13 December that year Richard Le Barbour was presented to the Lord Mayor of London in the Guildhall as Master of the Company of Barbers and he took an oath to maintain professional standards within the trade including a statement swearing that every month he would make scrutiny throughout the whole of his trade and if he found any of them to be keeping brothels he would distrain them.

In 1462 Edward IV granted a Royal Charter to the Barber's Company and in 1491 an informal alliance was formed between the Barbers' Company and the Fellowship of Surgeons. This was consolidated in 1540 when Parliament passed an Act uniting the Fellowship of Surgeons to the Company of Barbers. This union continued until the surgeons were separated from the barbers by another act of Parliament in 1745. In 1545 when our unknown barber-surgeon was working on board the *Mary Rose*, he was acting as barber, surgeon, physician and apothecary and his tools and equipment reflect all these skills. The surgeon's cabin was without any decoration and only sparsely furnished with a simple four-legged bench for preparing plasters or dressings and a large chest. The chest was undoubtedly the star find of the

A selection of objects found inside the barber-surgeon's cabin including wooden ointment jars, ceramic flagons for medicine, a pewter bleeding bowl, a large barber's shaving bowl, the metal base of a chafing dish which was used to hold hot charcoal, drug flasks, razors, a urethral syringe and a large wooden mallet. The mallet may have been used with an amputation knife.

1980 season of excavation. Deeply buried in soft silts and muds and apparently undamaged it was discovered late in the season and presented the archaeologists with a dilemma. Should we excavate it *in situ* in poor conditions with little light or should we try and package the box and bring it up to the surface intact? We settled for the former and sent one of the volunteers, Kirstin Taylor, to open the box and tell us what it contained, so that we could prepare the necessary containers to raise the contents to the surface. We had half-expected another chest of arrows but when Kirstin returned she reported that the box was full of clay pigeons. I dived immediately to check on this seemingly absurd report and as I gently lifted the lid I saw a row of circular discs with faint concentric grooves looking exactly like a row of clay pigeons. Gently I felt the discs and lifted one with my bare hand; a blob of air or gas rose from the box as I leant forward to look at the thing I was holding in my hand. It was the lid of a wooden ointment jar. Now I could see a row of similar wooden jars and behind them a row of ceramic vessels. It was a medicine chest.

Almost empty of silts and clearly undisturbed, the chest lacked any internal partitions except for a shallow lidded shelf on one of the short sides. It was made of panels of walnut jointed with dovetail joints at each corner and with a solid wooden bar pierced for rope handles at each end. Inside the chest lay 64 objects associated with medicine, including 9 lidded wooden canisters containing various ointments and a similar one containing peppercorns. Two of the ointments have been analysed by Hampshire County Public Analysts Gerald Thackray and D C Symonds and found to contain a resinous substance which may be frankincense, and it is interesting to note that a popular unguent used to cure ulcers and fistulas at this time was *unguentum apostolorum* which contained frankincense and rosin as well as other ingredients in a base of white wax. Woodall, the first Surgeon-General of the East India Company, says in *The Surgeon's Mate* (1617), the first medical manual written for practical use at sea: 'unguentum apostolorum, this unguentum serveth well to cleanse and scour ulcers and fistulae and to make good ground to healing. It is of temperament hot and dry, it was deified by anicine named apostolorum so that it consisted of twelve simples joined into one body.'

Peppercorns have been found in various chests throughout the ship but the largest single sample is in the container within the surgeon's chest. Culpeper in his seventeenth century herbal describes the use of pepper as an 'ingredient in the great antidotes' and specifies its use for agues and quinsy. Woodall in 1617 also describes the use of *pipernigram* (black pepper) to expel wind, to waste hard tumours, for treatment

ABOVE

A simple chess board incised with 'dimples' to indicate black squares found in a cabin in the bowcastle.

A folding backgammon board which was recovered complete with some of the counters. Backgammon was extremely popular in the sixteenth century and large sums were lost gambling at 'tables'.

ABOVE
Embroidered leather purse, one of several pouches found on the ship belonging to the officers.

Several dice and one domino were found strewn among personal possessions.

The head pieces of a barrel incised with two gaming boards: on the right, nine men's morris; the centre game is hitherto unidentified.

of agues and quinsies, as well as to 'aromatize meat'. From these references it would seem that this relatively expensive commodity may have been on board for medicinal rather than culinary purposes. The five carefully corked ceramic jars which once contained medicines have so far revealed nothing of interest to the scientists. They were all made at the same potteries at Siegburg in the Rhineland and are second quality pottery 'rejects', which may have been imported as non-returnable containers with medical supplies.

Several sausage-like rolls of unguents were found in the chest. Superficially some of them looked as if an amorphous clay-like substance had been applied to a thin fabric and then rolled into a cylindrical shape but X-ray examination failed to confirm this supposition and the question still remains open. A recipe book of Henry VIII's own salves and ointments survives in the British Museum; some of the preparations were formulated by the King himself and the formulae included instructions for preparing plasters and making them into rolls to keep ready for use as required.[1] 'When it has boiled enough which you shall perceive by the hardness or softness thereof when you drop a little of it on the bottom of a dish or saucer or on a cold stone then take it from the fire and when it is new cold make it into rolls and wrap them in parchment and keep them for your use.' It may well be that our amorphous rolls are the remains of carefully-prepared dressings of this type.

Syringes. Two metal syringes, one of brass and one of pewter with a bronze pipe, were also found, one in the the chest and one near by in the cabin. Both needles had small rounded nipples on the end and at first it was thought that these were used to draw pus from abcesses by aspiration. However, Ambrose Paré (1510–1590) refers to the use of a small syringe for urethral injections for the treatment of bladder stones and for gonorrhea. This latter use of the small syringe is confirmed by Woodall, in his book written 'chiefly for the benefit of young sea surgeons'. Woodall's compassion for those unfortunate enough to be sick or wounded at sea illuminates his book and one can only hope that he was reflecting a general attitude which was shared by the surgeon on the *Mary Rose*. He describes the use of the glister or large syringe for the treatment of the flux and constipation and he also describes the use of small syringes of the *Mary Rose* type: '. . . it might seem a vain thing to mention instructions herein, for what barber's boy is not practised in the use of the small syringe?'[2] He emphasised the need for cleanliness and described in detail the use of the syringe for treating patients with gonorrhea and he warned against over-use of mercury sublimate, although he recognised its efficacy in treating ulcers on the male sex organs. Woodall also described the use of the small syringe to treat wounds, ulcers and fistulae and recommended that every surgeon's chest must have 'at least two if not three each with three pipes to be ready in the chest upon any occasion'. Certainly the barber-surgeon on the *Mary Rose* was well prepared with his two syringes.

Surgical Tools. The blades of most of the fine steel surgical tools contained within the chest had completely corroded away – not even a fugitive stain is left to record their shape and suggest the range of surgical equipment in use on board. However it would be surprising if the surgeon attempted to do much more than let blood, extract teeth and cauterise wounds with a hot iron, except in emergencies when he may have amputated a limb to free a trapped man or to remove a dead body.

Eight small handles are similar to those of seventeenth century cauteries used to sterilise wounds and promote healing by the application of a hot iron, and a more robust handle $5\frac{3}{4}$in (0.14m) long with a ferrule for the blade at each end may have been the handle of an amputation saw or a large surgical knife.[3] A wooden mallet, eight razors and a whetstone completed the list of surgical equipment which survived. Around the box lay the other items of his professional equipment including a large brass shaving bowl with a recess to fit under the customer's chin and a small pewter bleeding bowl with the owner's mark 'WE' on one handle.

Other finds in the surgeon's cabin. A small brazier for warming a chafing dish and a heavy mortar for grinding drugs were also found in the cabin. Drug containers including turned wood jars and bottles, glass bottles and pewter cannisters and flasks also lay in the cabin alongside pewter plates, wooden bowls, leather shoes, combs and a purse of silver coins; these must have been the surgeon's personal possessions.

The most poignant find was a fine silk velvet hat: a simple coif with braid-covered seams at the nape of the neck and across the forehead. It was well worn when it was crumpled up and left behind by its owner, but after restoration by Howard Murray a glimpse of its original beauty can be seen. Fragmentary evidence of the silk ribbon ties which were used to fasten the cap beneath the owner's chin still survive and the reconstructed cap bears a remarkable resemblance to the head coverings worn by Thomas Vicary, Sergeant Surgeon, Sir John Ayleff, Surgeon to Henry VIII, and Nicholas Simpson the King's barber, in the contemporary painting of Henry VIII and the Guild of Barber-Surgeons, painted by Holbein in 1540.

See p187.

RIGHT

Glass bottle enclosed in wickerwork from a sea chest.

OPPOSITE, BOTTOM

One of several seamen's chests, recovered from the orlop deck at the stern.

BELOW

Gold coins, or 'angels' which were worth 8s (40p) when the ship sank in 1545. As a mariner was only paid 5s a month it is not surprising that relatively few of these gold coins were found on board and because the Mary Rose *is not a 'treasure ship' in a monetary sense, the site has never been ravaged by treasure hunters.*

The embossed leather cover of a book.

A fine set of bronze scales.

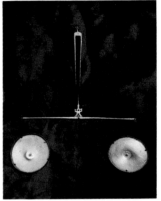

What does the examination of the surgeon's cabin tell us? Simply that Woodall in his treatise was writing about a regimen of hygienic medicine which had been practised at least 70 years earlier. The position of the cabin on the main gundeck close to action stations indicates that the surgeon intended to be close at hand when needed. The ready-to-use dressings and partially-used jars of ointment, with finger-marks showing where scoops of the ointment had been taken out, show that the surgeon had been busy and he was prepared for further action, but he was not trapped within his cabin and his chest was closed with everything in order. Was he below decks with the men lying on the ballast in the hold? We will probably never know but the group of objects he left behind does provide the earliest well-dated group of medical equipment for use at sea.

LIFE ON BOARD

Food stuffs, both fresh and preserved, were carried on board although as the King's ships were not anticipating a long voyage it is possible

Detail drawing to show the construction of a leather shoe with slash decoration, found on board the ship.

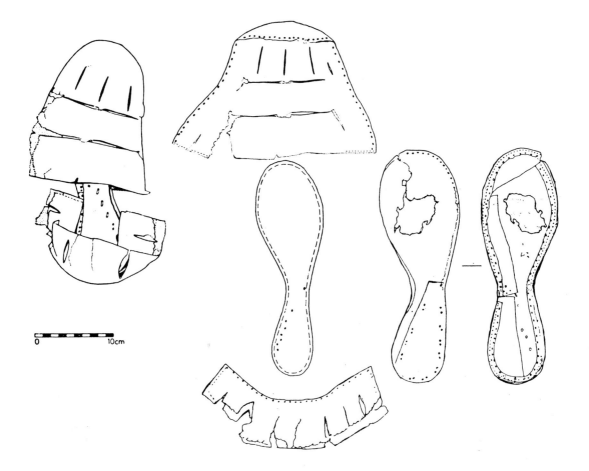

0   10cm

that they only carried light stores on this occasion. Carcasses of fresh pork and a basket of trimmed and headless fish indicate that good fresh food was readily available and most of the seamen's chests contained a hand line and floats showing that they were well able to supplement the ship's supplies when necessary. Fresh peas still in the pod and attached to the hulm were found in the stores at the stern of the ship and the stones of small plums or prunes have been found in several parts of the ship. Butchered venison, beef and mutton bones have already been identified, alongside more exotic animals such as a small whippet, a rat and a frog. Many more animal and fish bones found in barrels in the ship's stores await identification as do the insect remains, including flies, cockroaches and other beetles and mites. Bedding and packing materials have yielded samples of hay and cereal straw which often contain weed seeds and flower petals. Personal boxes contained herbs and spices, including peppercorns and bay leaves, either as part of a do-it-yourself medical kit or to add more flavour to the galley rations.

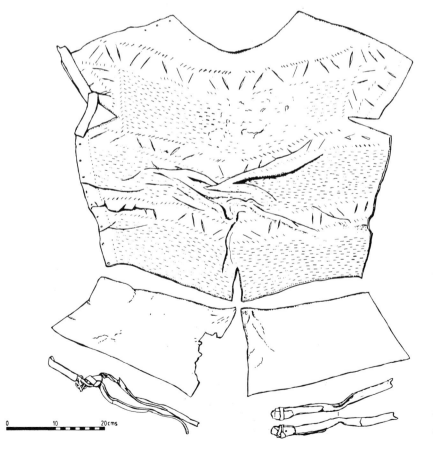

Sleeveless leather jerkin with a tie belt and a short skirt, and slashed decoration across the chest to allow easy movement. Several of the archers on board the ship wore jerkins of this type.

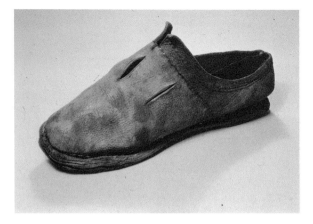

Leather shoe with high vamp and slashed decoration.

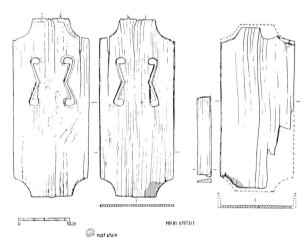

rust stain

ABOVE
Fragments of the sound box of a fiddle found on the orlop deck.

RIGHT
Margrethe de Neergaard, a finds assistant on board Sleipner *with an immaculate tabor pipe recovered in 1981.*

Pastimes included music and gaming. No trace of playing cards has been discovered but dice and gaming boards were found well stratified within the ship. A single domino may be a contaminant lost overboard from a later vessel but Henry VIII is recorded as losing £450, a colossal sum in 1530, gaming at dominoes at Greenwich and Whitehall and the single piece could have derived from the collapsed cabins high in the sterncastle and have been redeposited within the secondary silts. The finest gaming board is a folding backgammon table complete with counters. Gaming at tables was a popular pastime usually involving heavy stakes.

Music on board was lively, going far beyond the recorded requirements for a trumpet to convey orders from one part of the ship to another, to 'hail him (the enemy) with a noise of trumpets', or 'sound drums and trumpets and St George for England' as instructed by Captain John Smith in his *Sea Grammar* of 1627 under the heading of 'How to Manage A Fight at Sea'. No trace of a trumpet has been found on board, but objects of steel are not well preserved in the silts of the Solent. A wooden shawm lay in its stave-built case on the maindeck close to the surgeon's cabin and three tabor pipes and a tabor were found in the crew's quarters abaft the mainmast or among the storage chests on

One of several planes recovered from a carpenter's tool box. The steel blade has corroded away completely, but replica tools can be made and used to demonstrate the techniques employed on board the ship.

Court musicians, including a man playing a pipe and tabor similar to those recovered from the Mary Rose. *An illustration from Henry VIII's Psalter in the British Library.*

the orlop deck. The pipes and the drum were popular lively instruments much loved by court musicians and others. They were played by one man in the style of a present day street busker. He could tap the rhythm with one hand on the drum while piping the melody on the tabor pipe. The shawm was also used as a band instrument to provide an oboe-like melodic note. Several small reed pipes and bosun's pipes or calls were much more probably used to pipe orders over and above the noise of battle, although two of the bosun's calls were probably too small to be of practical use and they may have served as badges of office. A small wooden whistle and fragments of two stringed instruments, probably fiddles, were also found carefully stowed away by their owners. Eventually it is hoped that authentic replica instruments will be made and played so that visitors to the ship after she has been recovered will be able to enjoy the delights of Tudor music in an appropriate setting.

CLOTHING

Clothing on board ship must have been relatively simple and for most of the seamen a workaday tunic of worsted or leather and all-in-one hose, corresponding to modern tights, would have been sufficient.

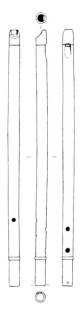

A tabor pipe found on the main gun deck.

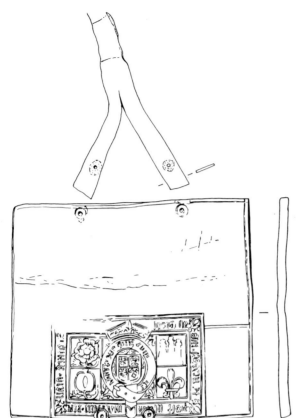

ABOVE

An archer's leather wristguard or bracer which served to protect the forearm from chafing as the string was released.

RIGHT

Many wooden combs have been found throughout the ship, suggesting that hygiene was taken seriously by the officers and the crew. This one was enclosed in a neatly fitting leather case.

TOP, RIGHT

A small fragment of print found bound into the cover of a leather book. The print has only been fully revealed by using ultra violet light and recording on infra-red photographic film.

Drawing to show the constructional details of one of several leather bottles found on board the ship complete with a wooden stopper.

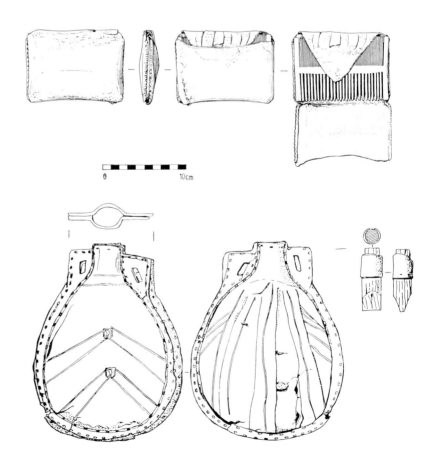

There are frequent references in the Royal Wardrobe accounts to purchases of coats of white and green at a cost of 34 pence each for the use of soldiers and others on board the *Mary Rose*, and we had always hoped that one of the chests within the orlop deck might have contained some of these spare uniforms — but unfortunately no trace of such a garment survives. However, many fragments of leather and woollen clothing have been excavated and recovered but conservation and study will now take several years.

The silk velvet coif recovered from the barber-surgeon's cabin is exceptionally well-preserved, but small satin-covered buttons and silk-embroidered purses hint at an elegance on board the ship more in keeping with the musical instruments than with the hurly-burly of the gundeck. A jaunty woollen knitted hat, resembling a flat brimmed beret, with a silk lining was found in on the orlop deck. Suitably decorated with a feather, it may once have belonged to one of the officers, who swaggered across the deck in his slashed leather jerkin, hose, and dainty leather shoes. Almost all of the garments found are simple sleeveless leather jerkins, often with lacing at the side and flared skirt pieces below the waist. Other jerkins were worn open to the waist probably to reveal an undershirt or stomacher. The programme of work is now in hand to make patterns or toiles of all the garments to enable us to assess how they were worn and reconstruct any of the missing parts. Around the waist, most of the men wore a simple girdle which served as an arrow holder and also secured the owner's pouch, or escarelle, and his knife or dagger. Often the pouches were elaborate, with embroidered decoration on the front and back.

Shoes vary enormously and many dozens have been found. Some of them are dainty leather slippers, cut so low across the toes that a strap was needed across the instep to hold them on the foot. Others were serviceable square-toed 'Chukka' boots with side lacings. An elegant pair of knee-length leather boots with folded-over tops were also found within a seaman's chest. They had been lined with felted worsted to protect the foot from chafing and leather laces up the sides ensured a snug fit.

Other leather objects found on board the ship included decorated leather comb cases, leather-covered books and leather bottles. Most of these objects await conservation and evaluation before they can be published, but eventually the comparative material recovered from inside the *Mary Rose* will help us to date individual and often fragmentary objects recovered from other underwater sites in Europe and throughout the world.

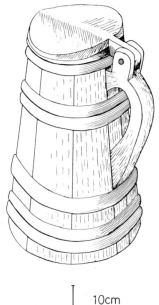

Reconstruction drawing of a stave-built drinking vessel. One of many found on board the ship.

CHAPTER 9

Salvage and Recovery

ANY ATTEMPT TO RECOVER a sunken ship presents a new challenge to salvage engineers, but whether it is a modern tanker, a fibreglass fishing boat or an ancient wooden warship, the basic choice of methods are limited and the salvage engineer has to modify and adapt existing and well-tried techniques to solve his particular problem. The basic choice is simple; either to make the structure buoyant by filling it with buoyant material; or to attach her to buoyant lifting bags, or camels; or to lift the vessel to the surface by attaching her to empty hulks and using the rise of the tides to effect a tidal lift; or by direct lift from the surface or a jack-up platform. The *Mary Rose* posed particular problems because although the weight of the empty hull was only estimated at some 45 tons in water it was quickly realised that this structure although coherent and sound had no athwartship strength and no tidy below-deck compartments within which we could insert buoyancy. In any case the threat of collapse would come not underwater but as the vessel passed through the surface into air and the weight of the structure increased by a factor of nine.

Since the earliest days of the project I had watched with admiration the work being done to rebuild and conserve the Swedish warship *Wasa* which sank outside the entrance to Stockholm harbour in 1628 on her maiden voyage. My first visit to the project was as an ordinary tourist in the summer of 1965 but even then it seemed to me that if we were ever going to find and recover the *Mary Rose* we would have to learn a lot from our colleagues in Sweden. In 1972 I visited Wasavarvet again and had long discussions with Edvin Falting, the chief diver who was responsible for the underwater work on the *Wasa*, Lars Kvarning, the archaeologist, and Lars Barkman, then head of the conservation unit. The comparison we made between the methods used to recover the *Wasa* and that which I thought we might use on the *Mary Rose* was invaluable but as work on the *Mary Rose* progressed we saw that our problems were almost entirely different.

The *Wasa* was built in Stockholm to a Dutch design and she sank on 10 August 1628 off Beckholmen in Stockholm harbour in 105ft

When first recovered from Stockholm harbour, very little of the Wasa survived above the upper gundecks. Since that time much of the superstructure has been reconstructed using the original timbers found around the ship. The view from the bow (bottom) looking along the reconstructed weather deck of the Wasa with work still in progress to restore the ship. A view along the starboard side of the Wasa (left) with the gunport lids replaced and showing considerable reconstruction, above the upper gundeck level. All of the internal structure dismantled from inside the half-hull of the Mary Rose will have to be restored to its former position by craftsmen and archaeologists working within the ship's hull within No 3 Dock in the Royal Naval Base.

The steel lifting frame being launched at Hythe on Southampton Water in March 1982. This steel frame was used to carry the weight of the hull when it was lifted from the seabed and placed underwater on a supporting steel cradle.

(32m) of water with a loss of about 55 lives. Although the ship was well-built, many of the iron bolts fastening the planks to the frames had been corroded away and much of the stern had been damaged by anchors. The underwater visibility in Stockholm harbour is even worse than in the Solent and the initial survey was limited to gloomy glimpses of iron-stained oak and an evaluation of the hull shape. She lay buried up to the original waterline in light mud with some 5–6m (16–20ft) of hull below the level of the seabed but with 5–8m (16–26ft) of hull and superstructure surviving above the seabed. Because the hull had only been exposed in cold, tideless, brackish water it had survived in miraculous condition. The cold temperatures and the low salt content had prevented infestation by many of the micro-organisms and wood-boring molluscs which destroy wrecks in warmer and more saline seas and the relative lack of tide had prevented erosion by current-borne sediments as has happened on the *Mary Rose*.

A decision was made to lift the *Wasa* intact, with most of the silts and muds still inside the hull concealing the objects and the heavy stone ballast. Six tunnels were dug through the silt and clays beneath the hull using a Zetterström water jet and an airlift was used to transport the loosened debris to the surface. The divers wore heavy-duty standard diving dress with air supplied to a helmet from a pump on the surface support vessel, and although this umbilical cord was supported by a communication link and a safety line it must have been distinctly hairy to tunnel beneath a ship of unknown strength with an unknown weight of ballast immediately above their heads. Be that as it may, these professional divers working in 30-minute shifts at a depth of 105ft (32m), dug the tunnels and passed six pairs of wire ropes beneath the hull and up to two pontoons moored on either side of the hull. The pairs of ropes parted and passed to either side of the pontoons *Oden* and *Frigg*, floating with their decks almost flush with the surface of the sea.

Slowly water was pumped out of the pontoons and gradually inch-by-inch the surface vessels rose above the waves and as they did so the *Wasa* came gradually and very carefully loose from the clay. In a series of eighteen lifts the *Wasa* was gradually brought into shallow water and in between each lift she grounded on her own keel! At a depth of 17m the divers replaced 6000 lost iron bolts with wooden trenails and passed metal bracing rods through the hull to stiffen her and brace her against any accidental compression during the lift. The hull was then fitted with a temporary transom, open gunports were sealed off and many tons of light mud infill were removed. Now the hull was ready to be lifted into air.

The usual flood of well-meant advice poured into Stockholm. Suggested methods varied from instant freezing and floating her to the surface as a seventeenth century iceberg, to filling her with ping-pong balls, but eventually it was decided to lift her on hydraulic jacks between the two pontoons *Oden* and *Frigg*. The Neptune Salvage Co, owners of the pontoons, repositioned seven 50-ton hydraulic jacks so that the lifting wires beneath the hull came up to the side of the pontoons. As the ship broke surface pumping started and eventually the *Wasa* was floating on her own keel. The whole operation took 20 months, but it was completely successful. A wooden warship had been recovered almost intact nearly three-and-a-half centuries after she had sunk.

The *Mary Rose* presents a different problem. In 1972, when I first discussed the matter with Edvin Falting, I believed that the *Mary Rose* might be as well-preserved as the *Wasa* and I thought that the best solution would be to lift the ship with all her contents into shallow water in Portsmouth or Langstone harbour and conduct the necessary underwater excavation to remove the contents in shallow water. Logistically such a plan had much to recommend it. At a depth of 9m (30ft)

The Swedish warship Wasa *after recovery, being brought into Stockholm on her own keel.*

Divers fitted with sonic communications equipment which enables two divers to converse with each other underwater and with a supervisor on the surface without any connecting wires which might snag on the delicate areas of the wreck. This equipment is extremely useful for rapid and efficient survey of large areas as the measurements can be recorded on the surface and erroneous measurements can be rechecked while the diver is still underwater.

or less in clear water we could work faster and use fewer divers, and I also believed that such an excavation could be less destructive. I now know that if we had followed this path in 1972 before the significance of the sediments in the scourpits outside the hull had been demonstrated we would never have understood what happened to the hull after it sank and the vital strategraphic and environmental evidence would have been destroyed.

It was only in 1974 that I began fully to understand the importance of the layers of sediments that lie in and around the wreck and learnt to apply these methods to other wreck sites. During the late 1970s many schemes were put forward to recover the hull and in 1978 it was agreed to remove all the contents and recover the half-hull with the decks still in position supported on the deck beams and the stanchions. As the timbers were mainly fastened together with wooden trenails it was believed that it would stay as a coherent structure if it was lifted on strops beneath a buoyant salvage vessel. A decision to purchase the diving salvage vessel *Sleipner* from the Neptune Salvage Co in January 1979 was made in the belief that she would not only serve as a stable diving platform but she would also be used as a pontoon to lift the *Mary Rose* with a tidal lift aided by hydraulic jacks. John Reid, an engineer, had joined the *Mary Rose* project in 1978 to coordinate the work of a team of consultants who were cooperating with the archaeologists to produce a plan on which the recovery programme could be based and a seminar was called in September 1978 to

The Wasa *supported between the* Neptune Salvage Co's *pontoons* Oden *and* Frigg *after recovery in 1959. It would be impossible to recover the* Mary Rose *using these techniques as only half the hull survives.*

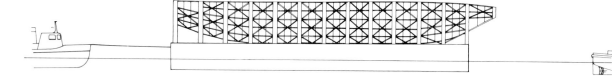

The Mary Rose *was lifted from the seabed and brought ashore on a barge cradled in a steel supporting structure. In order to achieve this, the programme of work was broken down into six operations.*

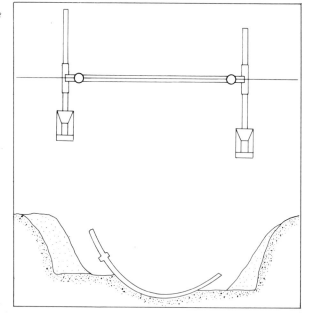

Stage One. *After excavation within the hull was completed, a tubular steel framework was placed in position above the hull. This underwater lifting frame stood on four legs firmly supported in the geological clay. It was towed out to site in June 1982 and gently lowered to the seabed from a barge on the surface.*

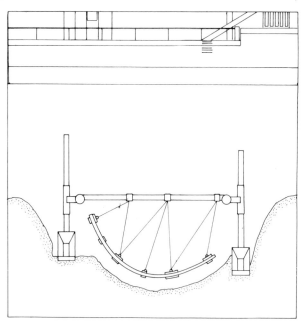

Stage Two. *Holes were drilled through the hull at predetermined points and steel bolts and backing plates were secured to the timbers. Eyebolts were fastened to the internal ends of the steel bolts, and from these points wire ropes were passed up to the cross-members of the underwater lifting frame. As each wire was firmly secured in position tunnelling could proceed beneath the hull.*

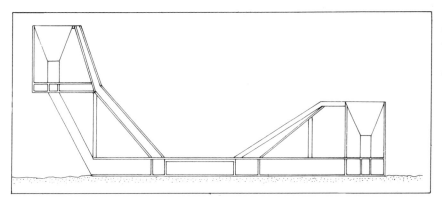

Stage Three. *A prefabricated steel cradle which was designed to conform with the lines of the* Mary Rose *was placed in position on the seabed close to the* Mary Rose *site.*

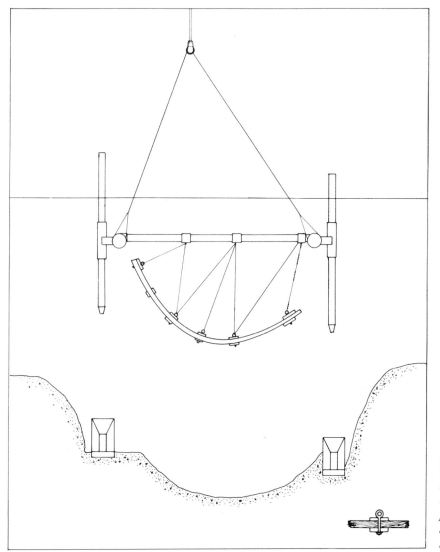

Stage Four. *The hull of the* Mary Rose *suspended from the steel wires was lifted from the seabed using hydraulic jacks in the legs of the underwater lifting frame. After the hull was free from the seabed, the frame was lifted by a crane barge and moved to a position immediately above the support cradle.*

Stage Five. *The underwater lifting frame within the suspended* Mary Rose *was moved into position above the steel cradle, and the legs of the frame were securely locked to the rising supports on the cradle. The space between the hull of the* Mary Rose *and the steel cradle was filled with a series of rubber bags filled with water, to accommodate the chain-wale and other features which needed special support.*

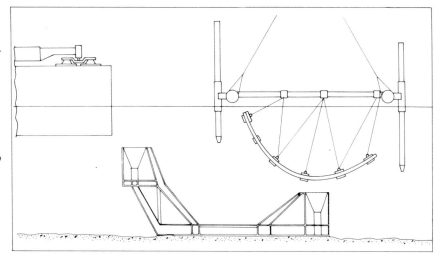

The late medieval merchant vessel excavated from the River Weser west of Bremen in 1962 has been reconstructed and is now being conserved in a stainless steel tank containing polyethylene glycol (PEG). The presentation of the tank echoes the shape of the vessel and the visitor gets an exciting view through the large plate glass windows, which in many ways echoes that of a diving archaeologist working underwater. As conservation using PEG will take a long time the presentation and interpretation of the ship plays an important part in the museum display.

consider possible methods for recovery of the hull. Many alternative schemes were considered but they fell into two main categories: one to move the hull complete with its contents to a wet dock and empty the hull under controlled conditions; the other to excavate the hull *in situ* and then remove the empty hull to a land site for conservation and display. Because of the unknown weight of the contents and the unevaluated structural strength of the hull, it was agreed that it would be impossible to lift the entire mass into air without serious risk of collapse. At the same time it was recognised that the shallow water at the narrow entrance to Portsmouth Dockyard precluded taking the ship into the wet dock fully submerged. Alternative schemes for recovering the empty vessel were also considered during 1979 including the construction of a submersible structure in steel and concrete which could be used as a floating dock to recover the hull, transport it

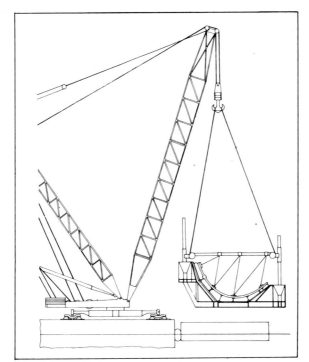

Stage Six. *The* Mary Rose *securely sandwiched between the supporting mattress, the cradle, and the underwater lifting frame was then lifted from the sea onto a barge for transport ashore. As the* Mary Rose *came through the surface, water inside the hull was pumped out and the water in the supporting mattress was replaced with air.*

The Mary Rose *is now in No 3 dock in the Royal Naval Base, Portsmouth. The historic setting is appropriate for the rebirth of the ship, being close to Nelson's flagship HMS* Victory *and the site of the dock where she was built in 1509.*

ashore and provide the shell of a museum ship as well. However this scheme involved breeching the sea defences to bring the hull ashore across an open beach and it was immensely costly. A more attractive scheme submitted by Clive Ward and Associates Ltd had the merit of supporting the hull structure from strops attached to a purpose-built jack-up platform and then towing the buoyant platform with the *Mary Rose* suspended beneath it to the beach. However this scheme also

Labels on image: Conservation, Ship Hall, Main Store, Car Park, Concourse, Visitor Services

Peter Ahrends of Ahrends Burton & Koralek has prepared this plan for a Tudor Ship Museum close to the beach at Eastney, Portsmouth. The centre point of the museum will be the ship hall, but great care has been taken to link the proposed exhibition galleries with views of the hull and the museum will, when complete, contain lecture theatres, a cinema, conservation laboratories and study facilities for visiting scholars.

required a canal to be dug through the sea defences to get the structure ashore and for this reason it was never pursued.

Finally a scheme was approved in principle and it was agreed to stiffen the hull of the *Mary Rose* with internal steel braces and a steel stiffening frame and lift it on strops using floating sheer legs. The hull would then be pumped free of water and residual silt as it broke through the surface and then it would be lifted onto a prefabricated steel support cradle on a barge for transport ashore.

I was always apprehensive about the terrible load that would be placed on the *Mary Rose* timbers as it swung from the water into the air. The strops alone did not seem sufficient to hold the hull with the external wales, chains and standards, together and I was afraid that the heavy weight of the proposed internal braces would deform the water-logged timbers. However these were details that remained to be defined and at the end of the meeting on 22 January 1980 it was agreed to accept this plan in principle but to ask John Grace of R J Crocker and Partners to study the possibility of transferring the hull onto a support cradle underwater where the load would be very much less.

In February 1980 the Trustee Board decided to postpone the recovery of the hull until 1982 and this gave time for more detailed study of the salvage method and allowed the archaeologists to complete the survey of the hull structure before the structural engineers needed to complete the detailed design of the support cradle. An initial advisory panel was appointed to review the salvage proposals

from time to time and met frequently in 1980 and 1981 to discuss the problems. In June 1980 John Reid wrote, 'The key to the successful raising of the *Mary Rose* will be the engineering which is done on the seabed to prepare the wreck for the lift. This work must be done based on a thorough engineering knowledge of the strength and the weight of the structure, the stresses that will be applied during the lift and an accurate analysis of the adequacy of the reinforcement to be applied. The underwater engineering itself will require a close integration of people who have an intimate knowledge of the wreck and a "feel" for its archaeological importance and people who will apply cool, analytical engineering techniques to the practical problems.' Unfortunately John Reid emigrated to California in July 1980 but before he went he recommended to the Trustee Board that the task of recovering the *Mary Rose* be done by a team working under direct Trust management with a land-based support team to undertake the design and fabrication work.

Martin Freeman, one of the Mary Rose Trust professional divers, being assisted with his surface demand diving equipment during the summer of 1982.

After being assisted with his diving equipment, the diver receives his final briefing from one of the dive supervisors, Jon Adams.

In August 1981 the Trustee Board appointed a salvage recovery team. It comprised: Colonel Wendell Lewis, Team Leader; John Grace, consultant structural engineer; Peter Paulin, heavy lift consultant; Commander Joe Evans, RN (Rtd), Salvage Adviser; and Captain John Brannam, representing the Royal Engineers, with Richard Harrison and myself of the Mary Rose Trust.

Colonel Lewis had considerable experience as a project manager for R J Crocker and his wide range of military and civil experience fitted him for the important role of coordinator; in addition, his innate good manners and personal integrity made him the ideal man to control the multi-discipline team of extroverts and experts who would be involved in the recovery programme. A team of professional divers was recruited from the experienced divers who had worked for the Trust since 1979 and under the leadership of Jon Adams and Chris Under-

The north-west stabbing guide of the cradle with the leg of the underwater lifting frame in position.

ABOVE
09.03am, 11 October 1982. The Mary Rose returns to the surface after 437 years underwater.

RIGHT
The Mary Rose viewed from the bow, safely supported on a mattress of inflated airbags within the steel cradle.

The transom planking of the Mary Rose *showing two of the steel bolts which reinforced the hull and secured the backing pads and steel channel bars in position. The hull was lifted from the seabed suspended from the lifting frame by steel wires secured to eye bolts on the inside ends of the bolts.*

Tog Mor *lowering the steel support cradle with the* Mary Rose *onto the barge* Tow One *with the DSV Sleipner dwarfed in the background.*

wood they became responsible for all the delicate work inside the hull and the assessment of the correct positioning of the internal hull stiffening braces which would be of such vital importance. They were also responsible for the excavation of the important archaeological deposits outside and beneath the hull including under the sterncastle where the standing rigging still lay attached to the chain-wale. The work of tunnelling beneath the hull would be done by divers from the Royal Engineers under the command of Captain John Brannam, the Army Inspector of Diving. Both teams used surface-demand diving equipment including Kirby-Morgan helmets and they had the benefit of a hard-wire communications link to the diving control centre on the ship above.

In January 1982 Colonel Wendell Lewis joined the staff of the Trust as Director of Salvage and Recovery responsible to the Executive Director Richard Harrison. As Director he chaired the meetings of the salvage recovery team and provided the essential link between individuals working within that team. In April I was invited by the Trustee Board to assume executive responsibility for the recovery programme. My acceptance did nothing to alter Wendell's overall responsibility but it did relieve Richard Harrison's workload and allow him to concentrate on the many problems of organising the shore support for 'Day 1', the recovery day, and for the ultimate housing and display of the hull once it was safely ashore. Work underwater had already started in early March but there had been innumerable difficulties with heavy lifting equipment and a new dive platform installed on the diving salvage vessel *Sleipner* during her winter refit. Amidst an overwhelming atmosphere of gloom and despondency the ship's master Sam Dooley had to bring his ship back to Flathouse Quay in Portsmouth for new deck equipment to be fitted. A new dive platform was fabricated and the old derrick which had been used during the previous three seasons was reinstated and tested. Jon Adams and Chris Underwood spent the time installing a decompression chamber loaned to the Trust by Comex Holder and establishing a dive control centre for the essential communications link to the divers underwater and to the chamber. The gift or loan of these essential items of equipment saved the Trust thousands of pounds and ensured that the professional diving team employed by the Trust was using the best equipment available. *Sleipner* was back on station on 22 April but it had been a bad start to the season and most of the *Mary Rose* staff on shore and at sea were demoralised.

Even then the troubles were not over and a completely new dive platform had to be designed by Jon Adams and Chris Underwood and fabricated by Fabweld before the diving programme could really get underway. Fortunately the large team of divers promised by the Royal Engineers did not materialise so the few army divers who did come in April could easily be amalgamated with civilian divers employed by the Mary Rose Trust. Work began on site to remove the backfill of the garbage and silt which had accumulated in the trenches over the winter months and divers from the Royal Engineers began to excavate the pits which would house the legs of the Underwater Lifting Frame (ULF).

This tubular construction had been launched successfully at Hythe on 31 March and Sappers from the Royal Engineers worked at the nearby military port at Marchwood to fit the legs to the frame and carry out underwater trials to rest its stability. A large Wimpey barge *GW71* was equipped with the winches, generators and other essential equipment which was necessary to convey the ULF to the *Mary Rose* site and install it on the seabed above the wreck. In June the original salvage scheme to lift the wreck on man-made fibre strops passed beneath the hull and attached to the ULF was finally abandoned when it became clear from a study of the archaeological survey that external strops might impose an excessive point loading on the hull. Such a loading would, at best, deform the wet wood, or, at worst, cause the futtock joints to open up.

Throughout May the archaeologists and John Grace the structural engineer worked closely together and eventually a new lifting scheme was devised and approved by the Salvage Advisory Panel at a meeting in June. The heavy internal steel struts which had been proposed as internal stiffeners within the hull were abandoned and it was agreed to strengthen the component timbers of the hull with iron bolts which would pass through holes drilled through the hull at 170 carefully selected points. Those bolts were backed with an expanded synthetic material and wooden spreader plates inside and outside the hull, and a section of steel channel on the outside of the hull served as a recess for the nut and to spread the load at each point over an area of 0.6 metres square. Inside the hull the bolt was capped with an eye bolt and to this end one or more steel wires were attached by a bottle screw and passed up to the transoms in the ULF. These steel wires were the only lifting medium. No fibre strops or wires passed beneath the hull; instead it hung in suspension from the lifting frame.

The preparatory work broke down into ten main phases. Phase 1 — removal of backfill and the excavation of four pits in the seabed to house the legs of the ULF. This work was timetabled for completion in mid-April but the ULF was finally installed on site on 15 June. This delay meant that the short programme of archaeological excavation and survey in May had to proceed without the benefit of the ULF and its sophisticated supply system of low pressure air and lights. Phase 2 — the

A close-up of the cradle holding the timbers of the Mary Rose. *The project received a major setback when one of the legs of the framework (left) was damaged and had to be removed underwater by Royal Engineer divers. Soon after the hull had been raised from the water another leg collapsed but luckily the hull was not affected. The framework was then loaded onto a barge and taken into Portsmouth Dockyard.*

archaeological programme of excavation was completed in May with the exception of the area of the complex brick-built galley in the hold where excavation continued throughout the diving season. Phase 3 – the removal of the secondary silts from the scourpits which had been formed alongside the port and starboard side of the hull. Phase 4 – the removal of the levels of the archaeological material beneath the starboard side of the hull and beneath the sterncastle. Phase 5 – determination of the best position for the steel hull bolts and the installation of these bolts and their backing plates. Phase 6 – excavation beneath the hull to position the external backing plates on the steel bolt. Phase 7 – connection of the underwater lifting wires to the ring bolts and to the ULF. Phase 8 – positioning of the prefabricated support cradle with its lining of rubber air bags on the seabed alongside the *Mary Rose*. Phase 9 – fixing the system of hydraulic jacks to the legs of the ULF and lifting the hull from the seabed by jacking the frame up its legs. Phase 10 – establishing a system of acoustic position fixing devices ('compatt' – Computer and Telemetering Transponder) on the cradle, the lifting frame and on the seabed to monitor the movement of the hull during the underwater transfer from the seabed into the support cradle.

Each phase was relatively simple and the individuals responsible for each separate task knew exactly what they had to do but many of the phases were interdependent and success depended on all those responsible respecting each other's problems and working effectively within the constraints imposed by working three dive systems concurrently. The role of coordinating the multi-discipline team was demanding and

ABOVE
The view from Sleipner *— seen flying the Royal Standard to indicate that Prince Charles was aboard. A flotilla of small boats turned out to watch the raising which was spread over two days.*

The steel cradle being placed in position on the seabed on 28/29 September.

BREAKDOWN OF DIVING TIMES IN HOURS AND INDIVIDUAL DIVES

	NUMBER OF DIVES			NUMBER OF HOURS ON SEABED				
	Mary Rose Trust Professional Diving Archaeologists and Volunteer Divers	Mary Rose Trust Professional Divers	Army Divers from Royal Engineers	Mary Rose Trust Professional Diving Archaeologists and Volunteer Divers	Mary Rose Trust Professional Divers	Army Divers from Royal Engineers	Total Number of Dives	Total Number of Hours
1979 Season	6,853	—	—	3,633	—	—	6,853	3,633
1980 Season	7,025	—	—	4,216	—	—	7,025	4,216
1981 Season	10,023	Dismantling Team 4 persons 787	256	8,302	S.D.E. 55.5 S.C.U.B.A. 723 Tot. 778.5	144	11,066	9,280
1982 Season	1,532	1,350	Not Known	1,048	S.D.E. 2,671 S.C.U.B.A. 112 Tot. 2,782 (ex. de-comp)	1,800 (ex. de-comp)	2,882 (excl. Royal Engineers)	5,631
TOTALS	25,433	2,137	256 + 1982 dives (no. unknown)	17,199	3,561 (ex. de-comp)	1,944	27,831 (excl. Royal Engineers 1982 dives)	22,710 OR 11.8 Man Years

Wendell Lewis was not helped by the fact that half his operational team had other loyalties and possibly wished themselves elsewhere during the months of the Falklands War. Soldiers and civilians do not work easily together and even the romance of the *Mary Rose* failed to make up for the soldiers' natural ambition to seek battle honours in a foreign field. Many of the diving tasks fell one by one to the dozen or so professional divers employed by the Mary Rose Trust and during the year they completed 1350 dives and spent 2782 hours on the seabed.

Towards the end of July after a long spell of good weather the preparatory work on site was nearing completion and it was believed that work on site would be completed in time to lift the hull on 28 September. The final lift was dependent on installing the cradle with its lining of rubber bags on the seabed, in time to transfer the hull to the cradle on or about 13 September when the tidal conditions were most favourable for this delicate operation. Progress in fitting out the barge which would support the cradle on its journey from Marchwood to the Eastern Solent was excruciatingly slow but by early August the cradle was complete and the work of installing the steel frames which would support the rubber air bags began. The airbag system was designed to cushion the water-softened timbers as they were lifted into air and special valves were fitted to relieve the pressures in the bag if it exceeded 0.5psi in the delicate area of the lightly-built sterncastle or 2.0psi beneath the more robustly constructed main hull. In spite of everyone's best efforts the cradle was not ready for installation on the seabed in time to do the transfer in early September, and high winds and incessant rain further slowed down work both at sea and on shore. Eventually on 25 September Captain Arthur King of Alexander Towing and Co left Marchwood in the tug *Sun* with a Wimpey barge *GW92* proudly bearing the cradle towed astern. On board *Tog Mor*, the giant crane barge, we watched anxiously in worsening weather, as tug, barge and cradle loomed into view but with winds approaching 35kts Captain King had to retreat from the open water and seek haven in Portsmouth harbour.

On the following day the weather was even worse and on board *Tog Mor* we contented ourselves with continuing trials with the sonar docking equipment which would be used to locate the legs of the underwater lifting frame in the stabbing guides of the leg sheaths on the cradle. By 15.35 the winds had reached 50 knots and sea conditions were distinctly hostile. We recovered the sonar compatts and on Captain Ian Bell's advice I leapt onto the tender *Tem How*, which was going ashore for supplies, and together with Adrian Barak and Jim Clark we made for Portsmouth harbour entrance. In an evil sea with short steep swells we were reluctant to leave the shelter of *Tog Mor* but the following day was my birthday and as we could not do anything useful at sea I much preferred to be ashore.

As *Tem How* lurched and tossed a line was swept off her deck and in a split second it had fouled the rudder. Gently, gently we edged our way into harbour with quiet faith in the skill of Captain Donald Macpherson to manoeuvre the crippled tender and avoid the worst of the waves. Safely in the Outer Camber Adrian Barak donned his scuba gear and went down to free the rope. It meant me hanging over the transom tending his life line with stand-by diving equipment ready. It was not the first time Adrian and I had spent Sunday evenings in foul weather repairing boats so that work could continue the next day and after it was over we reminisced for a moment or so about old times.

Throughout the next day *Sleipner* and *Tog Mor* weathered the storms and by midday *Sleipner* had lost one of her mooring wires and was lying back on the remaining three. We organised a large tug, the *Brockenhurst*, to stand alongside and waited for the storm to blow itself out. At 07.10 on the morning of the 28th a telephone call dragged me out of bed: the winds had abated and we stood a chance. Arthur King was prepared to bring the barge and the cradle out if the weather window held. By 04.28 hours the next morning the cradle was safely on the seabed in exactly the right spot manoeuvred into position by Arthur King, rigged with lifting wires, and dropped with superb precision alongside the *Mary Rose* by Captain John Suddes who operated the *Tog Mor* crane throughout this tricky operation.

It was only just in time and the stormy weather continued to hinder work on site throughout the following week. The next tidal window when conditions might be suitable for the underwater transfer of the hull to the cradle did not occur until 9 October but before that time the last bolts had to be fastened through the hull, the rigging wire tensioned and the hull had to be lifted a few inches free from the seabed and examined for any weaknesses.

The system used to raise the hull the critical first few inches was to install three hydraulic jacks on each leg of the underwater lifting frame and jack the leg sheaths on the underwater lifting frame up the supporting legs. To do this the steel pins which secured the legs and the leg sheaths had to be removed and the system was supported on three steel divadag bars. The scheme was well thought out and Bill Summers of Bygwik Telford who supplied the equipment was a dedicated enthusiast prepared to work day and night to get the job right.

At noon on 30 September Jon Adams and Chris Dobbs recorded the structure on our video cameras and we placed small plastic strips in position over dubious scarf joints to act as tell-tales and warn us of any movement in the futtocks or stringers. We detached two of the internal rigging wires and sent them away for destructive testing to be quite sure that the two months of service underwater had not degraded the metal bulldogs used to secure the bottle screws, and the eyes at the end of the wires. The answer came back – OK. Tested to more than six tons and still all right. With an estimated load of less than two tons per wire we were safe. At 16.05 the jack lift began and by 21.50 it was clear that the south-west leg was being driven down into the soft sediments beneath its foot. The pit for this leg had never been completely excavated in the spring and now we were paying the price.

The tell-tales on the starboard castle stringer were moving and the starboard rigging wires were bar taut while the portside wires had gone slack. We were in danger of bending the hull at its weakest point, the junction of the lightly-built sterncastle structure and the main hull of the ship. Dave Burden went into the water to monitor the rigging wires and report the situation. By carefully jacking down on the portside leg at the stern we managed to even out the tension in the rigging wires and at 23.45 our diver reported that he could feel the ship flexing in the current. Was she breaking up or was she coming free of the seabed in one piece? At 00.15 hours on the morning of 1 October we knew the answer. The hull was free of the seabed and all the wires were tight. We had lifted the structure in one piece. The Engineers went to bed, and we settled down to a night of diving to record the hull on video cameras and monitor any possible movement of individual timbers. As the ship hung in suspension she pumped the seabed gently and dust storms of silts puffed out into the camera lens. More fish than we had ever seen before swam in to feed on the debris in the silt and at times it was like filming in an aquarium but the ship looked good and our hearts were high. Little more could be done until after the spring tides but by 7 October we were back onboard to install the sonar docking equipment and to prepare for the underwater transfer scheduled to take place on 9 October.

Three other important jobs remained to be done. 1) The underwater weight of the underwater lifting frame and the hull of the *Mary Rose* had to be determined by lifting the complete package on the hydraulic jacks built into the legs and calculating the loads supported on the four legs. 2) The rubber bags had suffered some damage during the strong tides and the storms which swept the south coast after the cradle was placed on the seabed and every one of the eighty bags had to be inspected, reconnected to the airhoses and tied down securely to the supporting framework. 3) All long ends of the bolts which protruded through the channel bars outside the hull had to be cropped short and capped with a protective plastic cap to prevent the bolts tearing the rubber bags when the hull was placed in the cradle.

These tasks were time-consuming in bad visibility and the divers worked desperately to complete their jobs. The positions of the acoustic compatts on the two eastern cradle legs were then fixed accurately by reference on them to two compatts on the seabed east of the wreck to a transducer hung over the side of *Sleipner*. Depth measurements were recorded over several hours and all this information was fed into our tidal programme. Satisfied that the position of the cradle legs were accurately fixed we moved the compatts from the cradle legs to the corresponding legs of the ULF. The transfer of the ULF to the cradle could now be monitored by moving the legs of the ULF to the predetermined positions of the cradle legs.

Nigel Kelland and David Lawes of Sonardyne worked day and night with Jim Clark of British Airways to perfect the system but it was totally dependent on certain factors. 1) The legs of the ULF had to be fixed to a certain known length so that they would clear the top of the *Mary Rose* and the compatts had to be precisely positioned on those legs to measure the depth accurately. The legs also had to be reasonably vertical so they would engage the stabbing guides of the cradle. John Brannam of the Royal Engineers calculated the required leg lengths and arranged to fix the legs in their sheaths with solid steel pins after lift-off and before attempting to dock the hull in the cradle. 2) The water had to be free from any acoustic interference from divers' air bubbles or leaking air manifolds. Eventually we positioned the transponder between two compatts on the eastern legs of the ULF and we were then ready to go as soon as the bolt cropping was completed.

At 08.25 on the morning of 9 October the giant crane on *Tog Mor* lifted the ULF on polypropylene strops and began to move the *Mary Rose* to the north. The weight registered was 130 tonnes – far too high – something was wrong. Then the weight dropped to 114 tonnes and a few moments later to 94, and we heaved a sigh of relief. The feet had now dropped free of the legs and the ULF was completely free of the seabed. Later underwater inspection by Martin Freeman showed that the north-easterly leg had been dragged hard against the northern side of the pit which housed the feet and this drag may have accounted for the increased weight registered on crane hook.

Slowly and carefully the ULF was moved north and then west to bring it into line end to end with the cradle waiting on the seabed to the south. Small difficulties arose from time to time; a power failure on board *Sleipner* wiped out some of the vital position fixing information in the micro-processor and the constant tendency for the south-west corner of

View of the Mary Rose *in the steel support cradle in the Royal Naval Base during the preparatory work, which was necessary to secure the underwater lifting frame legs before the frame itself could be safely removed.*

The underwater lifting frame weighing 45 tons being removed from the cradle in the Royal Naval Base at Portsmouth.

the ULF to rise out of the water indicated that the ULF was not lying horizontal and therefore the legs were not as vertical as we desired.

At 11.30 the Sapper divers began to adjust the length of the legs and once this task was completed we began to move south. Our main concern was not to damage the hull by dragging the steel legs through the maze of deck beams inside the ship and all the time we had to monitor the depth of water and adjust the height of the ULF accordingly. By 19.00 it was clear that we could not dock all four of the ULF legs in the stabbing guide. Underwater inspection showed that three legs were in position but the fourth, on the north-east corner, was misaligned, 0.5 metres to the south of the stabbing guide. The sonar docking system was abandoned and brute force was called into play; divers attempted to force the recalcitrant leg into the stabbing guides with turfers and chain hoists, but by 03.50 on the morning of 10 October we knew that it was impossible to dock the fourth leg and a decision was made to remove it completely.

During the night a ring of guard boats had formed around the wreck site in anticipation of a salvage attempt at 07.30 hours but we knew that this could not happen and with sick disappointment we watched the sun rise on a perfect autumn morning. By 08.30 the President of the Trust His Royal Highness the Prince of Wales was on board *Sleipner* and decisions began to be made.

It was finally agreed to support the weight of the north-east corner on an auxiliary wire attached to the main crane hook and dock the hull down onto the supporting airbags as soon as possible. By early evening all was ready and Captain Arthur King moved the barge into position above the submerged ULF so that the polypropylene strops could be replaced with steel wires capable of carrying the weight of the full load.

The rigging operation continued for most of the night with divers from the Royal Engineers offering up the loops of the short strops attached to the cradle to the riggers on the barge. Steel wires capable of lifting the estimated load of 550 tons were then attached to these loops and the crane hook was ready for the big lift.

Wet cold rain swept the decks on the morning of 'Day 1', 11 October 1982. The weather forecast was appalling: 'South 4 backing south-east 5-6, veering west 5-7, occasionally gale'. The barometer registered 1008 and was falling and we were promised continuous rain. The only thing that was right were the tidal conditions, which would not exceed 0.5kts until early afternoon.

At 8.06 John Suddes began to lift the capsule and 57 minutes later the *Mary Rose* began to break the surface of the water. The sea became flat and calm and the wind fell away. Suddenly it seemed possible that we were going to get away with after all.

The wires inside the hull began to slacken as the hull bedded down onto the airbags which Chris Dobbs and Kestor Keighley had inflated beneath the bow and the midship section. At that moment all seemed well and I joined a small party onboard a combat support boat, with his Royal Highness the Prince of Wales, to go on board the *Mary Rose*.

As we came alongside it was obvious that the whole of the underwater lifting frame was under strain, acting as a great spreader to prevent the lifting strops bearing in on the hull. It was no longer a rectangle but there was no way it could be removed until the cradle was safely on the barge as it was necessary to spread the weight of the wire strops.

A few moments after we backed away there was an unforgettable crunch as the south-east corner of the underwater lifting frame slumped down to the level of the hull. A tubular pin used to restrain the leg had given way and the sheath or collar which connected the ULF to the leg had dropped by more than a metre. All hearts stopped but no damage had been done to the ship. The lift continued and by teatime the whole package was safely on the barge.

No-one felt entirely safe, champagne went undrunk and celebration cakes were uncut. Until we were safely into harbour no-one was happy. In the dark desperately tired, hungry and curiously unelated, we limped into harbour ahead of *Tow 1* with her unique cargo. As we came through the harbour entrance we became aware that the ancient walls built by the Tudor kings to defend Portsmouth were alive with a seething mass of people. We shouted at them and they cheered us and the cheers rose to a crescendo as the *Mary Rose* entered harbour. What a moment! She was back where she belonged and soon she would be safe in the Royal Naval base alongside *Hermes, Invincible* and Nelson's flagship, *Victory*.

Too tired for sleep we went to the Press Tent on Southsea Common to dance away most of the night to live 'country' music. REs, civvies and shore staff, we rejoiced together – the *Mary Rose* was home.

THE MARY ROSE MUSEUM

In March 1982 the Mary Rose Trust had decided to postpone the construction of the purpose-built museum at Eastleigh and concentrate all their resources into recovering the hull and bringing it ashore to a temporary location in No 3 dock in the Royal Naval base. In every sense this was a homecoming and it is appropriate that the initial work to restore the hull of the *Mary Rose* and prepare a long-term programme of conservation is taking place only a few yards from where she was built in 1509.

The wet dock provides excellent 'walls' and a 'floor' for the temporary ship hall and the ship is supported in the steel cradle which was used to lift her from the seabed. The archaeologists are supervising a task of reinstating the decks, cabins and companionways that they removed so laboriously underwater. It is necessary to keep the ship wet to prevent micro-biological decay and initially this is done by mist-spraying with chilled water. As the work progresses micro-biological contamination is monitored and localised applications of biocides are used to control biological degradation.

Scientists at the National Maritime Museum, Imperial College of Science and Technology in London and at Portsmouth Polytechnic have been monitoring the micro-biological infestations of samples of the timbers from the *Mary Rose* site since 1979 and their recommendations for the ultimate conservation of the hull will be followed once all the dismantled timbers are reinstated inside the hull.

The long-term plan for a Tudor Ship museum on a 12-acre site at Eastney has been pigeon-holed. At present the future of the Royal Naval base at Portsmouth is uncertain but if the run-down of the modern Royal Navy continues the development of a maritime heritage resource in the area around the main gate and No 1 Basin would be a rational use of the glorious storehouses, docks, mast-ponds and yards which have so miraculously survived the bombing raids of the 1939-45 war and the demands of modernisation. A unique range of late eighteenth century storehouses survive in the area around No 1 Basin, which itself dates from 1698, and although nothing survives of the timber-built dock within which the *Mary Rose* was built, the setting is appropriate and the proximity of Nelson's flagship HMS *Victory* in an adjacent dry dock only emphasises the relationship between the two most important warships in the world. It is right that the Mary Rose Trust should concentrate their resources on the preservation of the hull; their priorities are chosen for them and a decision is inescapable because the ship is unique in herself. Nevertheless, the real importance for future generations is the relationship of the people who lived and worked and died within that ship, to their personal possessions, their weapons, their tools and to the ship itself. Unless a vibrant, living museum can be originated and maintained to interpret those relationships the *Mary Rose* project will fail. One piece of wet wood, however large, looks much like another. People are interested in people and it is the How, Why and Where which is so exciting.

The architectural simplicity and the elegance of some of the store-

A photomosaic overhead view of the Mary Rose, *safely protected from drying out by layers of expanded foam.*

The Princess of Wales viewing the Mary Rose from a crane. In the background can be seen HMS Victory and No. 3 dock where the Mary Rose now lies.

houses near the dock where the *Mary Rose* will lie could be appropriate for the exhibition and interpretation of the objects from within the hull but the present constraints of running a museum within a naval base would limit any future development and prevent the growth of a living museum as we use that term today. Gone are the dusty unchanging rows of badly-displayed objects so often associated with museums in the past. Today a successful museum has public participation, theatre and interpretation inexorably linked. It is a place to enjoy and experience with all the senses. Life on board the *Mary Rose* was never dull and the understanding approach of a 'Williamsburg' or a 'Skansen' is necessary if the *Mary Rose* museum is to be worthwhile.

Appendix

REMOTE SENSING AND SURVEY METHODS USED ON
THE *MARY ROSE* SITE

'It is not the greater sophistication which the archaeologist requires, but the adaptation (which may sometimes mean the simplification) of highly sophisticated equipment and techniques for the particular needs of archaeology.'[1]

REMOTE SENSING

1966. A magnetometer made by Wardle & Davenport was towed across the site on two occasions.[2] The results were confused by the presence of metal cable in the vicinity of the supposed wreck area and the method was abandoned.

1967. An anomaly recorded in the supposed wreck area by John Mills of EG &G Ltd using a dual channel side scan sonar, with a range varying between 250ft and 1000ft, linked with a sub-mud acoustic profiler. The anomaly was recorded sub-mud and on the seabed and interpreted as a mound 4-5ft high above the seabed overlying a buried objects at a depth of 20ft below the seabed.[3]

1968. Professor Harold Edgerton of Massachusetts Institute of Technology conducted trials over the supposed wreck area with a 5k/c sub-mud sonar profiler and a 12k/c dual channel side scan sonar. Four sub-mud anomalies were found, but only one was in the area where the *Mary Rose* was believed to lie. This anomaly was interpreted as a large buried wreck with a scourpit on the western side and a mound on the eastern side. McKee deduced the sub-mud anomaly to be 'about 170 feet long'.

McKee combined the results of the sub-mud profiler and the side scan sonar as a 'three dimensional site map' with a buried feature at a depth varying from 5ft to 15ft below the surface.

1975 and 1976. Profiler surveys carried out on the known wreck site by the BP Group of Companies and David Viner failed to reveal the sub-mud anomaly recorded in 1968.

1975. New side scan sonar survey carried out by BP Group of Companies in advance of sonar ranging trials. Spoil dumps of excavation waste and wreck of diving pontoon shown in relation to the stern of *Mary Rose*.

1978. Stereo side scan equipment used on site by Dr Philip Denbigh of Birmingham University, to demonstrate relationship of structures revealed in the excavation trenches at the bow and at the stern, and to aid interpretation.[4]

The system used three arrays. The largest array operated at a frequency of 40KHz with a 3dB beam width of 20 degrees in elevation and 0.6 degrees in the azimuth and it transmitted acoustic signals in a narrow vertical fan beam. The along-track resolution was approximately 0.37m for ranges up to 37m and 0.01rm for greater ranges where r is the range. The other two arrays were used for reception and they were closely spaced one above the other.

This instrument was capable of measuring the time difference between the arrival of signals at each of the two receivers, and from this the declination angle relative to the boresight of the receivers was deduced and the depth was determined.

The information was displayed as a stereoscopic pair of side scan images which were generated simultanously in real time using two fibre-optic recorders. The stereo pairs were photographed and viewed with a standard pocket stereoscope and for the first time we had an overview of the trenches and the deck beams of the *Mary Rose* at the bow and the stern.

1979. Trials were undertaken with a sonic camera provided by EMI Electronics in an attempt to evaluate objects concealed beneath the mud in a trench over the area of the weather deck in the waist of the ship.

Sub-mud features were successfully recorded on black and white photographs of signals recorded on a TV type display system. The ultrasonic image converter tube used in this equipment was basically a cathode ray tube with a special face plate which was transparent to ultra sound and which supported a piezo electric sensitive layer (a quartz plate) and the signal electrode (a thin metallic layer) on the inner surface of the face plate.[5]

The inner surface of the piezo electric quartz receiver crystal was raster-scanned with a TV type display system. Objects buried beneath 50-80mm of fine silt were recorded successfully, but interpretation was difficult and the system would have been enhanced if we had been able to link it to a sonar location system or to a conventional wide-angle video camera.

VIDEO RECORDING

Video equipment for recording, processing, transmitting and displaying the underwater excavation of the *Mary Rose* was provided by Marconi Avionics, Sony UK, Rediffusion, Micro Wave Associates and British Airways and the result was of broadcast quality.

The camera chosen for routine use on the site was the Marconi V328, operating on the conventional 625-line 50Hz interlaced television standard. It was fitted with a 1in Newvican sensor tube which combined moderately high sensitivity with good signal resolution and shading uniformity.

Maximum use was made of signal processing to enhance display contrast and in practice the camera produced a better display contrast than the human eye. The lens used had a focal length of 6mm which produced an angle of view of 83 degrees in water and the optical focus was preset to give a depth of field of 14in to 355in at an aperture of f2.8.

Trials with a video colour camera were successful in 1980 and further trials were carried out with stereo mono-chrome and stereo colour cameras, but while these tapes were useful for public display they added little information to that produced by the conventional monochrome camera and both the colour system with its necessary battery of lights and the bulky stereo camera were considered too unwieldy for routine use.

Editing and copying facilities were provided by British Airways and playback and monitor facilities were available on board *Sleipner* and at the Trust Headquarters.

A microwave link was established between the base vessel *Sleipner* and Southsea Castle by Jim Clark of British Airways, using equipment loaned to the Trust by Micro Wave Associates. This enabled both live and playback displays of work on the seabed to be shown within the *Mary Rose* galleries in Southsea Castle, and also facilitated links with public service television.

1981. A sector scan sonar system was demonstrated on site by UDI Ltd but the inordinate amount of underwater 'noise' from air manifolds, airlifts and other air tools pre-vented its successful use for monitoring divers underwater.

SURVEY

The soft, featureless seabed which characterized the *Mary Rose* site in 1971 presented special surveying problems when a line of timbers was exposed as a result of tidal scour. Artificial datum points proved to be unstable if they were light (eg range rods rammed into the seabed) and they sank into the seabed if they were heavy (eg concrete sinkers with plastic antennae).

The survey was a two-dimensional problem as the frames were eroded to the same level and a simple plan was achieved by establishing a rigid datum (a straight 6m steel pole, 0.05m diameter) over the frame heads and fixing the position of frame, inboard and outboard planking by off-sets from the steel pole. The offsets were short measure-ments, limited to the visual range of the diver (usually 0.5m) and inter-frame distances and the distance from the

frames, centreline to centreline, were also recorded. As excavation proceeded north to expose the portside frame amidships, the steel pole was realigned over a selection of previously surveyed frames and newly exposed frames. The accumulated errors in the 'frame to frame' measurements and inherent inaccuracies in realigning the steel pole led to an artificial straightening of the slight curvature of the wreck structure.

In 1975 the British Petroleum Group of Companies agreed to assist with the survey and Nigel Kelland spent 5 days on site conducting a rangemeter survey using an instrument developed by John Partridge of Sonardyne Limited.[6] Before the survey was carried out the site was resurveyed using side scan sonar to ensure that the trans-ponders used in the survey would be neither screened by underwater obstructions nor too close to any obstacle which might cause multipath reflections of the acoustic signals.

Four transponders, supported on steel tripods, were placed on the western side of the wreck and their relative positions were fixed using the rangemeter. Twenty selected points on the wreck were surveyed during two dives each of 30 minutes duration. The hand-held rangemeter was held over each point to be surveyed and each transponder was interrogated in turn by an acoustic signal from the rangemeter.

The time interval between the emission of the acoustic signal and the return of the signal to the rangemeter was measured in milliseconds and this time interval was directly proportional to the distance between the rangeme-ter and the transponders. The temperature and salinity of the seawater were recorded at 15-minute intervals throughout the survey in order to determine the velocity of acoustic propagation accurately and a computer plot of the survey was prepared and co-related with the National Grid.

The range measured during this survey varied from 75m to 200m and the relative positional accuracies were better than 0.15m over a 200m range.

After this survey all other datum points on the wreck were correlated using short distance trilateration from the prime datum points fixed by the rangemeter and further points were surveyed by Kelland in 1979 using a rangeme-ter manufactured by Sonardyne.

As the trenches became deeper, horizontal measure-ments using a plumb bob became impossible and the entire wreck was surveyed using a three-dimensional cartesian co-ordinate system based on the National Grid and the depth below the original seabed level.

A system of direct measurement from any four fixed points was introduced by Nic Rule and from 1981 all survey measurements were made from a series of DSM points established within the hull by attaching small labelled iron hooks to the main timbers. The cartesian co-ordinates of the DSM points were established from the original rangemeter survey using trilateration and a simple underwater level, and a computer programme was written to establish the co-ordinates by a series of measurements from any 3 points of which the cartesian co-ordinates are known. In practice measurements were usually made from four DSM points enabling the surveyor to reject spurious measurements and quantify the error of each point.

The computer programme enabled any spurious measurements to be eliminated rapidly and it revealed unsuspected areas of weakness, such as careless transposition of numbers written underwater and divers with poor eyesight apparently unable to read a tape measure underwater. To overcome the former difficulty a system of through-water sonic communications was used on site between 1980 and 1982. This single side band system was developed by UDI Limited for the Home Office and it is widely used by the British Police Force divers. Its use enabled divers to communicate with each other and with a supervisor on board *Sleipner*. The acoustic quality was excellent and survey measurements could be read directly to the supervisor and recorded in air.

It would have been possible to link diver, supervisor and micro-processor operator using this communication system, and plot the survey measurements while the diver was still in the water, thus enabling spurious measurements to be rejected and retaken. The aim of the survey was to fix each main hull timber and every object or group of objects found within the ship in three dimensions, the x and y co-ordinates being the National Grid reference points and the z co-ordinates being the depth below chart datum.

When the ship is raised we will transform the co-ordinates to give new values relative to the axes of the ship and to reconstruct the relationship of the hull with the associated object. A secondary programme has been devised to enable us to use the co-ordinates to produce an 'instant catalogue' of associated objects found within the vessel.

The criteria which dictated survey methods on the *Mary Rose* site were low cost, speed underwater and the ability to accurately quantify any error in each position fix. The DSM system came nearest to fulfilling these requirements as even the most casual measurements produced an accuracy of c10cm in a 3m cube and careful workers consistently produced measurements c2cm in the same area.

References

Chapter 1

1 Cuncliffe B 'The British Fleet', *Fifth Report on the Excavation of the Roman Fort at Richborough, Kent* (Society of Antiquaries, London 1968 pp55-71)

2 *Letters & Papers Henry VIII* I. 67

3 *Letters & Papers Henry VIII* I. 287

4 *Letters & Papers Henry VIII* I. 145-6, 709

5 *Inventory 1514. PRO State Papers of Henry VIII* 1/7 including a list of ordnance remaining in Flanders the 8th day of April the 5th year of the Reign of our Sovereign Lord King Henry VIII. Published in Blackmore, H C *The Armouries of the Tower of London* (HMSO, 1976 p1259)

6 *Letters & Papers Henry VIII* III. 1370

7 *Letters & Papers Henry VIII* V. 296, 306. In 1531 Baude was paid for 42 guns made for the King and for a third share of 36 guns made by him with Robert and John Owen.

8 *Regent* inventory. Published in full in Oppenheim, M (ed) *Naval Accounts and Inventories of the Reign of Henry VII* (Navy Record Society, 1896, pp218-291)

9 *Sovereign* inventory *ibid*, pp161-218

10 *The Mariner's Mirror* 45 (1959), pp94-99 and 47 (1961), pp81-90

11 *Sovereign* inventory *ibid*, pp143-161

12 *Ibid*

13 *Ibid*

14 *Letters and Papers of Henry VIII* TR MISC Books. I, f46 RO. Daunces Accounts. 16 November 1511. William Asteley, John Eawteles, John Aleyn and other merchant adventurers, by charter party for freight in the *Peter Poundegarnade* to Borrowe and back to London.

15 *Letters and Papers of Henry VIII* TR MISC Books. I, f25. RO. 29 July 1511. To Robert Brygandyne, clerk of the King's Ships, for the conveyance of two new ships, *The Mary Rose* and the *Peter Granade*, from Portsmouth to the Thames £120.

16 *Ibid* 24 September 1511. To Richard Palshidde, one of the King's Customers at Southampton for 24 coats of white and green for 24 soldiers employed for the safe conduct of the *Mary Rose* from Portsmouth to the 'Temmys of London', and six similar coats of white and green for the master, 4 for the quartermaster and boatswain, at 6s 10d a coat.

17 *Letters and Papers of Henry VIII* TR MISC Books. I. f29. RO. October 1511. To Cornelius Johnson, gunmaker, towards new stocking and repairing divers pieces of ordnance in the King's ships now in the Thames viz *The Mary and John,* the *Anne of London*, the *Mary Rose* and the *Peter Granade*, £20. To the same for 8 loads of elm for stocking the said ordnance at 4s the load.

18 *Ibid* 18 October 1512. To Thomas Sperte master and David Boner purser of the *Mary Rose* for decking and rigging the same £66 13s 4d.

Note: A month later Thomas Sperte and David Boner were paid £66 13s 4d for decking and rigging the *Peter Poude Granada* which suggest that these officers were responsible for both ships at this time.

19 *Ibid* 17 December 1512. To William Botrye of London, mercer, upon a bill signed by Sir Edward Howard for tukes, bokerums, Brussels cloth and chamletes to make streamers and banners for the *Mary Rose* and the *Peter Pounde Gernade* £50 19s 2d. To John Brown of London, painter, upon a book of parcels signed by Sir Edward Howard for painting and staining banners and streamers for the same £142 4s 6d.

20 Webb, J et al (ed) *Margaret Hoad: Hampshire Studies* (Portsmouth City Record Office, 1981, pp17-20). Miss Hoad dismisses reputed earlier charters and presents a strong case for the charter of King Richard I 'retaining in our hand our borough of Portsmouth' being the earliest given to that town, and attributes the foundation of Portsmouth as a 'new town' to John de Gisons who forfeited it to King Richard after supporting the aspirations of Prince John while the King was in the Holy Land. The charter gave the town the right to hold a weekly market and undoubtedly this contributed to the growth of the town.

21 Corney, A *Fortification in Old Portsmouth — A Guide* (Portsmouth City Museums).

22 *Letters and Papers of Henry VIII* V. 338

23 *Archaeologia* 28. Narrative eye-witness account of the battle by Sir Peter Carew. Republished 1979 as a reprint of Horsey, S *The Loss of The Mary Rose* (Hunnyhill Publications, Corner Cottage, Hunnyhill, Brighstone, Isle of Wight)

24 Oglander, Sir John *Diary of a Royalist* (1610)

25 Lediard, T *The Naval History of England* (Wilcox, 1735)

26 *Archaeologia* 28

Chapter 2

1 *PRO State Papers* 1831 I 794. Lord Russell to Sir William Paget, Secretary of State; Bodnam, 23 July 1545:

'I am sorry of the unhappy and the unfortunate chance of the *Mary Rose*, through such rechenes and great negligence, should be in suchwise cast away, with those that were within her, which is a great loss of the men and the ship also.'

[2] McKee, A *History Under the Sea* (Hutchinson, 1968, p203)

[3] Davies, R H *Deep Diving and Submarine Salvage* (St Catherine Press, 1936)

[4] Portsmouth Evening News

[5] *International Journal of Nautical Archaeology* 2 (1973), pp385-388

[6] *The Mariner's Mirror* 62 (1976), p184

Chapter 3

[1] Barker, B D, Kendell, K, and O'Shea, C 'The Hydrogen Reduction Process for the conservation of Ferrous Objects' *Proceedings of the Conservation of Iron Symposium National Maritime Museum, 1980*; Slade, J 'Analysis of the Corrosion Products on a rudder pintle from the *Mary Rose*' (BSc Applied Chemistry Project, Portsmouth Polytechnic, 1978); Kendell, K 'The gaseous reduction of archaeological ironwork' (PhD Thesis, Portsmouth Polytechnic, 1982)

Chapter 4

[1] Salisbury, W (ed) *A Treatise on Shipbuilding circa 1620*, SNR Occasional Paper No 6.

Chapter 5

[1] Portrait in Ashmolean Museum, Oxford. Published in Waters, D W *The Art of Navigation in England in Elizabethan and Early Stuart Times* (National Maritime Museum, 1978)

Chapter 6

[1] Chapter House Book XIII, 1514

Chapter 7

[1] Anderson, R C *The Mariner's Mirror* 45 (1959), p90

[2] *PRO State Papers of Henry VIII* I. *12/6*

[3] *Letters and Papers of Henry VIII*, I. 537

[4] Acts of Parliament 33 Henry VIII C1X

[5] De Commines, P *Les Memoirs de Messire* (Paris, 1580)

[6] State Papers of Venice, A1, Part 2, 1047

[7] Hardy, R *Longbow* (Patrick Stephens, 1976, p135)

Chapter 8

[1] *A Book of Plaisters, Spasmadraps, Ointments and Pulses devised by the King's Majesty, Dr Butts, Dr Chambre, Dr Cromer and Dr Augustine.* Manuscript, British Library. A spasmadrap was a plaster made by dipping strips of linen in a melted dressing and smoothing out on a flat surface.

[2] Woodall, J *The Surgeon's Mate* (1617, reprinted Kingsmead Press, 1978, p21)

[3] Bennion, Elizabeth *Antique Medical Instruments* (Sotheby Parke Bernet, 1979)

Appendix

[1] Blackman, D J *The Underwater Cultural Heritage* (Council of Europe, 1978).

[2] Blackman, D J (ed) *Marine Archaeology*: *Proceedings of the 23rd Symposium of the Colston Research Society* (Butterworths, 1973).

[3] *Ibid.*

[4] Denbigh, P N 'Stereoscopic Side Scan Sonar', *Acoustic Letters* 2 (1979), pp108-112.

[5] Clayden, R T & Brown, P H 'A simple high definition ultrasonic imaging system for the location and inspection of submerged objects in turbid conditions', *Oceanology* (1978).

[6] Kelland, N C 'A method for carrying out accurate planometric surveys underwater', *The Hydrographic Journal* 2, pp17-30.

Glossary

Within the definitions, references to other words in the Glossary are set in italics.

Athwartships. Across the ship, from one side to the other; or in that direction.

Bar shot. A form of dismantling shot fired mainly against masts and rigging, consisting of a ball cut into two halves and connected with an iron bar.

Battens. Flexible lengths of light timber. See also *seam ribbands*.

Beakhead. A platform over the bows, forward of the bowcastle, serving as the crew's latrine, and also to give access to the *bowsprit* and *spritsail*.

Bonadventure mizzen mast. The fourth mast of a ship, positioned abaft the mizzen proper; usually carrying *lateen* sails.

Bowsprit. The heavy spar projecting forward from the ship's bow from which the *spritsail* was set.

Carling. Part of the structure of the decks; smaller timbers running fore and aft between deck beams proper.

Carrack. A late-medieval ship-type, possibly originating in the Mediterranean. It is impossible to be specific about its characteristics, but the carrack was probably the largest ship of its day.

Carvel planking. A type of construction where the strakes of timber are laid edge to edge, which produces a smooth surface; usually contrasted with *clinker* construction.

Cascabel. The moulding at the breech end of a muzzle-loading gun.

Caulking. Material, usually oakum, driven into the seams between planking to render them watertight.

Chain boom. A strong chain rigged across the mouth of a harbour as a defensive measure to prevent the passage of enemy vessels.

Chainplates. Sometimes shortened to 'chains', the plates were links of iron that fastened the *deadeyes* to the hull.

Chain-rails. The lower rigging of sixteenth century ships was set up over *chain-wales*, but an auxiliary rail ran fore and aft above it. Since there is no traditional term for this feature, it has been referred to in this book as a 'chain-rail'.

Chain-wales. Later shortened to 'channels', the term normally referred to the wide platforms that spread the lower mast rigging. See also *chain-rails* and *deadeyes*.

Clew line block. A distinctive block, with a 'shoulder', used to haul the corners of the sails up the yards.

Clinker planking. A form of construction involving overlapping strakes of timber; usually contrasted with *carvel* construction.

Cross bar shot. Another form of *bar shot*.

Culverin. A long-barrelled, medium calibre gun, principally designed for long-range firing.

Curtow. Large calibre, relatively short-barrelled cannon, firing a very heavy shot of about 80lbs.

Deck clamp. Strong timber fastened continuously along the inside of the frames and under the ends of deck beams to give the ship longitudinal strength.

Deadeyes. A form of block with a pattern of holes through which lanyards are passed; set up in pairs, they are used to tension the *shrouds*.

Footwales. Interior planking over the frames; also called 'ceiling', although 'footwales' usually applies to the larger strengthening timbers, as with the exterior *wales*.

Forepeak. The extreme forward space, or compartment, in the hold.

Fore yards. The transverse spars of the foremast, from which the sails are set. The fore yard proper is the lowest yard, which carries the *foresail*.

Foresail. The lower (and therefore principal) sail of the foremast; also called the 'Fore course'.

Frame heads. The upper ends of the floor timbers (frames); called 'rung heads' by shipwrights.

Futtocks. Individual parts of the composite timbers that made up the frames of a wooden ship.

Gaff sail. A quadrilateral fore-and-aft sail, spread by a spar at its head, attached by its forward edge to the mast, and often extended at its foot by a boom.

Galliass. Usually refers to a type of warship combining sail and oar propulsion, but in Henry VIII's day it was also applied to small, low-built ships that depended entirely on sails.

Gudgeon. Iron fittings on a ship's sternpost which is part of the 'hinge' on which the rudder moves. The gudgeon is a brace containing a hole into which a pin or *pintle* on the rudder is located.

Gunwale. See *wales*.

Halyards. Ropes or tackles used to hoist or lower sails.

Hawser. A large rope or cable.

Headrails. Slender timbers extending along the side of the *beakhead* from the bowcastle to the forward extremity of the beak.

Hood ends. The ends of the planks which fit into *rabbets* of the stem and sternpost.

Keel. The principal longitudinal member at the bottom of the hull. On large ships it consisted of a number of pieces *scarfed* and bolted together.

Keelson. A heavy longitudinal timber, which in effect is the internal equivalent of the keel; it is fitted over the frames, immediately above the keel.

Knee. An angled timber chock or brace, used to connect beams to the frames of a ship; principally divided into 'hanging' knees which are fastened in an up-and-down direction, and 'lodging' knees which fit fore and aft; there are also 'rising' which are inverted hanging knees, and 'dagger' knees which are fitted obliquely.

Lanyards. Short pieces of rope with various functions in the rigging and fitting of a ship; lanyards to the *deadeyes*, specifically, are used to set up a form of tackle to tension the *shrouds*.

Lapped planks. See *clinker planking*.

Lateen sail. A triangular sail set from a long yard, thought to originate in the Mediterranean; useful for balancing the square sails of larger ships, but also used on their own in smaller craft.

Mast partners. A frame of strengthening timbers around the apertures in the decks through which the masts pass.

Mast-step. A baulk of timber fitted with a rebate into which the shaped end of the mast was inserted.

Mizzen mast. The aftermost mast of a three-masted ship. At the period under review it usually set a *lateen* sail.

Ordnance. A generic term for artillery, and all matters associated with it.

Orlop deck. The lowest proper deck of a man-of-war; usually divided into storerooms and cabins.

Parrels. A form of collar used to attach yards to the mast so as to allow a swivelling movement of the yards; it consisted of multiple strings of bead-like *trucks* separated by wooden spacers called *ribs*.

Pintles. Iron pins fastened to the forward edge of the rudder on which it pivotted; pintles fitted into *gudgeons* on the sternpost.

Plain shot. Round shot, or ball.

Rabbet. A shipwright's version of 'rebate'; the notch cut in keel, stem or any other timber to take the ends of planks.

Restraining tackle. A system of ropes used to dampen the recoil of naval guns.

Rider. Heavy strengthening timbers; usually refers to the internal ribs fitted over the interior planking.

Rove. Small metal plate or ring on which the point of a nail is 'clinched' or beaten down.

Running rigging. The assemblage of ropes, blocks and tackles used to control the yards and sails, as opposed to *standing rigging* which supports and steadies the masts.

Scarf. A method of joining two pieces of timber at their ends by overlapping; there are many forms of scarf joints, some very elaborate.

Scuppers. Channels, pipes or openings through a ship's side to allow water on the decks to drain into the sea.

Seam ribbands. Lengths of chamfered battening covering the seams of carvel planking to give additional strength and watertightness.

Serpentine. A relatively small calibre, long-barrelled gun.

Sheave. The pulley, or wheel, inside a block, over which the moving part of a rope or tackle runs.

Shot line. A line permanently fastened to the seabed by a sinker; used by divers as a method of finding and leaving the site quickly.

Shrouds. Multiple ropes that give lateral (*athwartships*) support to the masts. They are tensioned with a system of *deadeyes* and *lanyards*.

Spritsail. Small sail set under the bowsprit; also used for a sail set by a diagonal spare.

Stanchions. Upright pillars supporting the ship's structure.

Standing rigging. The assemblage of ropes, set up more or less permanently, to support the masts; usually contrasted with *running rigging*.

Stave-built guns. An early form of gun manufacture in which the barrel was constructed of individual lengths of wrought iron forged or welded together; strengthening hoops were then shrunk over the barrel.

Stays. Large ropes, part of the standing rigging, which supports the masts from forward.

Strake. A longitudinal line of planking.

Stringer. Internal strake of timber, usually under the ends of the beams where it is known as a 'shelf' or 'shelf piece'.

Studding. The light woodwork panelling used to line a room or cabin.

Topgallant. The mast fitted above the *topmast*, or the sails set from the topgallant.

Topmast. Masts of sailing ships were divided into separate sections; the topmast was fitted above the main, or lower, mast section. See also *topgallant*.

Topsail. The sail set from yards on the *topmast*.

Transom stem. A square, flat stern. The 'transoms' were the *athwartship* timbers that framed the stern.

Trenails. Wooden dowels (originally 'tree-nails', but pronounced 'trunnels') used to fasten the frames and planking of ships in addition to bolts and nails; they were usually fashioned from oak.

Trucks. Round pieces of wood, either cylindrical or spherical; hence the term came to refer to the solid wheels of naval gun carriages, the bead-like elements of *parrels*, and the 'button' at the very top of a mast or flagstaff.

Trunnions. The short cylinders fixed at right angles to the bore of a gun, which served to support it on its carriage, and also to allow the barrel to be elevated or depressed.

Tumblehome. The narrowing of the ship's breadth above the point of maximum beam – the ship's side describes a convex curve inwards from this point to the *gunwale*.

Waist. The area of the open upper deck between the bowcastle and the sterncastle.

Wales. Thickened strakes of planking running along the outside of the hull; structurally the most important of these is the 'main' or 'lower' wale; the uppermost is called the *gunwale* (pronounced 'gunnel') which has come to mean the capping rail on top of the bulwarks.

Weather deck. The uppermost continuous deck; the one 'exposed to the weather'.

Wire-linked shot. An early form of chain shot, in which two cannon balls are linked together; it was particularly effective against masts and rigging. See also *bar shot*.

Bibliography

ABELL, Sir W *The Shipwright's Trade* (1948, reprinted Conway Maritime Press, 1981)

ANDERSON, R & R C *The Sailing Ship: 6000 Years of History* (Harrap, 1927)

ASCHAM, R *Toxophilus* (1545, reprinted SR Publishers, 1969)

BARTO ARNOLD, J *Beneath the Waters of Time* (Texas Antiquities Committee Publication No 6, 1978)

BATHE, B W *Seven Centuries of Seafaring* (Barrie & Jenkins, 1972)

BIRINGUCCIO, *Pirotechnia* (1540, reprinted MIT Press, Cambridge, Mass, 1972).

BLACKMAN, D J (ed) *Maritime Archaeology: Colston Papers No 23* (Butterworths, 1973)

BLACKMORE, H *The Armouries of the Tower of London: Ordnance* (HMSO, 1976)

CARMA, W Y *A History of Firearms* (Routledge & Kegan Paul, 1955)

COAD, J *Historic Architecture of HM Naval Base Portsmouth 1700-1850* (Portsmouth Royal Naval Museum)

CORNEY, A H *Fortification of Old Portsmouth* (Portsmouth City Museum)

FALCONER, W *A New and Universal Dictionary of the Marine* (1780, reprinted David and Charles, 1970)

FRANZEN, A *The Warship Wasa* (Norstedts Banniers, 1960)

HARDY, R *Longbow* (Patrick Stephens, 1976)

HOGG, O F G *English Artillery 1326-1716* (Royal Artillery Institution, 1963)

HOWARD, F *Sailing Ships of War 1400-1860* (Conway Maritime Press, 1979)

LANDSTROM, B *Sailing Ships* (George Allen & Unwin, 1961)

LEES, J *The Masting and Rigging of English Ships of War 1625-1860* (Conway Maritime Press, 1979)

LAVERY, B (ed) *Deane's Doctrine of Naval Architecture, 1670* (Conway Maritime Press, 1981)

LONGRIDGE, C N *The Anatomy of Nelson's Ships* (Model & Allied Publications, 1955)

MCKEE, A *King Henry VIII's Mary Rose* (Souvenir Press, 1973)

MILLIKEN, E K *Archery in the Middle Ages* (Macmillan, 1967)

MUCKELROY, K *Maritime Archaeology* (Cambridge University Press, 1978)

OCLEY, J E *The Fletchers and Longbowstring makers of London* (Worshipful Company of Fletchers)

OPPENHEIM, M *A History of the Administration of the Royal Navy 1509-1660* (Navy Records Society, 1899)

PADFIELD, P *Guns at Sea* (Evelyn, 1973)

SANDAHL, B *Middle English Sea Terms* (University of Uppsala, Sweden, 1952 vol I, 1958 vol II)

SAUNDERS, A D Hampshire Coastal Defence since the Introduction of Artillery *Archaeological Journal* CXXIII: 136-171

SMITH, Capt J *A Seaman's Grammar* (1627, reprinted Michael Joseph, 1970)

SPONT, A *The French War of 1512-13* (Navy Record Society, 1897)

UNESCO *Underwater Archaeology: A Nascent Discipline* (1972)

WATERS, D W *The Art of Navigation in England in Elizabethan and Early Stuart Times* (National Maritime Museum, 1978)

WILKES, W St J *Nautical Archaeology* (David & Charles, 1971)

WOODALL, J *The Surgeon's Mate* (1617, reprinted Kingsmead Press, 1978)

Index

References in *italics* refer to illustrations

A
Ackland, Percy 57, 59
Adams, Jon 83, 213, 216, 222
Airlift *75*, *81*, *83*
de Andreas, Peter 39, 40, 153
d'Annebault, Claude 31, 34
Anne 23
Anthony, Anthony 28
Anthony Roll *26/27*, 28, *39*, 120, 125, 136, 137, *138/139*, 152, 153, 156, 163, 164, 168, 172, *174/175*
Arcanis, Francesco 15
Arcanus of Cesene 156
Archery equipment
    Arrows 118, 172, 174-181, *176*, *180*, 186
    Bows 118, 168, 172, *176*, *177*, *179*, 181-183
    Bracers 172, 173-174, *200*
Ascham, Roger 176-177

B
Baker, Matthew *128*, 135, 146, *146*, *147*
Baldwin, Alan 58, 60, 61
Ballard, Barry 58
Barak, Adrian 83, 101, 175, 186, 221, 222
Barber, John 60
Barber-surgeon 122, 186, *187*, *188*, 189
Le Barbour, Richard 188
Barkman, Lars 202
Barrels *94*, 148, *192*
Barrett, Jack 68
Baude, Peter 14, 164
Bax, Cdr Alan 54, *54*
BBC Chronicle unit 67, 102
du Bellay, Martin 34
Blindage *123*, 125, 128, 153
Boner, David 24
Books *195*, *200*
Botrye, William 24
Bottles and tankards *187*, 193, *194*, *200*, *201*
Boyne 49
Brandon, Charles, Duke of Suffolk *14*, 32, 39, 40
Brannam, Capt John 216, 224

de Briez, Marshal 31
British Petroleum 74, 96
British Sub-Aqua Club 47, 59, 60, 67, 74, 80
Brown, John 24
Brygandyne, Robert 24, 109
Burden, Barrie 101

C
Calshot Castle 29
Camber Castle 29
Carew, Sir Gawain 35, 37, 38
Carew, Sir George *31*, 33, 37, 38, 117
Carew, Sir Peter 37, 38, 39
Carraquon 31
Catherine of Aragon 13, 29, 173
Catherine Forteleza 25
Charles, HRH Prince of Wales 67, 69, 74, *88*, 226, 227
Charles V, Emperor of Spain 13, 29, 30
Christ 25
Clark, Jim 95, 101, 221, 224
de Clermont, Admiral René 25
Clothing 193, 199-201, *196*, *197*, *198*
Cloudesdale, Reg 59
de Commines, Philip 173
Computer 103, *103*
Conservation 90-93, *91*, *94*, *95*, *180*, *185*
Cowdray engraving *32/33*, *137*
Crothall, Alan 76

D
Dahl, Ian 98
Deane, John & Charles 42, 43, 45-47, *42*, *43*, 49, 50, 51, 55, 62, 110, 122, 153, 156, 157, 159, 163
Descharges 19
Diving safety 81, 100-101
Dobbs, Chris 85, 222, 227
Dobbs, Peter 100
Dooley, Sam 76
Drake, Sir Eric 74, *88*, 102
Dudley, John, Viscount Lisle 32, 33, 39, 40, 117, *117*, 118

E
Edgerton, Prof Harold *51*, 52

Edwards, William 46
Elizabeth I 23, 121, 176
Echyngham, Sir Howard 125, 128
Evans, Cdr Joe 213

F
Falting, Edvin 202, 205
Fielding, Andrew 81, 85, 101
Fiennes, Edward, Lord High Admiral 121
Food 148, 196, 199
Francis I, King of France 30, 31, 168
Frigg 205

G
Gabryell Royal 25
Games 190, 191, 198
George 172
Giles, Simon 15
Glover, Tony 61
Grace, John 104, 212, 213, 216
Grande Louise 25
Green, Sue 90
Greenhill, Dr Basil 74
Gun carriages 118, 128, 159-162, *158*, *160*, *161*, *170*, *181*

H
Hardy, Robert *177*, 183
Harrison, Richard 73, 74, 216
Harvey, Dr John 89
Hawkins, Sir John 23, 184
Henry VII 13, 109
Henry VIII 13, 15, 19, 20, 24, 25, 28-34, *32/33*, 36, 37, 38, 77, 152, 153, 156, 157, 165, 168, 172, 173, 176, 192, 198
Henry Grace à Dieu 33, 38, 118, 136, *138/139*
Hildred, Alex 101
Holder, Gwen 60
Howard, Sir Edward 24, 25
Hurst Castle 29

I
Imperial College, London 183, 228

J
James IV, King of Scotland 13
James V, King of Scotland 29
Jesus of Lubeck 39, 40, 110

K

King, Roy 183
Kvarning, Lars 202

L

Lewis, Col Wendell 213, 216, 221
Levy, Prof John 183
Louis XII, King of France 13, 24

M

McKee, Alexander 47, 48, *48*, 49, 50, 51, 52, 54, *54*, 55, 57, 58, 60, 64
La Maitresse 31
Majer, W O B 54, *54*
Marie la Cordelière 25
de Marine, Peter 39, 40, 153
Maritime Trust, The 67
Mary 46
Mary Fortune 147
Mary James 25
Mary Rose, Princess 13, *14*
Mary Rose
    Anchor 128, *134*, 153
    Cabins 120-123, 186, 193, 196
    Castle deck *118*, 133-135
    Galley *101*, *107*, 107-109, 117
    Hull 20, 22, 73, 93, 97, 103-116, *112/113*, *118*
      Maindeck 72, 106-107, 110, *118*, 120-124, 145, 184
      Orlop deck 72, 106, 107, 110, 116, *118*, 117-120
      Sterncastle 66, 105, *118*, 128-133
      Upper deck *118*, 124-133
Mary Rose (1967) Committee, The 54, 67, 72, 73, 96
Mary Rose Development Trust, The 98
Mary Rose, Court of the 98
Mary Rose Trading Company, The 100
Mary Rose Trust, The 74, 75, 76, 98, 102, 216, 217, 221
Mason, Edward 73
Medicine 186-196
Michel, Giovanni 173
Miller, Major General Sir William 45, 46
Mills, John 52
Monsom, Sir William 41
Mortlock, Berit 83, 175
Muckelroy, Keith 68
Mudie, Colin 105
Mulford, Louise 100-101
Murray, Howard 92, 93
Musical instruments 198-199, *198*

N

National Maritime Museum 67, 228
Netley Castle 29
Navigational instruments 120-121, *119*

O

Oden 205
Oglander, Sir John 34
Ordnance 13, 15, 17, 20, 21, 41, 45, 46, *46*, 56, 62, 120, 122, 128, 133, 135, 149-168, *154*, *155*, *157*, *158*, *159*, *163*, *165*, *169*
O'Shea, Chris 55, 90
Owen, John & Robert 133, 162, 164-168, *165*

P

Paget, Sir William 39, 40, 110
Palshidde, Richard 24
Panter, Ian 90, 93
Paré, Ambrose 192
Pasley, Col C W 43, 47, 49
Pasqualio, Lorenzo 13
Paul, Peter 41, 153
Paulin, Peter 213
Peter Granade 24
Peter Pomegranite 22, 23, 152
Pikeman, Henry 168
Plates, wood and pewter 117-118, 193
Poppenruyter, Hans 15
Portsmouth *12*, 22, 24, 25, 28, 31, 32, 34, 36, 45, *46*, 49, 66, 72, 73, 100, 122, 152, 153, 156, 206, 221
Portsmouth Dockyard 28, 210, *211*, 227-229
Powell, Peter 58
Pratt, Prof Peter 183
'Project Solent Ships' 47, 48, 49

R

Raleigh, Sir Walter 39
Rangemeter 96
Recording methods 89, 98, *80*, *84* 85, *90*, 218-220
Regent 15, 24, 25, 109, 145, 147
Reid, John 73, 207, 213
Rigging, Standing & Running 118 135, 136-147, *140*, *141*, *142*, *143*
Roger Grenville 59, 60, 61
Rose Slype 172, *174*
Royal George 42, 45, 49, 51
Rule, Nic 97, 104

S

Samson 40, 110
Santa Catharina do Monte Sinai 149

Science Museum 74
Sharp, Douglas 57
Shaw, Artie 60
Sheringham, Cdr 50
Shot 162-166, *166*
Sleipner 23, *74*, 75, 76, 77, 81, *82*, 96, 100, *130/131*, 206, 216, 222, 224, 226
Sonar 52, *53*, 54, 93, 95, 101, *207*
Southsea Castle 29, 32, 50, 51, 55
Southworth, Henry 168
Sovereign 15, 16, 21, 25, 69, 151, 152
Sperte, Thomas 24
Spithead 62
Stewart, Bob 85, 89
Stirland, Anne 184, 185
Surveying techniques 62, *64*, 65, 85, 89, *92*, 103-104
Symonds, D C 189
Symsom, Robert 186

T

Taylor, Joan du Plat 52
Taylor, Kirstin 189
Thackray, Gerald 189
Tidbury, Charles 98
Towse, John 50, 51
Tudor Ship Museum 72, 216, 217

U

Ughtred, Capt Anthony 25
Underwater acoustic camera 95, *95*
Underwood, Chris 81, 97, 100, 128, 213, 216

V

Veneti, ships of the 19
Vernon 28
Victory 125, 160, 217
Video camera, Marconi Blue Ball 81, 86, 87, 96

W

'WA', Flemish artist 17, 18, 140
Walker, Humphrey 13, 15
Waller, John 183
Walliker, John 101
Wasa 66, 75, 76, *121*, 122, 202, *203*, 204-206
Wolsey, Cardinal 29
Woodall, John 189, 192, 193, 196
Woolwich Ship 22, 23, 69, *69*, 151, *151*
Wryothesley, Sir Thomas 30
Wyndham, Sir Thomas 24, 25, 186

Y

Young, Morrie 59, 60, 64
Yonge, Henry 186